EXPERIENCING DAVID BOWIE

The Listener's Companion
Gregg Akkerman, Series Editor

Titles in **The Listener's Companion** provide readers with a deeper understanding of key musical genres and the work of major artists and composers. Aimed at nonspecialists, each volume explains in clear and accessible language how to *listen* to works from particular artists, composers, and genres. Looking at both the context in which the music first appeared and has since been heard, authors explore with readers the environments in which key musical works were written and performed.

EXPERIENCING DAVID BOWIE

A Listener's Companion

Ian Chapman

ROWMAN & LITTLEFIELD
Lanham • Boulder • New York • London

Published by Rowman & Littlefield
A wholly owned subsidiary of The Rowman & Littlefield Publishing Group,
Inc.
4501 Forbes Boulevard, Suite 200, Lanham, Maryland 20706
www.rowman.com

Unit A, Whitacre Mews, 26-34 Stannary Street, London SE11 4AB

British Library Cataloguing in Publication Information Available

Library of Congress Cataloging-in-Publication Data

Chapman, Ian, 1960–
Experiencing David Bowie : a listener's companion / Ian Chapman.
pages cm. – (Listener's companion)
Includes bibliographical references and index.
ISBN 978-1-4422-3751-3 (cloth : alk. paper) – ISBN 978-1-4422-3752-0 (ebook)
1. Bowie, David–Criticism and interpretation. 2. Rock music–History and criticism. I. Title.
ML420.B754C53 2015
782.42166092–dc23
2015010350

∞ ™ The paper used in this publication meets the minimum requirements of
American National Standard for Information Sciences Permanence of Paper
for Printed Library Materials, ANSI/NISO Z39.48-1992.

Printed in the United States of America

For Ben, Mia, and Arlo

CONTENTS

SERIES EDITOR'S FOREWORD

The goal of the Listener's Companion series is to give readers a deeper understanding of pivotal musical genres and the creative work of their iconic practitioners. Contributors meet this objective in a manner that does not require extensive music training or any sort of elitist shoulder-rubbing. Authors of the series are asked to situate readers in the listening environments in which the music under consideration has been or still can be heard. Within these environments, authors examine the historical context in which this music appeared, exploring compositional character and societal elements of the work. Positioned in real or imagined environments of the music's creation, performance, and reception, readers can experience a deeper enjoyment and appreciation of the work. Authors, often drawing on their own expertise as performers and scholars, are like tour guides, walking readers through major musical genres and the achievements of artists within those genres, replaying the music for them, if you will, as a *lived* listening experience.

I still recall a day in the 1970s when my tween-aged self swiped an older brother's copy of *Circus* magazine long enough to ogle at the striking image on the cover. I had never seen anything like the penetrating stare and spiked orange-rust hair of pop star David Bowie. He looked out from the cover—sickly, gaunt, brutally sincere, unapologetically rakish, and deliciously attractive to my twelve-year-old sensibilities. He was a beautifully young non-American and I, without any sullied adult ideas blocking the doorway, knew immediately that to look and act just like him was the epitome of cool. I even went so far as to take the picture with me on my next trip to the barber and ask: "Can you make my hair look like that?" The reply: "What do you think you are, kid, Japanese?" Racial insensitivities aside, the barber's comment aligned with a common issue among the music journalists, fans, and record companies in those days—just how do you categorize the Bowie package? He embraced, some might even say defined the essence then of what it meant to be a "rock star." And yet his music would eschew many of the most recognized elements of rock. He dangled his thoughtfully marketed persona for all the world to see but the general public knew little about him offstage. And throughout his career, he would cross and blur the lines between acting, producing, songwriting, recording, and performing. He bedded the various aesthetics like so many enamored and willing concubines. David Bowie was and remains a singular entity in the history of rock music, one of the few to successfully avoid any sort of ossified categorization while simultaneously topping the charts of those same categories. In the movie version of *Hedwig and the Angry Inch*, its angry protagonist describes the importance of Bowie among his contemporaries:

> Late at night I would listen to the voices of the American masters: Tony Tennille, Debby Boone, and Anne Murray—who was actually Canadian working in the American idiom. And then there were the crypto-homo-rockers: Lou Reed, Iggy Pop, and David Bowie—who was actually an idiom working in America and Canada.

The description, couched in satire, is wickedly precise in referring to Bowie as his own idiom. Categories of art bend and distort in order to accommodate Bowie's work—and not the other way around, as is so often the case with pop-star success stories. Conveying Bowie's unique standing in the development of popular music requires the deft hand of a writer keenly skilled at bringing together the full story of the artist's work and delivering it to the reader within its proper contemporaneous context. As a fan of Bowie's music for over forty years, I can say that Ian Chapman nails it. A full-time professor of music at New Zealand's University of Otago, Chapman has delved into the iconography, history, and social implications of popular music at great length, resulting in excellent writing on Bowie, Kiss, Bow Wow Wow, and various Kiwi-related topics. I had the pleasure of serving as first reader of his drafts and anxiously devoured each new submission. I never did get Bowie's hair, but the music is still with us, and Chapman has now made it all the more approachable for all of us.

Gregg Akkerman

ACKNOWLEDGMENTS

As a lifelong fan my primary acknowledgment most gratefully goes to David Bowie. Over the course of decades you've had me alternately inspired, bewildered, delighted, intrigued, disappointed (once or twice), gob-smacked, alarmed, amazed . . . but never, ever, uninterested. You have provided a soundtrack to the lives of millions of people, resplendent with twists, turns, and thought-demanding "crunchy bits." I'm thrilled to be among their number.

Sarah Williamson has been a crucial ally in the preparation of this book and I am indebted to her for her support, her enthusiasm, her witty repartee, and her multifaceted help. Dallas Synnott-Chapman, Shirley Chapman, Carol and Brian Foy, Maureen Rice, Peter Adams, Ian Loughran, Greg Platt, David Harrison, Rob Burns, Graeme Downes, Mary-Jane Campbell, Nick Hollamby, Suzanne Little, Henry Johnson, Ian and Kath Oreibow, and Mike and Miriam Lynch have all helped in ways both direct and indirect. Thanks to you all. "Love-on ya!" (David Bowie, *Pin Ups*, 1973).

TIMELINE

January 8, 1947	David Robert Jones born in Brixton, London, England.
June 12, 1962	Debut live performance with his first proper band, the Konrads, at the Bromley Tech PTA School Fête.
April 14, 1964	First live performance with the King Bees at the Jack of Clubs, Soho, London.
May 9, 1964	First live performance with the Manish Boys at the Star Club, Maidstone.
June 5, 1964	Debut single release, "Liza Jane," by the King Bees.
March 5, 1965	Single release, "I Pity the Fool," by the Manish Boys. The B side, "Take My Tip," marks Bowie's first singer-songwriter credit.
April 8, 1965	First live performance with the Lower Third at the Working Men's Club, Minster.
August 20, 1965	Single release, "You've Got a Habit of Leaving"/ "Baby Loves That Way," by Davy Jones and the Lower Third. Both songs written by Bowie.
January 1966	David Jones changes his name (unofficially) to David Bowie.
January 14, 1966	Single release, "Can't Help Thinking about Me"/ "And I Say to Myself," released under the new band name David Bowie and the Lower Third.

February 10, 1966	First live performance by David Bowie and the Buzz at the Mecca Ballroom, Leicester.
April 1966	Bowie signs a five-year management deal with Kenneth Pitt as a solo artist.
June 1, 1967	Debut studio album, *David Bowie*, is released.
July 11, 1969	"Space Oddity" is released as a single, eventually reaching number five on the UK singles chart.
November 4, 1969	Second studio album, *David Bowie*, is released (in the US this was retitled *Man of Words/Man of Music*).
February 22, 1970	Bowie and backing band, the Hype—a precursor to the Spiders from Mars, and featuring guitarist Mick Ronson—perform at the Roundhouse, London.
May 10, 1970	Bowie receives the Ivor Novello Award from the Songwriters' Guild of Great Britain for "Space Oddity," deemed the most original song of the year.
November 4, 1970	Third studio album, *The Man Who Sold the World*, is released in the US (six months earlier than in the UK).
December 17, 1971	Fourth studio album, *Hunky Dory*, is released.
February 10, 1972	The first Ziggy Stardust tour opens at the Toby Jug, Tolworth, London.
April 14, 1972	"Starman" is released as a single, supported by an appearance on the iconic BBC television show *Top of the Pops*.
June 6, 1972	Fifth studio album, *The Rise and Fall of Ziggy Stardust and the Spiders from Mars*, is released.
September 22, 1972	First US tour begins with a performance at the Cleveland Music Hall.
April 13, 1973	Sixth studio album, *Aladdin Sane*, is released. Advance orders total over one hundred thousand copies.

July 3, 1973   To the surprise of almost everyone in attendance, including most of his band, Bowie announces his retirement over the public announcement system at the conclusion of the final concert of the Ziggy Stardust tour at London's Hammersmith Odeon.

October 19, 1973   Seventh studio album, *Pin Ups*, is released.

April 11, 1974   Disembarking from the SS *France*, Bowie arrives in New York. He immediately begins assembling a new band and will remain in the US for almost two years.

April 24, 1974   Eighth studio album, *Diamond Dogs*, is released.

March 7, 1975   Ninth studio album, *Young Americans*, is released.

August 1, 1975   "Fame" is released as a single, reaching number one in the US.

September 26, 1975   "Space Oddity" is rereleased as a single in the UK, reaching number one.

January 23, 1976   Tenth studio album, *Station to Station*, is released.

May 9, 1976   Movie *The Man Who Fell to Earth* is released, directed by Nicolas Roeg and featuring Bowie as the lead, in his first major acting role.

October 1976   Bowie takes up residence in Berlin.

January 14, 1977   Eleventh studio album, *Low*, is released.

October 14, 1977   Twelfth studio album, *"Heroes,"* is released.

May 18, 1979   Thirteenth studio album, *Lodger*, is released.

July 29, 1980   Bowie makes his serious acting debut in Denver, playing the lead role of John Merrick in *The Elephant Man*. Extremely well received by critics, he would follow this with seasons in Chicago and also on Broadway in New York.

September 12, 1980   Fourteenth studio album, *Scary Monsters (and Super Creeps)*, is released.

March 2, 1982   Bowie makes his television acting debut, performing the title role in Bertolt Brecht's play *Baal* (1918) for the BBC.

April 14, 1983   Fifteenth studio album, *Let's Dance*, is released. Bowie's most commercially successful album, it reached the top of the charts in many countries around the world and spawned several equally successful singles.

September 1, 1984   Sixteenth album, *Tonight*, is released, to a generally poor critical reception.

June 17, 1986   Ever-popular children's movie *Labyrinth*, directed by Jim Henson, is released, featuring Bowie as Jareth, the Goblin King.

April 27, 1987   Seventeenth studio album, *Never Let Me Down*, is released, to the most unfavorable reception ever given to a Bowie album.

May 22, 1989   With Bowie temporarily retired from being a solo artist, his side project, Tin Machine, releases their first (self-titled) album.

September 2, 1991   The album *Tin Machine II* is released.

April 5, 1993   Bowie resumes his career as a solo artist, releasing his eighteenth studio album, *Black Tie White Noise*.

November 8, 1993   Nineteenth studio album, *The Buddha of Suburbia*, is released but largely ignored, being poorly promoted and misconstrued by critics and fans alike as a soundtrack album for the television series of the same name, to which Bowie contributed the title track.

September 26, 1995   Twentieth studio album, *1.Outside*, is released.

February 3, 1997   Twenty-first studio album, *Earthling*, is released.

October 4, 1999   Twenty-second studio album, *'hours . . .'* is released.

June 11, 2002	Twenty-third studio album, *Heathen*, is released.
September 16, 2003	Twenty-fourth studio album, *Reality*, is released.
July 2004	Bowie undergoes emergency heart surgery in Germany to clear a blocked artery after suffering pain onstage during a concert.
January 8, 2013	Bowie releases the surprise single "Where Are We Now?" on his sixty-sixth birthday and announces his forthcoming album, *The Next Day*.
March 8, 2013	Twenty-fifth studio album, *The Next Day*, is released.

INTRODUCTION

An extraordinary marriage of sound and vision underpinned by constant evolution and change lies at the heart of the work of David Bowie, the most enigmatic performer in popular music. Still active in a career now well into its fifth decade, Bowie has had vast influence. No other major music artist has intersected with other disciplines as effectively as Bowie has. His influence is found in fashion, film, gender studies, theater, performing arts studies, and, of course, cultural studies. Bowie's approach has always been that of an actor who plays various roles upon the vast stage of popular music, a defining trait evident even very early in his career. This sits in total opposition to romantic notions of rock artists being seamlessly authentic beings of superhuman ability chosen to channel some kind of divine inspiration. Because of this, Bowie has worn many faces, and listeners contemplating his large body of work are confronted with a bewildering array of musical styles including music hall, heavy metal, glam rock, ambient, avant-garde, soul, funk, electronic, and drum and bass, to venture just a few descriptors. Bowie's innovation and legacy has included the creation and abandonment of a succession of performance personas, each charged with performing one of these musical styles on record, on the concert stage, on film, and in interviews and other promotional situations. The images of these personas, each carefully crafted to mirror its respective musical style, have been calculatedly assembled from an amalgam of references from popular culture and borrowings from art history, film, literature, and other sources. In order to truly experience David Bowie, an appreciation must be gained for this interdisciplinary montage that he assembled time after time to provide the appropriate conduit for his music.

My personal journey of experiencing David Bowie began in 1972 when I was twelve years old. It was Kenneth's fault, although undoubtedly I'd have found Bowie by some other route sooner or later. The older brother of my teenage sister's boyfriend, Kenneth was in his early twenties and a music fanatic. There were a lot of Kenneths around in the early seventies: young men (mainly) absolutely consumed by rock music who applied themselves with single-minded determination to the task of accumulating as much vinyl treasure as they possibly could. Everybody had a record collection, and "let's see your vinyl, man" was as sure a way of gleaning a newcomer's worth as two dogs slowly circling and sniffing each other's nether regions. Just as it was for so many others, rock music was Kenneth's way of making sense of the world and it was the face he wore when he went out into that world. With his long straggly mane, facial hair, and ever-present denim, he could have slotted seamlessly into any number of late-sixties/early-seventies hippy bands. But he wasn't a musician, he was a baker, and he would spend every dollar left over after paying his rent and buying food each week on albums. Sometimes, I recall, both landlord and stomach had to wait. Rock music, still the wayward son of decent society at the time and the only game in town in terms of a unifying youth medium (no computers, no Internet), was Kenneth's way of demonstrating rebellion even as he clocked in for work on time each day. Kenneth's record collection took over the walls of his lounge, the custom-built floor-to-ceiling shelving (aka bricks and planks of wood) an ever-growing shrine. Living the unsociable lifestyle of a baker, he'd rise (forgive me) and head off to work at a ridiculously early time every working day, six days a week, well before the birds began clearing their throats in anticipation of the coming day. By the time I emerged from the gates of Peachgrove Intermediate School at 3 p.m. he'd be back at his flat, his day's work completed, and almost certainly lying on the couch while his stereo blasted out his latest acquisition. Routinely I'd drop by on my way home. Walking in through the always-open front door, I'd grab a Coke from his fridge on my way past the kitchen, head into the lounge wordlessly, saying gidday with a grin and flick of the head like well-acquainted Kiwis are wont to do, and settle myself into one of his huge, brown, swallow-you-whole,

1970s velvet armchairs. There I'd stay until around 5 p.m., working on my education, before heading home.

One day, following the dying shrieks, rumbles, and buzzes of an Emerson, Lake and Palmer album, Kenneth pulled out of its sleeve a shiny new record bearing the distinctive bright-orange RCA label. "See what you think of this," he muttered, and with the care of a connoisseur he placed his just-purchased copy of *The Rise and Fall of Ziggy Stardust and the Spiders from Mars* upon the turntable, handing me the cover to peruse before resuming his position on the couch. Like watching Neil Armstrong step onto the surface of the moon on a grainy black-and-white television placed precariously upon a chair on the stage of our packed-out school hall three years earlier—like hearing and feeling the impact of a fatal car crash on the corner of our street when I was five and pulling back the curtains of my window to see the frightening aftermath—listening to David Bowie for the thirty-eight minutes and thirty-seven seconds that it took to experience the *Ziggy Stardust* album for the first time remains indelibly etched into my memory. When the needle lifted from the vinyl at the completion of "Rock 'n' Roll Suicide," Kenneth, a hairy hippy on the cusp of his comfort zone with David Bowie, was grudgingly appreciative. I, however, was changed.

I didn't know then how or why it had impacted me as it did, of course, but now, having had four decades to come to understand it, I do know. I understand why I "got" David Bowie. And it is this experience I hope to impart to those who read this book. It is a deep engagement and a lifelong passion. No other artist or band in the history of popular music has made a mark upon me as great as has David Bowie, and it is a wonderful thing.

Oh yes, you can listen to David Bowie and simply *like* him, never buying an album or attending a concert but tapping your toes or fingers when you hear his distinctive voice on the car radio. Millions of people have done exactly that, and that's fine. But to truly "get" David Bowie is an experience that goes far beyond mere listening, far beyond even music itself. David Bowie is a conduit for many things. The most important of these for me personally, at least, has been his knack for bringing into the mainstream that which would have otherwise languished in the barren wastelands of unacceptance, of marginalization. To me, David Bowie has been, and remains, a lightning rod for the acceptance of difference, and I—like many others—owe him a lot for that.

In these pages I seek to unpack how such a thing is possible; how it is that an avid David Bowie fan such as myself can relate on such an intensely personal level to the art of a man I have never met. I am in no doubt that millions of Bowie fans around the world are absolutely avid in their fandom. Ardent, fervent, passionate . . . such adjectives are most certainly not an exercise in "over-egging the cake," as my wife would say. Personally, I have met many, many fans as avid as myself, people who genuinely feel that David Bowie has made a real, tangible impact upon their lives.

In recent years there has been a wave of renewed interest in David Bowie. The world-renowned Victoria and Albert Museum in London, with its proud history of over a century and a half of displaying the best arts, culture, and more that the world can offer, held its most successful exhibition ever in 2013. Three hundred eleven thousand visitors attended *David Bowie Is*. I was lucky enough to be one of them, and I include an account of this at the end of the book. Kings, queens, philosophers, and artists of every description have been exhibited at the V&A over its many years, but it was a self-confessed actor-playing-at-rockstar, born less than five miles south of the V&A in unfashionable Brixton, that trumped them all.

It is not just in the public domain that interest in David Bowie has soared recently. Within academia a highly interdisciplinary field of scholarship known as Bowie studies has emerged. In 2012 the University of Limerick, Ireland, hosted a three-day conference titled "Strange Fascination: A Symposium on David Bowie," at which academics from all around the world, including myself, gathered to deliver papers and join in group debates. There were musicologists, psychologists, psychiatrists, sociologists, and scholars from gender studies, film studies, theater and performing arts studies, and cultural studies, as well as industry people, media people, and even curious fans.

As I write, I know of two academic publishers that are currently in the process of preparing edited collections of papers that will become foundational texts for Bowie studies at universities and colleges around the globe.

All things considered, this is not a bad effort as far as legacies go for a rock star now in his sixty-ninth year. And to top it all, completely out of the blue after a ten-year hiatus, in 2013 *The Next Day* topped album charts all over the world and received glowing reviews.

Today, undoubtedly assisted by generous amounts of time for reflection (aka getting older), Bowie's "people"—fans, scholars, whatever and whoever they may be—are more vocal than ever before in acknowledging and/or analyzing Bowie's impact upon the world that they, and he, have lived in. Bowie's points of difference—the factors that have set him apart from other artists and acts throughout his career—have been largely identified by numerous biographers, critics, and journalists. These include the unprecedented changeling qualities of his musical style and visual image, his problematizing of gender signification (most especially through the early to mid-1970s), his multifaceted presentations and critiques of alienation, his exposing of rock stardom as mere construction, and—allied to this—his actor's approach to his art (within an art form where, previous to Bowie, any admission of such artifice was tantamount to rock 'n' roll suicide). To reduce Bowie's most unique quality to a single word that encompasses the points raised here, and more, he is inherently *other*. Pop musicologist Simon Frith put it well when he suggested, "Bowie's fans have always identified with him particularly intensely, because no one else has captured so well their sense of difference."[1] This trait will become evident in this book. Through tracing the sound and vision of his studio albums I seek not only to uncover this most significant point of difference, but also to come to understand how he has meant, and does mean, so much to his enormous worldwide fan base.

The book is ordered chronologically for the most part. Forty-six years of Bowie's extraordinary career are considered, with his self-titled debut album of 1967 the earliest work and *The Next Day* the last. His studio album recordings—as opposed to live albums and the many compilations and greatest-hits packages available—are the primary means by which I got to know David Bowie, and, with no disrespect to his many film-acting credits and other artistic endeavors, this is the case for the majority of his fans. (One exception being my nine-year-old daughter, Mia, for whom Bowie will always be first and foremost the Goblin King from *Labyrinth*.) This body of recorded work comprises twenty-seven studio albums, including his two-album foray into being "just" a member of the band Tin Machine in the late eighties and early nineties. Because of the sheer size of this output it was not possible to compile a song-by-song critique of all twenty-four albums. With that said, however, I have done exactly that up to and including 1980's *Scary Monsters (and Super Creeps)*. My justification for allotting more space to these earlier works is that it is within this career-establishing decade-and-a-bit that the performative palette that would sustain him throughout his career can best be unpacked. That is, all of the thematic concerns that became cornerstones of his work were brought to the fore during this period, and his unique penchant for stylistic change became firmly cemented. While I certainly do not regard Bowie's post-1980 works as being any less deserving, the artist was at the peak of his influence and potency during the 1970s. Therefore, tasked with providing a "way in" to the recorded legacy of David Bowie, I believe it is justifiable to focus most attention upon this period. For the thirteen post-1980 albums, instead of track-by-track analysis I focus upon key tracks. Of course, subjectivity in making such determinations is inevitable; music is just like that. So, to those readers offended by my slim treatment of certain works or concentration on others, I apologize in advance. However, I sincerely hope we will share *some* common ground.

As mentioned earlier, Bowie's albums are examined chronologically for the most part, but not entirely. After much soul-searching I decided to break from this clean and neat, if predictable, ordering system briefly at the beginning of the book. My justification is that the overwhelming majority of fans did not discover the artist through his debut album, *David Bowie*, in 1967, which was a commercial failure. His second album, released in 1969 and also self-titled, suffered the same fate. His third album, *The Man Who Sold the World*, 1971, also failed to meet expectations despite garnering some promising reviews. More widespread interest in David Bowie began to grow with the release of his fourth album, *Hunky Dory*, in 1972. However, it was his fifth album, *The Rise and Fall of Ziggy Stardust and the Spiders from Mars*, released later that same year, that truly elevated him to the level of star, a fact reflected in commercial success for both the album and the enormous international tour schedule that accompanied it. Therefore, given that my task is to impart to others how best to experience David Bowie, it would be irresponsible of me to insist that readers begin with his debut album—or indeed the handful of albums that followed—simply to adhere to a strict, tidy, chronological ordering. In truth, almost none of us experienced David Bowie that way.

In order to mirror the real-life experience of Bowie fans worldwide, I begin the book with *The Rise and Fall of Ziggy Stardust and the*

Spiders from Mars. Following this breakthrough I turn my attention in chapter two to the album that immediately preceded it, *Hunky Dory*, in a similar attempt to mirror the trajectory taken by Bowie's nascent audience at the time. As the fledgling fans of *Ziggy Stardust* looked to see what else their new favorite artist had in the shops, *Hunky Dory* quickly gained a new lease on life, becoming the second purchase for many fans. Indeed, borne on this wave of fervor, it eventually eclipsed its successor in terms of sales. These two albums, then, were the dual means by which an enormous number of people initially experienced David Bowie, and this as-it-really-happened order of things is something I have tried to replicate.

Following *Hunky Dory* I step backward in time in chapters three and four to consider Bowie's earliest days. Once this retrospection is complete, from chapter five onward the albums are considered chronologically, beginning with *Ziggy Stardust*'s successor, *Aladdin Sane*, of 1973.

A word on how it is that I am fortunate enough to be writing this book. My particular academic specialization is music iconography; that is, I am interested in how musicians and music making are represented in visual art. I consider album covers to be works of art in their own right, and the best popular-music artists ensure that the messages they seek to impart through their music are also made clearly visible on their album covers. Bowie is one of the finest exponents of this, and therefore, while his songs remain at the forefront of this book, consideration of the album covers that housed them is woven into the mix in order to further contextualize Bowie's work and explain its innovation and importance. For Bowie fans, it has never *just* been about the music. I also seek to locate the songs within the social climate in which they were created. In iconographical terminology, it is the application of art historian Michael Baxandall's "period eye." Nuances and inferences inevitably change over time, so I have tried to consider both music and album art in ways that are sympathetic to their time.

David Bowie has been the subject of a great many biographies, several of which are extremely detailed and comprehensive. As this is a listener's companion I have made no attempt at compiling any kind of biography here. Nevertheless, as I progress through a chronological analysis of his recording career, at times it is appropriate to include brief biographical information in order to further consider the music.

One of the more enjoyable and creative components of this Listener's Companion series is the "imagine you are there" re-creations, whereby events such as the first playing of a Bowie album are re-created using a touch of artistic license. While these sections are, by their very nature, fiction informed by fact, as a lifelong Bowie fan I do have firsthand knowledge in such matters. On twenty-seven memorable occasions I have had the pleasure of experiencing a new David Bowie studio album for the first time.

Though a music academic, I am, above all, a fan. Sometimes, too, I am a performer, and I have frequently performed Bowie's music, regarding myself as privileged to be able to gain insight into the artist's compositional and performative genius from the inside, so to speak. In keeping with having written this book largely "away from the office," I have endeavored to avoid unnecessarily jargonistic or academic language. Part of Bowie's attraction, after all, is his expansive inclusivity, and to couch his work in scholarly language, which by its very nature excludes many, would be un-Bowie-like. It would also not be in keeping with the aims of this series of books, admirably concerned, as they are with breaching the academic/popular divide.

I freely admit that being asked to write this book about a subject so close to my heart is one of the highlights of my career. Bowie fans are ardent fans, and if you are a reader who hasn't yet "got" Bowie, then I am hopeful this book will help to rectify that situation. And if you do already "get" Bowie, then I sincerely hope the listening experiences I describe will resonate as keenly with you as they have with me.

IS DAVID BOWIE RIGHT FOR YOU?

> News-guy wept and told us, Earth was really dying. —David Bowie, from "Five Years," 1972

> They can't get enough of that Doomsday song. —David Bowie, from "The Next Day," 2013

It's 1972. You are twelve years old, and bored. You are also vaguely unsettled, although if someone asked you outright why it was so, you wouldn't even know it to be true, let alone be able to ascertain why, because, simply, you've never felt any different. Deep within you, however, and shared with your generation, a latent fear sits at the most fundamental core of your being. It's a fear you shouldn't have to bear at age twelve. It is a fear of death.

You've grown up during the Cold War. Ever since grasping the basics of language, you've overheard your parents, your parents' friends, your older siblings, news reporters, academics, and politicians talk about nuclear warfare, nuclear testing, nuclear fallout, and nuclear winter. Nuclear this, and nuclear that. Has there ever been a generation of kids so fearful of the seemingly innocent term "big red button"? Of course, since the beginning of humankind generations of children have experienced the horrors of war, because, sadly, we are undeniably a warring species. But war, however distasteful, has always previously been somewhat localized. Death made manageable by the limitations of transportation and the realities of geographical distance, if you like. But the war that threatens now, during your childhood, World War III, would not be contained, would it? The existence of ICBMs (intercontinental ballistic missiles) means that warring countries are no longer bound by the necessity of being close to whomever it is they are seeking to kill. Developed and refined under the diversionary skirts of the space race, these odious devices can rain devastation anywhere and everywhere on the globe. Casualties in such a conflict will not be limited to the armed forces but may wipe out everyone in the entire world, including you and your family and friends. Through the late 1960s and early 1970s you've seen maps of the world on television and in newspapers and magazines that show calculated projections of how cities, countries, and continents may be wiped out in a matter of minutes or even seconds. There would be no escape. If the blasts didn't get you quickly then the radiation fallout would get you slowly, or the nuclear winter that followed would get you even more slowly.

In 1972, with the shadows of Hiroshima and Nagasaki still clearly visible over the shoulders of your parents as they lean in to hug you at bedtime, you know for an absolute fact that all life on Earth could be wiped out with the push of "that" button.

Yes, you are a child of the Cold War. Being obliterated along with all of your kind and everything else on Earth is a fundamental fear that previous generations did not have to contend with. The arms race and the closely allied space race have been yours to witness but not to understand. Weren't adults supposed to be sensible? Weren't they supposed to protect the likes of you? Are you the only one who can see, through your increasingly less innocent twelve-year-old eyes, the immense stupidity of a conflict in which it doesn't matter who pushes the button first because all that is really at stake is who will die first and who will die later? Missiles, schmissiles. All you know as you drink your glass of milk and get tucked into bed each night is that nuclear conflict between the USA and USSR, maybe next week, maybe next year, will in all likelihood destroy the world. "Good night, son. Sleep well." "Good night, Mum. Good night, Dad."

Of course all of this depressing nuclear business does not sit at the forefront of your mind each and every day. You get on with life. You *are* a kid, after all, and you know how to have fun, play games for hours on end, worry your parents, goad the family cat until you wear stripes, watch TV, construct plastic Airfix or Revell models . . . and you've got a rapidly developing passion for pop music. But nevertheless that fear is there, partially repressed, sitting down deep and out of sight.

How did the human race get to this point where war can be waged so devastatingly without even having to look one's enemy in the eye? It is because of the rapid advancement of technology. We are living in the so-called space age. How we love the good things it brings us, but how we fear what it might do. Technology has put televisions in our living rooms and stereo systems in the bedrooms of us kids. Technology brings us our much-loved *Doctor Who*, *Star Trek*, and *Top of the Pops* every week. And, just a few years earlier, weren't we held in thrall every bit as much as our parents by the dramatic unfolding of the space race between the Sputnik and Apollo space programs? Didn't we cheer just as loudly as they did when the Apollo 11 astronauts made their successful moon landing in 1969? And remember, although you weren't really into music back then, some guy had that catchy "Ground Control to Major Tom" novelty song that everyone sang along to? Whatever happened to him, I wonder? OK, that triumphant "one small step" rah-rah-for-technology stuff was all very well, but did you *see* what HAL 9000 did when he had the chance? HAL, the onboard computer of the *Discovery One* spacecraft in Stanley Kubrick's *2001: A Space Odyssey*, turned traitor, didn't he? With his red, glowing, all-seeing eye and calm, emotionless voice, HAL killed all but one of the astronauts on the ship in cold blood, and he'd have killed that last one too if he could have. Why should we assume that technology will always meekly work for us and not turn, or *be* turned, against us? Oh yes, on the surface of it, you love technology. But deep, deep within, just what such advanced technology might actually lead to looms large among your subconscious fears.

Notwithstanding the fact that you love them, of course, your family is, well . . . boring. Dad, Mum, and your older brother—they're on different planets from you, aren't they? Dad goes to work, watches football on the telly, reads the newspaper, and maybe goes to the pub. That's his life, right there. Mum works part-time at the grocery store and looks after the house, but subtract football from the equation and substitute knitting and *Coronation Street*, and her life is otherwise pretty much the same colorless, repetitive affair as your dad's as far as you can see. Your seventeen-year-old brother is in his last year of school and only cares about his girlfriend, football, and crusty old hippy musicians and bands from the 1960s like the Beatles, the Rolling Stones, the Doors, Jimi Hendrix, and Janis Joplin. He doesn't seem to care that most of them are either dead or disbanded now. There's not much of a revolution going on there anymore, is there? "Don't you know it's gonna *be*—alright!" the mop-tops had assured everyone. But it wasn't all right, was it? With all due respect, love was not, evidently, all you needed, and you only had to look to the never-ending Vietnam War to know that. So much for the flag-bearers of the counterculture. Indeed, so much for the counterculture itself, no matter how well intentioned it might have been. "Turn on, tune in, drop out" . . . and then, er, what came next, exactly? No, your brother is only five years older than you but it might as well be fifty, you have so little in common with him. Without your radio and *Top of the Pops* you'd have gone stark raving mad by now.

Nothing interesting ever happens around here. Life in the burbs is dull and gray; as dull and gray as your school uniform. How you crave some color. If girls are allowed to dress up and brighten their world, why can't you? Who decided that boys should be limited to blue, black, gray, and brown anyway? What's with that? Adults will tell you that being a kid is the best part of your life. Really? That can't be true. What would they know? There has to be more to life than this, surely?

You are twelve years old and staring down the barrel of teenagehood. You are simultaneously excited by and fearful of technology and all the potential for good and evil it possesses. You are all too familiar with the terms "apocalypse" and "Armageddon." You have a burgeoning passion for pop music, but are completely bored by the tired old music your older brother revels in. You feel alienated from him, and even more so from your parents. School is dreary, and you are increasingly bored with your life in the suburbs. No one understands you.

[A small, back-of-the-hand, theatrical cough] "Ahem . . . excuse me, but have you heard about David Bowie? He's new. I think you'd like him."

I

ROCK AND ROLE

The Rise and Fall of Ziggy Stardust and the Spiders from Mars, 1972

It's the morning of July 7, 1972, and you're in the schoolyard. Barely twelve hours have passed since David Bowie performed "Starman" on the BBC's top-rated television music show, *Top of the Pops*. That performance is now dominating conversations on this midsummer weekday morning, a scene being repeated in schoolyards throughout the country. Pop music dominates the youth culture of the day and *Top of the Pops* is television's pop flagship in the UK, number one on everybody's weekly must-view list. Inevitably, however, a few kids missed it due to summer football practice or other commitments that they'd been unable to wriggle out of, or perhaps crueler-than-cruel parental retribution for dishes unwashed or rooms not tidied. Whatever the reason, these poor souls now find themselves suddenly the most un-hip, uninformed kids in school. Just like you, the vast majority *did* see it, of course, and now cannot shut up about it, their eyes bright with excitement at witnessing such an unexpected and knee-knockingly edgy revelation. Deep in the bowels of the staff room the teachers too are talking about David Bowie. How they tut-tut, shaking their heads as they wipe away biscuit crumbs, drawing comfort from their shared disapproval while administering, with hands unsteady, further mouthfuls of tea—more heavily sugared than usual—in a doomed attempt to forget the glimpse of the future they had witnessed. How they fear for the nation if the likes of this David Bowie character—a strutting peacock of no fixed gender—is set to replace healthy, sanctioned role models, such as footballers, cricketers, and *real* musicians like those nice Beatles, in the affections of the youth of the day. Older brothers and sisters back at home with their Beatles and their Stones records are also less than impressed: "Did you see that bloody poof on the telly last night? What a *poseur!*" But the kids, the *kids*, know that something amazing took place on *Top of the Pops* that magic night.

As *Top of the Pops* beamed into the temperamental old television set that sits on its four spindly legs in the corner of the living room, last night started out just like any other Thursday night. Your mum was enjoying another quiet evening in with her knitting—click click click knit-one purl-one knit-one purl-one knit-one purl-one and then a sip of sherry—and your dad was in his comfy chair all but hidden behind his beloved newspaper, a cup of tea balanced precariously at his elbow on the arm of the chair. Your older brother was watching *Top of the Pops* at his girlfriend's house, which was great because it meant you wouldn't have to be subjected to the derogatory comments he always made about the bands you loved the most, such as T. Rex and Slade.

Tonight, acts came and went on the show as they always did. "Ooh, I like that one," your mum might have said once or twice in her usual lighthearted, not particularly interested appraisal. And then it was David Bowie's turn. It came out of the blue, didn't it? You had never seen David Bowie before—none of you had—although the name rang a bell; was he the guy that did that "Ground Control to Major Tom" song a few years back at the time of the Apollo 11 moon landing? Regardless, your expectations weren't high, and why would they be when the song he was evidently about to sing, something called "Starman," was currently sitting at a lowly forty-one on the chart? But then, he began. Even if the sound had been completely turned off you'd still have been transfixed because nobody went on TV looking like that in 1972 . . . *nobody*. Bowie wore a tight-fitting gold, red, and blue quilted jumpsuit that accentuated his skinny, androgynous frame, and his hair was red and rooster-styled, teased up and spiky on top and long and feathered at the back and sides. If his look was designed to get attention, it was working. Even more than that, however, he wore an indefinable look on his face that was not what you were used to seeing on *Top of the Pops*. The performers usually bore expressions designed to convey the impression that their right to be on the UK's hottest music show was a given. They were stars and that was that. But Bowie seemed highly amused to be there, certainly self-assured, but not in an off-putting way. Rather, his obvious amusement—even bemusement—drew you in, despite not being privy to why he might have felt that way. It was impossible not to be attracted to him. Well, that's how it was for you anyway. What about others? Before so much as ten seconds had passed, the ever-present sound of knitting needles had stopped and your mum was glued to the TV screen despite her better judgment. And when you sneaked a sideways look at your dad, there he was peering over the top of his partially lowered newspaper, his glasses pushed up onto his forehead and a face on him like the devil himself had come into the lounge and sat down to file his nails in the corner. "Don't tell your papa or he'll get us locked up in fright," sang the devil antagonistically with accompanying smile, looking straight across the room at your dad as he did so.

In contrast to your parents, you sat there watching in complete thrall throughout Bowie's performance, goose bumps rising on your skin, your heart racing and breathlessness growing. Oh yes, you were well aware of your parents' mounting discomfort just feet away. To say they merely disapproved would not do their feelings justice; they were threatened and disturbed. But their recoiling made you love what was unfolding all the more, didn't it? As the song went on you began to feel more and more that Bowie was speaking directly to you, and then he proved beyond doubt that it was so. Dispensing with the mimed strumming of his bright-blue acoustic guitar, he pointed, smiled, stared straight down the throat of the camera and into your lounge, nailing you firmly to the couch while singing, "I had to phone someone so I picked on you, ooh, ooh." Sleep came slowly that night.

And now here it was a mere twelve hours or so afterward and your "this is big!" instincts had been proven correct. There was a buzz going around the schoolyard that you could reach out and touch, it was so strong. In the days and weeks to come the girls in your class would begin wearing glitter and as much makeup as they could get away with, and the boys would begin booking themselves in at the local barber to request rooster cuts that those who wielded the clippers in such establishments as yet had no idea how to create. "Can ya cut it like Bowie's, please?" would soon be heard on a daily basis. In no time at all, you'd be saying it yourself. Everywhere in the days that followed you'd hear kids singing, "There's a Star-*man* waiting in the sky." You sang it too. The world, for us kids, had changed. Suddenly, color was everywhere.

Of course, you and all your school friends simply *had* to buy this song. You couldn't rely on randomly catching it on the radio; you had to be able to play it again and again whenever you wanted. So that week's pocket money was quickly exchanged for the "Starman" single, completely sold out at the first two shops you visited but triumphantly procured at the third. When you got it home you found the B side was also brilliant, the barnstorming "Suffragette City" surely the best bonus to a 45 purchase that you'd ever encountered. Within no time the amateur renditions of "Starman" on the school playground were joined by ascendant adolescent cries of "Ohhhhhh . . . wham bam thank you ma'am!" accompanied by behind-cupped-hands speculation pertaining to the meaning of the phrase. And the talk was all over school that "Starman" was not just a single but had come from a full-length album with the crazily long title *The Rise and Fall of Ziggy Stardust and the Spiders from Mars*.

The album had been released on June 6, exactly a month before *Top of the Pops*, but it wasn't until July 7 onward that a phenomenon for which Bowie had striven during the frustrating early years of his career finally took place: fans were walking into record shops all over Britain, determinedly ignoring the myriad other offerings on display, and plucking *his* album off the shelves and out of the racks before heading to the till. You were one of the many thousands who did this, and your combined efforts culminated in pushing the *Ziggy Stardust* album to number five on the album chart and "Starman" to number ten on the singles chart. Without a doubt, David Bowie had arrived.

THE RISE AND FALL OF ZIGGY STARDUST AND THE SPIDERS FROM MARS, 1972

> Of course there's nothing Bowie would like more than to be a glittery super-star, and it could still come to pass. By now everybody ought to know he's tremendous and this latest chunk of fantasy can only enhance his reputation further. —James Johnson, *New Musical Express*, June 1972

Bowie's bid for stardom is accelerating at lightning speed. —Michael Watts, *Melody Maker*, July 1972

Side One	**Side Two**
1. Five Years	1. Lady Stardust
2. Soul Love	2. Star
3. Moonage Daydream	3. Hang on to Yourself
4. Starman	4. Ziggy Stardust
5. It Ain't Easy (Davies)	5. Suffragette City
	6. Rock 'n' Roll Suicide

A concept album consisting of eleven songs, *The Rise and Fall of Ziggy Stardust and the Spiders from Mars* reveals its story in a way that is, while largely thematically coherent, fragmented enough in terms of its flow to require assembly on the part of the listener.

The opening track, "Five Years," creeps gradually and unhurriedly into audibility as drummer Woody Woodmansey's simple, restrained triple-time (6/8) pattern of hi-hat, snare, and kick drum fades in from complete silence. As the drums reach their full volume, piano, bass guitar, and autoharp enter in unison on an emphatic, declamatory major chord that sustains throughout Bowie's opening vocal line: "Pushing through the market square." With the exception of the constant and almost metronomic drums, these instruments are used sparingly throughout most of the first verse, reserved mainly for the beginnings of lines. Their long sustains give an impression of spaciousness and allow full attention to be paid to Bowie's scene-setting description of a populace in turmoil at the news of its forthcoming destruction in just five years' time. With heavy reverb supporting this impression of spaciousness, the strategic use of echoes at the end of some of Bowie's lines lends gravitas to his emotive words ("sighing," "dying," "lying"). Bowie relates each of the fragmented scenes he witnesses as he continues on his way, building in the listener's mind an almost filmic overview so that we too bear witness to an unfolding catastrophe. In 1972, with the possibility of nuclear conflict a very real and constant presence in the minds of Bowie's generation, such a scenario seemed an all-too-possible one and readily accessed a deeply felt universal fear. While initially matter-of-fact and dispassionate, as the first verse proceeds, Bowie's vocal melody shifts to a higher register and a new intensity becomes evident in his voice as strain and emotion betray the fact that, although an observer, he too is caught up in the events he is relaying; just one of many similarly scared people. This increased intensity is supported by an instrumental accompaniment that incrementally becomes more expansive, until it is almost too much to bear: "My brain hurt like a warehouse—it had no room to spare." At the beginning of verse two, however, with his voice dropping away again in both register and emotion, Bowie regains control. Strummed acoustic guitar and plaintive strings join the mix, the latter high and fragile at first but gaining in strength and breadth as the action continues. Bowie's voice once again becomes more strained and emotive as he relates a series of vignettes involving individuals including an unnamed girl, a black, a cop, a queer, a priest, and, most tellingly, "a soldier with a broken arm" seemingly contemplating suicide as he "fixed his stare to the wheels of a Cadillac." Moving on, he recognizes somebody he knows in an ice-cream parlor who is seemingly unaware of the catastrophic events unfolding. Here Bowie unexpectedly employs a Brecht-like distancing device as he steps back from the action to comment that the person didn't know he/she was appearing in a song. Just two lines later he repeats this distancing effect by suggesting that he feels like an actor. From this point on Bowie remains in his higher, emotion-laden register, and when he begins to sing of returning to his mother it is clear he has moved irreconcilably from observer to protagonist, as swept up in the unfolding events as anyone. As he repeatedly cries his message of doom, that Earth has but five years until annihilation, now joined by backing vocalists, the instrumental accompaniment begins to ominously swirl up and around him. His voice now at breaking point, he finally becomes overpowered by the musical backing. The music here is expertly and most emphatically painting the action, Bowie himself overcome by events beyond his control. With the reaching of this tumultuous point, the music seems to start collapsing under its own weight, the previously highly unified strings giving way to chaotic free-form lines. With one final overwhelming chordal crescendo, sustained just for a moment and joined by the futuristic wail of a heavily effected electric guitar, the wall of accompaniment suddenly gives way to nothing, the drums left exposed and alone to usher the song out in the same way it began.

"Five Years" is an emphatic, highly theatrical, expressive, and poignant opener to the album. As effectively as one might expect to see in the opening scenes of a movie, the stage has been set for the action that will follow. To its 1972 audience, Bowie had opened up a conduit to very real fears and emotions held either consciously or subconsciously. What if a similarly apocalyptic event were to be announced on our own TV screens? Would we experience exactly these kinds of chaotic scenes in the streets that we walked down every day? The imagined experience conveyed through "Five Years" was therefore a highly transferable, universal one, inviting us all to imagine the same scenario in our own towns and cities wherever in the world we lived.

In the second track, "Soul Love," Bowie initially muses over the futility of and pointless loss created by war, described through the actions of a distraught mother at the grave of her fallen son: "Stone love, she kneels before the grave. A brave son who gave his life to save the slogan." In 1972, with World War II less than three decades in the past, the effects of war were still very much in evidence in the London that Bowie had grown up in. A third of the city had been destroyed during the German bombing campaign known as the Blitz, and sixteen thousand Londoners had been killed. Personal loss through the ravages of war, whether through civilian or armed-forces casualties, was still a very real experience in 1972, certainly for those who had lived through it, but also for the children born in the decades after the war who would hear of family members or friends who "never came home." Following this poignant opening, the allied emotion of human love is then critiqued in verse two with a description of two young lovers caught in a world of their own. Could love truly be the answer—an effective and comprehensive means of banishing loss and fear? Could the Beatles have been right after all? Up to this point in the song, both verses have been sung over an unobtrusive backing dominated by bongo drums and acoustic guitar. However, at the first chorus the instrumentation becomes much more dense, with electric guitar destroying the contemplative images of the grieving mother in the graveyard and of the young lovers. With his vocal melody rising in pitch and an emerging edge of desperation in his voice, the chorus takes an unmistakably cynical view of what Bowie now refers to as "idiot love," relegating it to a mere balm; a last resort for those who are otherwise defenseless. The intensity then drops away again to allow a languid and ironically beautiful saxophone solo, at the end of which the key unexpectedly changes, moving up a tone in a heavenward step that paints the new subject of faith in God, introduced in verse three. This notion in turn receives a similarly cynical dismissal, the return of the chorus taking its dismissive cue from the final line of the verse, which depicts a priest enveloped by blindness. This time, due in part to the key change, Bowie's rendition of the chorus sounds desperate, with his voice higher again, strained and emotive. The intensity then drops away again, for the final time, with electric guitar supported by a "la la la" backing vocal taking over the verse melody as the track fades out.

Each of the belief systems in which mankind has traditionally sought comfort—those belief systems that would, come news of impending Armageddon, be tested—has been summarily dismissed. Within the first two songs Bowie has set up an apocalyptic scenario and then effectively removed our means of coping with it. If not God, then where might we find a savior?

Daa Da Da! begins "Moonage Daydream," with a loud, aggressive fanfare of electric guitar power chords that rudely interrupts the dignified fade-out of the previous song. In the most emphatic way possible, Ziggy Stardust has burst through your speakers and into your bedroom, warning, "I'm an alligator! I'm a mama-papa coming for you!" before continuing on, "I'm the space invader!" While these opening words are potentially ominous, as the track unfolds it becomes clear that Ziggy's goal is simply to rock; more precisely, to be a "rock 'n' roll bitch" for us. Science fiction terminology remains at the fore throughout "Moonage Daydream," with terms such as "ray gun," "space face," "electric eye," and the frequently repeated song title sitting in complete contrast to the earthbound context and language of the previous two songs. There's a touch of sixties psychedelia in the invitation to "freak out," and the extended guitar solos do exactly this. An aggressive and very electric song, "Moonage Daydream" is the track that establishes for the first time on the album a raw sonic vibe and distinctly science fiction–styled timbres and effects, most especially in the extensive use of echo in the final chorus that mimics pulsating sound waves, and the wildly phased strings that feature during the extended concluding guitar solo. The concept of daydreaming about the moon, space, and, indeed, space invaders is one very easily identified with by a generation whose imaginations have been fed on the space race.

A vague familiarity comes to the mind of the listener as the softly toned introduction to "Starman" begins. As was the case with "Space Oddity" three years earlier, the introduction features a strummed acoustic guitar pivoting between two chords. One of them is the same spacious, mysterious, F-major seventh chord used in that earlier and similarly space-themed song, although the tempo here is somewhat faster. In the latter stages of this tranquil beginning, Bowie, his voice soft and oddly quiet in the mix, delivers two short, unintelligible lines of lyrics that the ear strains to decipher but cannot, giving the impression that he is singing from some distance. A drum fill then announces the arrival of the rest of the band at the start of verse one and, as if he is suddenly much closer, hereafter Bowie's voice is clear and at the forefront as he relates the story. From a first-person perspective he tells of relaxing while listening to rock 'n' roll on his radio, an activity almost universal among British teens and preteens in 1972 and therefore extremely easy to identify with. However, he notices that the music starts to fade before the "hazy" voice of a starman, presumably Ziggy Stardust himself, begins communicating with him, borne on the airwaves and through his speakers. Four of the six lines of the verse end with a very catchy technique whereby the final syllable is repeated two further times: "low-ow-ow," "radio-o-o," "fa-a-ade," and "ph-a-ase" in a simulation of echoes. This quickly establishes itself as an important hook, while in addition providing an aural inference of distance and cavernousness consistent with a voice traveling across the vast distances of space. A highly distinctive and imaginative linkage between verse and chorus then follows, with the instruments in unison playing long, successive, descending chords that sustain for a full bar each, while over the top of this a synthesizer stabs rapid single staccato notes that resemble Morse code, with the message then immediately repeated: *ta-ta ta-ta ta-ta ta-ta taa taa, ta-ta ta-ta ta-ta ta-ta taa taa*. It is as if Ziggy Stardust is again attempting to communicate with Earth's inhabitants.

The chorus then starts with an emphatic harmonic and rhythmic statement whereby, preceded by the two set-up words, "There's a," the first syllable of the song title, "Star–," is timed to fall with the most emphatic emphasis possible on beat one of the chorus, pitched equally emphatically in a harmonic sense upon the root note of a chord in F major, the home key of the song. Further, in a melodic trick that Bowie has frequently acknowledged borrowing from "Somewhere over the

Rainbow," from the 1939 movie *The Wizard of Oz*, he splits the two syllables of the word by assigning each a different pitch, soaring up a full octave to sing the second syllable, "–man." It is a simple and enormously effective piece of word-painting, drawing the mind's eye of the listener heavenward to precisely where "a starman waiting in the sky" would be. In addition, the sound of a string section swirls ever upward during the chorus, further supporting the lyrical content. Through the words of the unnamed protagonist with whom Ziggy communicated in verse one, the chorus lyrics go on to reveal that, while the extraterrestrial visitor would like to physically land on Earth, he is afraid that the experience might be too much for the human population to comprehend. Here Bowie utilizes an expression drawn from the sixties counterculture, suggesting that landing might "blow our minds." He also makes it clear in this relayed communication that it is the children of Earth who are the focus of interest rather than the adults. As if to demonstrate his mastery of a musical language able to be understood by, and specifically pertaining to, this young section of the populace, when the chorus concludes a new instrumental section comes in, wherein the electric guitar of Mick Ronson plays a simple melody, accompanied by handclaps accentuating the second and fourth beats of each bar as if it were a schoolyard sing-along.

In verse two the song's protagonist excitedly phones his friend: "I had to phone someone so I picked on you." (You will never be able to listen to this line without remembering that it was at this precise moment on *Top of the Pops* that Bowie pointed straight at you as you sat on the couch in your living room.) Finding out that his friend heard Ziggy's message too, the singer suggests that the starman might try to communicate through the televison set next, specifically, "on channel two."

In the latter half of verse two, Ziggy becomes more than just a hazy disembodied voice on the airwaves as his light becomes visible out the window, causing the excited youths to speculate that "if we can sparkle" brightly enough, Ziggy may actually land that very night. This line has a quintessential glam rock quality to it, with glam rock fashion being so in vogue at the time and encompassing a plethora of sparkling fabrics and accessories, sequins and glitter.

At the conclusion of verse two, the Morse code signals again usher in the chorus, which is repeated. Subsequently, the sing-along section also returns, extended this time, before fading out to end the song. Further bearing out the threefold reference to children made in the chorus, on this final occasion the electric guitar surrenders the melody to Bowie, who sings a "la la la" passage similar in style to what one might have heard at the time in songs popular with children, such as, for instance, "Hot Love" by T. Rex, with its similar "la la la" section at its conclusion. (NB: In the Ziggy Stardust live concerts, during "Starman" Bowie would make this association more overt by name-dropping the song "Get It On"—a number-one UK hit from 1971 by T. Rex—in the first verse.)

As well as being the crucial hit single that engendered such widespread interest in the *Ziggy Stardust* album, "Starman" is a vital song to the album's conceptuality. You and the rest of the younger brothers and sisters of the countercultural generation had watched the space race unfold throughout your childhoods during the 1960s, as the Americans and Russians repeatedly sent men into space, edging closer to the ultimate goal of putting a man on the moon. Children of this momentous era were drawn repeatedly to wondering whether there might not be other beings, aliens, *starmen*, already up there. "Starman" therefore brought to life a universal fantasy. But the song's impact went even beyond that. With its conspiratorial "don't tell your papa," the repeated appeal in the chorus to "the children," and allied associations to the sound and look of glam rock, the song created a separatist, generational rallying call, as the existence of Ziggy Stardust was a secret that only kids were invited to share in. Young fans of David Bowie circa 1972 felt keenly this sense of being a part of an exclusive, new, and supremely exciting "in crowd." Disinterested in riding on the worn-out coattails of the 1960s with its tired sycophants and equally tired soundtrack, an exciting new artist who looked, acted, and sounded different from anything that had gone before—a pop-cultural package tailor-made for you and your friends *only*—was just exactly what you desired more than anything. David Bowie was sexily cool and instantly made obsolete everything around him in the world of pop music.

The fifth and concluding track on side one is "It Ain't Easy." The only song on the album not written by Bowie, it was penned instead by little-known American songwriter Ron Davies. While it is frequently considered one of the lesser moments on the album, the lyrics seem relatively consistent with one of the album's central themes, that of personal transformation. This is perhaps clearest in the opening lines with their daydreaming imagery: "When you climb to the top of the mountain—look out over the sea. Think about the places perhaps, where a young man could be." A futuristic synthesizer blip is the first sound heard in the song, although, echoing and fading away to nothing, it is not heard again.

Side two begins with the piano ballad "Lady Stardust." Again tapping into the aesthetic of glam rock, here the style's playful disruption of gender signification is at the fore, as "people stared at the makeup on his face." Later, the wrong pronoun is provocatively used when Bowie sings of the themes addressed by Lady Stardust: "Lady Stardust sang *his* songs of darkness and dismay."

While having no obvious role in forwarding the *Ziggy Stardust* narrative, the song is aligned to the wider context of the album through its theme of transformation, by "gender-bending," as the androgynous aspect of glam rock costuming and fashion was termed at the time. Bowie had Marc Bolan in mind as the subject of this song, and an earlier demo recording of "Lady Stardust" was titled "He Was Alright," with the alternative title "A Song for Marc." On occasion, in concert, a photograph of Bolan was projected above the stage during the song. Clearly, then, "Lady Stardust" plays a significant role in solidifying the album's glam-esque concept of personal transformation and star construction.

The next song, "Star," exemplifies the foundational reinventive ethos of glam rock: the promise of deliverance from conformity, oppression, and the daily humdrum through personal reconstruction, thereby elevating oneself from being one of the masses to the exalted and rarified heights of a sparkling glam rock star. To what is easily the fastest tempo of the album thus far, the song's unnamed subject begins by musing upon the failed efforts of his friends to transcend the environment into which they were born: Tony by joining the army, and Rudi by staying at home and doing nothing. This is a situation the song's subject intends to avoid by transforming himself into a star. "I could play the wild mutation as a rock 'n' roll star," he jubilantly claims. There is no suggestion that he will become a real, bona fide rock star, or indeed that such a thing is even necessary. Rather, he would be content to "send my photograph to my honey, and . . . c'mon like a regular superstar." "Star," then, is a pivotal track in that it holds a mirror up to Bowie's own methodology. With telling candidness he effectively says, "Ziggy Stardust is me, David Bowie, *pretending* to be a rock 'n' roll star—and you can do it too!" With the benefit of hindsight, wasn't this notion of playacting exactly the indefinable quality that you'd seen on your TV screen when Bowie played "Starman" on *Top of the Pops*? Remember how the expression on his face—especially at the start of the song—had been one of inexplicable amusement/bemusement, setting him apart from the many other performers you'd seen come and go on the show? The norm on *Top of the Pops* was to emphatically present one's star credentials, but hadn't Bowie distanced himself from all that? Hadn't he "come on like a regular superstar"? He'd as good as given you a nod and a wink. And if Bowie could do it—and it was very clear, given the fact that his name was today on everyone's lips, that it *could* be done; that you could fake it till you made it—then couldn't you, perhaps, give it a try too? Small wonder then that you and your friends, from this point onward in your lives, had a new respect for the power of image and of fantasy, and for the paramount importance of not surrendering your dreams, no matter what. David Bowie was living proof that you didn't have to just accept what life may have handed you. You could design and construct your own super-charged version of yourself. You would never have learned such a thing at school or from your parents. Bowie was a living testament to the fact that life really could imitate art, as before your very eyes he was becoming a real rock star through pretending to be one. Magic!

With the up-tempo "Star" critiquing the notion of stardom, the following song, "Hang on to Yourself," then explores the temptations that come with rock stardom. Most specifically, it concerns the traditional rock-star perk of gratuitous sex with groupies, hardly a topic not of interest to you, with your teenage years beckoning and testosterone flowing through your veins. "She wants my honey not my money she's a funky thigh collector," sings Bowie in the first verse. "If you think we're gonna make it you better hang on to yourself," he warns in the chorus, the frenetic tempo barely under control and underscoring the likely difficulty of himself and the Spiders from Mars being able to hold things together as their fame grows.

The title track, "Ziggy Stardust," follows immediately. It is at this point on the album that we hear Ziggy has been destroyed by his fame—the fall following the rise as foretold in the album title. The song begins with a magnificent chordal fanfare figure on electric guitar and, although moderately paced, the track is dense and emotive, with Bowie singing high in his register and evincing strain, particularly in the chorus, in keeping with the subject matter. Written from the perspective of a jealous band member witnessing the destructive effects of Ziggy's all-consuming ego, the lyrics document the rift that has developed between the star and his backing musicians, because Ziggy "made it too far," becoming "the special man, then we were Ziggy's band." Accused of "making love with his ego," Ziggy has overstepped the boundaries and been killed by the adulation of the very children he sought to lead. The dream of Earth's salvation by the messianic alien rock star is now over, the Spiders from Mars disillusioned and disbanded, their leader thrown irrevocably off his mission by overindulgence in the seductions of fame. The triumphant and subsequently tragic extremities of his failed quest are summarized in the two-word descriptor of the hero as a "leper messiah," with "messiah" representing the very essence of one who promises salvation and "leper" undercutting it to invoke the lowest possible level of societal hierarchy. That the song is bookended by a summative statement couched in the past tense is proof of Ziggy's demise. Rather than *playing* guitar, "Ziggy *played* guitar."

The following track, "Suffragette City," is problematic for anyone determined that Bowie's concept should follow the narrative convention of chronology. Despite what we learned of the demise of the star and his band in the preceding track, here Ziggy Stardust is found fit and well and fully indulging once again in the sexual benefits of stardom. "Suffragette City" is the most celebratory, straight-out rocker on the album, and the only hint of trouble exists in the line "my work's down the drain," due to his obsession with "this mellow-thighed chick." A less than convincing argument could be made that here we find Ziggy indulging in sexual solace in order to assuage his failure, but given the extremely high-spirited nature of the song, this is clutching at straws in order to forcibly impose a narrative flow that simply doesn't exist at this point. "Suffragette City" would have made far more narrative sense had it come before "Ziggy Stardust." Nevertheless, with its theme of rock 'n' roll excess befitting the rock 'n' roll lifestyle, the song makes thematic sense within the album overall. "Droogie don't crash here," sings Bowie, in a clear reference to Stanley Kubrick's violent, highly controversial 1971 movie, *A Clockwork Orange*, the protagonists of which were called droogs. This introduces to the song an element of danger-by-association.

The final track on the album is "Rock 'n' Roll Suicide," during which Ziggy's fall from grace is completed, and the listener finds out what has become of the would-be hero. Reverting to the same 6/8 time signature as the opening "Five Years," and thereby providing a sense of closure, an unnamed observer describes Ziggy's aimless stumble through the city streets as dawn arrives: "Chev brakes are snarling as you stumble across the road, but the day breaks instead so you hurry home." Burned out, alone, probably dangerously coked out and completely alienated, he is the epitome of the washed-up rock star. Despite this graphic depiction of the failed hero, however, the lengthy coda takes on a surprisingly positive, empathetic air: "Give me your hands 'cause you're wonderful . . . Oh give me your hands."

And there it is. The needle lifts from the vinyl and the arm withdraws, settling back into its cradle with a familiar clunk. You've just heard the most definitive work of Bowie's career up to this point. The promise you gleaned from seeing and hearing him perform "Starman" on *Top of the Pops* has been borne out in the fullness of the album that spawned it. The album might not always have been logical in terms of the flow of its story line, but Ziggy Stardust, androgynous alien glam rock superstar, has undeniably risen and fallen as promised. Certainly, the album is bookended by songs that neatly frame the work, with "Five Years" being a most effective, almost filmic scene-setter, and "Rock 'n' Roll Suicide" providing a clear conclusion. While you've gleaned some semblance of narrative flow at times, the album is clearly more conceptual in terms of its commononality of lyric themes than in the order in which the events have unfolded.

The front cover, which you've been perusing with varying degrees of intrigue throughout the thirty-eight minutes and thirty-seven seconds of the album's passing, now warrants closer attention. Given what you have now heard, Bowie looks every bit Ziggy Stardust on the front, a starman who has beamed down from his spaceship to a nondescript urban-industrial street somewhere in the middle of London. That the location is London is clear because one of the cardboard boxes at the front right of the picture bears the handwritten words "L. I. CO. LONDON No. 2003." While the writing confirms where Ziggy has landed, "2003" also subtly suggests a date thirty-one years in the future. Bowie/Ziggy's physical stance is particularly supportive of the album's story line. With his head held high, his electric guitar held casually at his side, and his left leg raised, his presentation is recognizably that of a heroic figure. Traditionally, statues of famous military figures throughout the world are posed in a comparable stance, with the primary tool of their trade, usually a sword or gun, at their side, their head facing forward and held erect and their expression serious and unsmiling, with one foot before the other as if stepping into a new frontier. Explorers too are pictured like this, with perhaps a rolled-up map or a staff at their side in lieu of a weapon. As a starman, Ziggy's primary frontier is clearly Earth; however, his small size within the frame and the manner in which the drab urban scene surrounds and dominates him ensure the picture has a highly alienating quality, with the city itself posing a challenge of its own. Urban alienation—the notion that a large industrial city can present a daunting threat to the well-being of the people that live in it—can readily be observed. With the dark, inhospitable sky above, the reflective shine of recent rainfall upon the concrete footpath, and the bright light of the neon sign above him, the image bears close resemblance to a film noir set, a genre of film that has urban alienation at its core. Exacerbating this impression, the photograph is hand-tinted, with over-brightening of parts of the scene, a technique frequently used in film noir posters. Barbara Mennel suggests of such films that "lonely characters in empty, urban spaces evoke a sense of urban alienation. The city is usually shown at night and in the rain."[1] And Andrew Spicer confirms, "Film noir's iconography consists of images of the dark, night-time city, its streets damp with rain which reflects the flashing neon signs."[2] During the hours of darkness, city streets change in nature, from the domain of daytime workers to sites of leisure and entertainment, rich with the potential for crime and deviance, for furtive, under-cover-of-darkness activities. Ziggy faces the potential for such dangers in this image, and, as alluded to earlier, there exists a strong parallel with Stanley Kubrick's movie *A Clockwork Orange* from the previous year: the notorious, violent critique of urban alienation, set in future London. This followed hot on the heels of his previous work, *2001: A Space Odyssey*, which was influential upon Bowie when he was writing his breakthrough song "Space Oddity," as he has said: "For me and several of my friends, the seventies were the start of the twenty-first century. It was Kubrick's doing on the whole. With the release of two magnificent films, *2001* and *A Clockwork Orange*, within a short period, he pulled together all the unarticulated loose ends of the past five years into a desire of unstoppable momentum."[3]

Flipping the album cover over, the rear picture of Bowie in a phone box contains its own popular-culture connotations, with an instant connection to the *Doctor Who* television series that was at its peak of popularity during the 1970s. The Doctor's means of transport, the TARDIS, was surely science fiction's strangest-ever spacecraft, being a police phone box notorious for its unreliability and frequent habit of setting down in the most unlikely and inhospitable locations. Such space transport was light-years away from the sleek, state-of-the-art starship the USS *Enterprise*, of rival US science fiction series *Star Trek*. At the time of *Ziggy Stardust*, the incumbent actor playing the Doctor was John Pertwee, who introduced a camp irony to the role. The picture of Bowie posed in a phone box, his left arm raised and right hand campily positioned on his hip, tapped effortlessly, whether intentionally or not, into this peculiarly British experience.

Much has been written about the *Ziggy Stardust* album from the time it came out until today. It is the most picked-over of all Bowie's work, with numerous critiques to be found in magazines, books, biographies, academic journals, film documentaries, Internet fan sites, and many other forums. Debates have raged as to how cohesive the concept of the album is, how much of that concept Bowie actually intended, and whether too much has been read into the work by commentators overreaching themselves to find meaning where there may have only existed happenstance. But such brow-furrowing misses the point. There can be no absolute, single "right" reading of the album. If somebody sees a clear narrative spine that runs through the work, then that is the correct reading for them, whereas if someone else sees the work as a group of songs with little narrative flow that are nevertheless bound by the existence of thematic commonalities, then that too is correct. And just what Bowie intended or not is immaterial because, once a work of art is put in the public domain, the artist relinquishes control over its reception and consumers are free to make of it what they will. Rather, the album's strength is that it demands that the listener think. Bowie has said, "All I try to do in my writing is assemble points that interest me and puzzle through it and that becomes a song and other people who listen to that song must take what they can from it and see if information that they've assembled fits in with anything I've assembled."[4]

Before we leave discussion of the album that made David Bowie, it is important to consider *Ziggy Stardust* within the wider context of glam rock: the popular-music style within which Bowie was, quite rightly, considered to be the preeminent artist, surpassing in both commercial and critical senses even his friend, rival, and oft-held originator of glam, Marc Bolan, of T. Rex fame. Glam was widely considered to be a simple, escapist style of music packaged for young teens and preteens, and this is almost certainly true for the majority of the main progenitors, including Gary Glitter, Slade, Sweet, Alvin Stardust, Suzi Quatro, etc., and even T. Rex. Glam was based upon short, catchy pop songs written about nothing in particular but containing superb hooks. Absolutely crucial to glam rock was the visual means of selling the music. Image was of utmost importance. Certainly Bowie presented a bona fide glam rock image—the most glam of them all, arguably. And his songs on the *Ziggy Stardust* album frequently adhered to glam rock song-writing convention in their short, hook-based, pop catchiness. In terms of theme, however, Bowie did not write about nothing in particular. On the contrary, as *Ziggy Stardust* attested, he wrote songs that were focused, perceptual, and often concerned with weighty issues outside the traditional domain of glam rockers. Renowned cultural theorist Dick Hebdige has suggested that Bowie's "meta-message was escape—from class, from sex, from personality, from obvious commitment—into a fantasy past (Isherwood's Berlin peopled by a ghostly cast of doomed bohemians) or a science-fiction future."[5] However, such an appraisal does Bowie a disservice. Gary Glitter might have invited simple escapism, but Bowie's message went far deeper, requiring that his young listeners confront issues, including the biggest of all—apocalypse—at the same time as they found comfort and self-empowerment in the proffered notion of reinvention of the self and transcendence of one's environment and social station. Glam rock, in Bowie's hands, acknowledged such fear while offering a means of coping with it at the same time.

Finally, with Bowie and his young fans the natural successors to the sixties countercultural generation, and their embracing of artifice and fantasy so antithetical to that previous generation, it is tempting to read into the rags-to-riches-to-rags story of Ziggy Stardust an analogy for the failure of rock 'n' roll to lead a new world order, as had seemingly appeared possible to the idealistic hippies of the late sixties. By the time of the release of Bowie's career-making album, Janis Joplin, Jim Morrison, and Jimi Hendrix—the triple-J flag-bearers of a generation's hopes and dreams—were all dead, while the indisputable gods of the era, the Beatles, were disbanded and dysfunctional. Like Ziggy, the sixties had risen and fallen. But in Bowie's case, he was only *playing* "the wild mutation as a rock 'n' roll star." Ziggy's demise was not Bowie's demise. Indeed, he was just getting going.

2

THE ACTOR EMERGES

Hunky Dory, 1971

As the needle settles into the groove of your shiny new copy of *Hunky Dory*, purchased just minutes ago on your way home from school thanks to an advance of your pocket money after much groveling to your mum and dad, your expectations of the next three-quarters of an hour or so are very high indeed. It is less than a week since you watched "Starman" on TV, purchased the *Ziggy Stardust* album, and felt a quantum shift occur in your world. *Ziggy* now leans up against the left speaker of your stereo system, taking pride of place at the front of your small but rapidly growing album collection. Tucked in behind it are *Electric Warrior* and *Bolan Boogie* from T. Rex, the self-titled debut album by Roxy Music, Elton John's *Honky Château*, Gary Glitter's *Glitter*, and Rod Stewart's *Every Picture Tells a Story*. Each record thrilled you when you first got it, and you still play each of them often. But nothing has ever hit you as hard as *Ziggy Stardust* did. It was as if David Bowie had materialized before you, placed his hands upon your shoulders, looked you straight in the eye, and said, "I'm writing about *you*." And so, atremble with the thrill of anticipation, what delights might *Ziggy Stardust*'s predecessor, *Hunky Dory*, now deliver?

HUNKY DORY, 1971

> With his affection for using intriguing and unusual themes in musical settings that most rock "artists" would dismiss with a quick fart as old-fashioned and uncool, he's definitely an original, is David Bowie, and as such will one day make an album that will induce us homo superior elitist rock critics to race about like a chicken with its head lopped off. . . . Until that time, *Hunky Dory* will suffice hunky-dorily. —John Mendelsohn, *Rolling Stone*, January 1972

> David Bowie is a million different people and each one is a bit more lovely than the one before. But for Christ's sake don't think he's a gimmick or a hype! Instead, enjoy him as he is; a surreal cartoon character brought to life for us all to enjoy. . . . It's very possible that this will be the most important album from an emerging artist in 1972, because he's not following trends—he's setting them. —Danny Holloway, *New Musical Express*, January 1972

Side One	Side Two
1. Changes	1. Fill Your Heart (Rose/Williams)
2. Oh You Pretty Things	2. Andy Warhol
3. Eight Line Poem	3. Song for Bob Dylan
4. Life on Mars	4. Queen Bitch
5. Kooks	5. The Bewlay Brothers
6. Quicksand	

The first track, "Changes," begins softly in almost stately fashion, with four bars of slowly ascending piano and lush, expansive strings that usher in the rest of the band. With a quiet "oh yeah" from Bowie, the band then enters together, playing a jaunty five-bar call-and-response sequence with the saxophone and piano swapping lead duties bar by bar. At the beginning of verse one, the driving rhythm drops away with the exit of the drums and the backing once again reverts to the far more sparse sonic territory of the opening, again dominated by piano and strings. "I still don't know what I was waiting for," begins Bowie in contemplative confession. As the verse progresses you increasingly relate to his quiet disclosure because his words artfully sum up a truism of your youth. Isn't it one of the inevitable conditions of one's early years and adolescence that you're always in a state of high impatience as you wait to grow older/wiser/bigger—all manner of things that you are not *yet*—so that you might step through a door and gain access to the myriad things that kids who are more mature than you, or adults, are evidently free to do? Always looking forward and upward, feeling marginalized by your age/size/social status as a "kid," it's almost impossible to be content with being in the now when you are so shackled. And yet "every time I thought I'd got it made it seemed the taste was not so sweet." That rings true as well, doesn't it, because every time you've actually reached one of those sought-after milestones that you have long imagined will make life so much better, the reality has not matched the dream. By the end of verse one, Bowie has reached even further into universal youth psyche in exploring the notion of feeling false, candidly referring to himself as a faker. Whether pretending we are tougher than we are, saying and/or doing things in order to be liked, or suppressing our real selves in order to fit in with peers or family, in our younger years, such protective cloaking rituals are commonplace.

In verse one, then, Bowie has summed up with startling perception deeply rooted feelings that you believed lay only within you and not in others. Listening to "Changes" you may have started to realize on some amorphous level that your bubbling, seething, ever-changing feeling of discontent and instability may in fact be a shared condition. Well, you certainly share it with David Bowie anyway. Otherwise, how could he possibly know?

The stuttered enunciation of the beginning of the title word at the beginning of the chorus, "Ch-ch-ch-ch," underpinned for emphasis by the reentry of the full band, paints quite literally the notion of multiple changes coming at you thick and fast. Immediately after, the step-by-step descending bass line draws the chorus forward, creating a sense of tonal inevitability, as if the changes Bowie sings of are absolutely unavoidable. You can't, or shouldn't, run from them, Bowie tells us, as these challenges are best dealt with by turning to face them head-on. He then employs a clever trick to support the two lines that conclude the chorus. While singing about the inevitable changes that time brings about, he alters the time signature of the song from 4/4 (four beats per bar) to 3/4. Further, he activates this change via a fleeting 2/4 bar inserted between the last bar of 4/4 and the first bar of 3/4, thereby creating three consecutive bars of changed time: 4/4, 2/4, 3/4. Tongue in cheek, Bowie's musical joke is that just as time may change him, he, in turn, *may* change time.

On the *Ziggy Stardust* album, Bowie revealed the starman's presence to the children of Earth but not to the adults. Here, in the earliest moments of *Hunky Dory*, we see clear evidence that this theme of championing youth existed before *Ziggy Stardust*. During verse two he emphatically turns his attention to advocating for your generation, imploring your elders not to spit on you and your peers as you try to change the world you live in. In the chorus that follows, his tone toward the previous generation turns decidedly accusatory, suggesting that the reason things need to be changed at all is due to the mess they have created, which has, to their shame, left the young up to their necks in trouble. The message is spelled out very clearly that, rather than simply being told to "grow up" (a standard adult response to youth angst), the young should be allowed to get on with the task of changing things because they are completely aware of their situation and of what needs to be done to rectify it.

The generational divide is here being brought to life with considerable sophistication in opposition to any sort of brash revisitation of the Who's chain-rattling "Talking 'bout My Generation," because that was last decade's news perpetrated by those who are now by dint of the passage of time part of the problem. Indeed, Bowie even issues a warning for their kind. "Look out you rock 'n' rollers," he cautions, gently poking fun at the established sixties-era rock stars while clearly distancing himself from them in favor of siding with the children of the seventies. A year later, in September 1972, Marc Bolan and T. Rex would visit similar generationally divisive territory in the anthemic UK number-two hit single "Children of the Revolution," a phrase that Bowie must have wished he'd thought of first. "You won't fool the children of the revolution," sang Marc in total accord with the sentiment of "Changes."

"Changes" is insightful and empathetic, like nothing else you have heard. Couched in beautiful and sophisticated musical language in both song writing and instrumentation, and quite different from the brash electric attack of *Ziggy Stardust*, "Changes" is not what you were expecting at the beginning of *Hunky Dory*, and yet you are far from disappointed. It is not lost upon you that an intelligent, talented, and controversial rock artist is taking you, a kid, and your kind seriously, and not talking down to you. Just as *Ziggy Stardust* did, "Changes" demands of you that you think. It is not a mere musical salve. The good-time escapism of "Come on! Come on!" by Gary Glitter is all very well, and T. Rex's "Hot Love" will always have a place in your heart as the song that hooked you into music in the first place, but what Bowie is doing is clearly in a different league.

In youth, change is a constant and normal state of being, and here, in the very first song of *Hunky Dory*, David Bowie has related to you and your young peers on a profound, personal, intellectual level. "Pretty soon now, you're gonna get older," he warns us, but it's all OK because, just as he assured us in the final lyrics of the *Ziggy Stardust* album, we are not alone. In "Changes," Bowie delivers to his fans a potent feeling of belonging, introducing the concept that their deeply felt feelings of generational alienation actually bond them to others of their ilk rather than separating them.

The conclusion of the track is given over to the emotive, soft, contemplative musings of a solo saxophone, freed up from the limitations of playing with other instruments and timing constraints. The melody is like a trail of abstract thoughts drifting slowly upward into the ether to where answers may lie. You look at the cover at this point, noticing that Bowie's image encapsulates exactly such deep, search-for-enlightenment thought processes. His face is lifted heavenward as if seeking divine inspiration, his eyes focused on something far beyond physical reach while his hands cradle his head absent-mindedly, the way we might unconsciously touch our own heads or cradle our chins in the act of deep contemplation. And didn't the opening bars of the album, too, suggest exactly this, with their slow but deliberate upward momentum? Similarly, while the verses began low in Bowie's vocal register as he spoke of his doubts and fears, the melody moved higher in the latter half of these sections before reaching its highest point of all in the no longer doubting, but triumphant and empowering chorus.

"Changes" is the most personal and reflective song you have ever heard from Bowie, but it is not just about him. It contains universal truth and is just as much about you. You are kindred spirits, you and he.

If the first song on *Hunky Dory* felt like a highly personal exchange between Bowie and his young audience, the second, "Oh You Pretty Things," extends the notion further. The instrumentation used for the introduction and throughout the first two verses is solo piano, presented with minimal reverb and sounding very close, as if being played by someone right there, just across the room. Similarly, Bowie's vocals when they enter have minimal reverb, achieving the same effect. It's hard to tell from the first two verses, presented back to back as they are with no chorus in between, just what the song is about, although the imagery is rich with talk of nightmares, strangers, and "the Golden Ones," whoever they might be. Later you may learn that Bowie's inspiration for the song came from the work of Friedrich Nietzsche, the German philosopher, critic, composer, and poet. Nevertheless, even without this level of cognizance, there are touches of imagery in these early verses that are consistent with the celestial and messianic imagery of *Ziggy Stardust*, for instance in the description of the sky cracking open and a hand reaching down.

Through the first two verses the harmony has been unswervingly busy underneath Bowie's melody, with the chords changing at least twice during every bar. Sometimes there have been as many as four chords, one for each beat of the bar in the song's 4/4 time signature. Even the song's tonic chord of G-flat major is never allowed to sustain for more than two beats at a time. However, in the final bar of verse two, at the point where Bowie warns that the strangers may be "here to *stay*," the harmony finally halts its continual, restless movement. Beneath the final word the G-flat chord is allowed to remain unchallenged for an unprecedented entire bar, literally staying put, while Bowie's melody note too hits the note of G-flat in an emphatic tonal statement. Along with the length of time allotted to this point in the song, the notion of remaining stationary is implicit because the tonic chord by its very nature allows no implication of imminent harmonic movement as we are already "at home." No other harmonic configuration—no other chord at Bowie's disposal—could have conveyed such a sense. But Bowie has not yet finished making his point. The next bar marks the start of the chorus and, although here the full band emphatically kicks into action at last to join the solo piano, significantly raising the intensity of the song, the harmony is still not permitted to progress: the G-flat chord is forced to linger on through the first two beats of the chorus, before finally being released to go elsewhere at beat three. Six beats of the same harmony have ensured that the strangers stay put, just as Bowie predicted, the music providing a quite literal underlining of the text.

As the chorus proceeds, Bowie once again emphatically revisits the theme of generational alienation by addressing the children with the same directness as in the opening song: "Oh you pretty things. Don't you know you're driving your mamas and papas insane?" To young glam rock fans such a concept could be instantly identified with, as they were indeed the pretty things of their day, transcendently groomed, dressed, and adorned in clear homage to their glittery heroes. Glam rock fashion was intensely challenging to many parents, particularly those worried about the implications of their sons' burgeoning interest in makeup and the wearing of fabrics and clothing items that were traditionally the domain of women. Is it not part of the rite of passage of all youth to challenge the morals, beliefs, and traditions of the generations that have gone before? This simple question, then, was Bowie's clearest rallying call yet to the youth. As was their wont, the kids were indeed driving their parents insane. In the concluding lines of the chorus, however, Bowie speaks of making way for "homo superior." Is this a further description of the coming generation of children, or might it be a reference to an as-yet-undefined new race of beings?

With the first chorus over, in verse three Bowie switches to directly addressing the parents of the children. He begins by turning a sense of alienation back upon the parents with the threat that their children are no longer their own: "Look out at your children—see their faces in golden rays. Don't kid yourself they belong to you, they're the start of the coming race." This clearly links back to the notion of the "homo superior" just mentioned in the chorus. And personally, don't you *feel* like you are indeed the start of a coming race, as different from your parents as chalk and cheese? Sure, you are their biological child, but you are so estranged from them in every way you might just as well be of a different race. Immediately, Bowie goes on to address again the theme expressed in the previous song, that the legacy the older generation will leave the young is a damaged, vulnerable Earth, here referring to the planet as "a bitch."

In verse three not only has it been made clear that the parents/adults must make way for the next generation to usurp them, but it seems these children are a new breed of superior human being completely unreliant upon those who spawned them, the homo sapiens, because these forerunners are no longer of any practical use and have wrought major harm upon Earth. While the Nietzschean concept of *Übermensch* (a superhuman—a new generation) as espoused in his book *Thus Spake Zarathustra* (1883–1885) was Bowie's subsequently acknowledged subject here, for Bowie's new generation of music fans, there was much to identify with and the song took on an anthemic quality. There had never before been youth quite like the glam rockers of the early 1970s. The pretty young things were unique and well they knew it. And Nietzschean or not, with the nuclear-weapon testing of the Cold War and the actual usage of these weapons of mass destruction during World War II, the idea that the previous generation(s) had damaged the planet and would indeed leave a scarred Earth as their legacy was seemingly entirely correct.

For many of Bowie's fans hearing *Hunky Dory* for the first time, listening to "Oh You Pretty Things" proved to be an unusual experience because six months earlier the song had been a number-twelve solo hit for Peter Noone of the band Herman's Hermits. While Bowie himself had played piano for Noone, the song had taken on a very different nature, being faster and more obviously pop-oriented, with handclaps, and so on, and little of the depth of Bowie's album version. Some of the words, too, had been altered in this sugar-coated treatment, and it is hard to reconcile the two songs, such is their vastly different rendering.

The third song of the album, "Eight Line Poem," is two and three-quarter minutes of unfathomable weirdness in three quite distinct sections. Repeating the pattern of the album thus far, the song begins with solo piano, but here the pulse is very slow and the piano lines fragmentary. Quickly joined by more fluid and melodic lead guitar lines, the two instruments hold a lengthy conversation as they interact. It is over a minute before Bowie's vocals join them, beginning with the impenetrable "tactful cactus by your window surveys the prairie of your room." This sets the tone for the mostly unfathomable lyrics to follow. The guitar drops out almost completely to leave Bowie alone and exposed with just the piano as he sings his eight lines, ending with "but the key to the city is in the sun that pins the branches to the sky." Perhaps Bowie is here opining that even in the man-made urban environs of the city, man is still reliant upon nature for survival—the claustrophobic image of him surrounded by the inner-city gloom on the front cover of the *Ziggy Stardust* album coming to mind—but this line, like all in this unusual song, is wide open to speculation and individual interpretation. It is Bowie requiring much work from his audience; perhaps even too much. As he finishes, the guitar rejoins the piano for the song's coda, comprising a revisitation, with subtle variances, of the beginning.

The simple solo piano chord that begins the fourth song, "Life on Mars," confirms that the instrumental timbre of *Hunky Dory* is very different from that of its successor, as has become increasingly clear with the passing of each track. With no electric rock ensemble at the core of the sound, such as was provided so convincingly by the Spiders from Mars, coupled with an obvious dominance of piano, this album finds Bowie in very different stylistic territory.

On first impression, the title of "Life on Mars" immediately locates listeners turned on to Bowie by "Starman" and the *Ziggy Stardust* album—notwithstanding the much earlier "Space Oddity"—in the very familiar thematic territory of space. However, from the first lyrics it is clear that the geographic location of the action is most decidedly on Earth. The mousy-haired girl about whom the song is written is placed in a succession of mundane situations of depressing urban boredom and/or conflict with which we can all too easily empathize, being the kind of events we either experience ourselves or, at the very least, hear about with regularity. We learn immediately that she has had a serious fight with her parents, the result of which is that her father has thrown her out while her mother yelled "No!" The theme of generational alienation has therefore been introduced once again as a foundational concern of Bowie's. Tellingly, the power imbalance lies in favor of the older generation or, at least, of her father, who has the authority to evict her from the family home. She is then stood up by her friend, from whom she would presumably have received solace, and subsequently goes to the cinema alone in order to find temporary escape from the stresses of her personal situation. But then the movie proves to be "a saddening bore, for she's lived it ten times or more." Stereotypical Hollywood-type film scenarios are then described, like "sailors fighting in the dance hall" or a scene from an unnamed Western where a lawman is observed "beating up the wrong guy." Bowie depicts humankind as predictable, unenlightened, and unimaginative, in reality but also even in the fantasies created for our own entertainment on the movie screen. "Oh man, look at those cavemen go," he observes, and you can almost see the accompanying shake of his head as he muses on the virtual freak show that modern life has become. The essence of the song is easy to distill: Is this *really* all there is? Surely, there *must* be more! There's a continuation of the theme of "Oh You Pretty Things" to be discerned here as well, because if this is really all homo sapiens can aspire to, then it is time indeed to step aside for the "homo superior."

In the title line of the song Bowie employs the same trick he used in "Starman" on *Ziggy Stardust*, his voice soaring up a full octave on the word "Mars" and thereby once again creating an implication of movement through the pitching of his melody, drawing the listener heavenward. The notion is very much of its time as, with the question of life on the moon having been so recently answered, mankind had to determine to look farther afield in the quest to find out if we are alone in the universe.

The following song, "Kooks," was written for Bowie's recently born son, Zowie, and dedicated as such by the words "For small Z," handwritten next to the track's listing on the rear cover. Acoustic guitar, trumpet, and barrelhouse piano provide almost a front-parlor family-sing-along setting while, as befitting a children's song, the lyrics are the most direct of anything encountered on the album thus far, with no obfuscation or ambiguity of any kind and the mood throughout being celebratory and lighthearted. While "Oh You Pretty Things" presented a typical generational divide between parents and children, here Bowie offers a picture of an alternative, far more positive kind of relationship. Nevertheless, clearly positioning himself and his wife, Angie, as outcasts, as freaks who don't fit in with regular society, he jokingly forewarns his new son of what he might expect if he stays with his parents, going so far as to buy him "a book of rules on what to say to people when they pick on you. 'Cause if you stay with us you're gonna be pretty kooky too." Such is the solidarity between parent and child that Bowie assures him that, should he ever have to go to school—inferring that he won't *make* him do so because, as he clearly states, school messed him up because he didn't fit in—if the homework gets him down, "we'll throw it on the fire and take the car downtown." The possibility of being picked on for being different is further tackled when Zowie is warned to stay away from bullies, ostensibly because his father is himself no good at standing up to their ilk. Although lighthearted and consciously child-like in its sing-along melody and crystal-clear language, the song still serves to strengthen underlying issues of alienation and otherness, ensuring that these factors that are fast becoming evident as Bowie cornerstones remain at the fore.

The song that follows to end side one could not be more of a contrast. "Quicksand" completely dispenses with the jaunty innocence of "Kooks," painting a picture of a man consumed with and tortured by deeply existential questions that cause him to drown in his own thoughts. Amid the dilemma of being "torn between the light and dark" and fearful of which direction he might take, Bowie name-drops historical figures both notorious and famous, such as Aleister Crowley, Winston Churchill, and Heinrich Himmler. He rails against his own inadequacy to fathom the big questions, derides the ability of religious "bullshit faith" to provide answers, and, taking up again the topic of mankind's obsolescence such as was expressed earlier in the album, despairs at being "tethered to the logic of homo sapien." The chorus conveys the belief that someday man *will* understand the mysteries of the universe, but that this will only transpire at the very end, when "knowledge comes with death's release." Beginning with acoustic guitar but building steadily in intensity, the song progresses to become a dense amalgam of rock instruments, piano, and strings, and at over seven minutes might well be considered a progressive-rock track, a stylistic world away from anything on *Ziggy Stardust* or elsewhere on *Hunky Dory*.

Just as "Quicksand" immediately obliterated the jaunty vibe of "Kooks," the opening song of side two, "Fill Your Heart," just as quickly dispenses with the overwhelming cerebral calisthenics and underlying desperation created by "Quicksand." The only non-original track on the album, the up-tempo, unerringly cheerful song, written by Americans Biff Rose and Paul Williams, is perfectly placed to directly address what has just preceded it. "Fear's just in your head . . . so forget your head and you'll be free," sings Bowie, and in what seems to be a nod to the Beatles and the countercultural generation's well-intentioned, naïve, yet—as time had come to show—fundamentally flawed notion that love was all one needed, Bowie goes on to suggest, "Love cleans the mind and makes it free!" The chorus melody ensures that the highest note Bowie sings is on the word "free," again arrived at via an octave leap from the previous word and literally a depiction of the singer being set free.

Via segue, the second track on side two, "Andy Warhol," finds Bowie paying homage to one of his heroes. After a playful false start where the pronunciation of Warhol's name is laughingly debated between Bowie and studio engineer Ken Scott, the song begins with an acoustic guitar

scale run over strummed acoustic guitar chords, and this simple, sonically spacious two-guitar acoustic flavor prevails throughout the track,
joined only at the end by flamenco-styled syncopated handclaps. Enthusiastic applause greets the song's finish. Several of his subject's well-
documented approaches to art and life are espoused, including the
notion that the key to discovering who people *really* are lies in an
appraisal of their surface rather than what lies within: "Dress my friends
up just for show—see them as they really are." Bowie applies the same
treatment to Warhol himself, reducing him to two dimensions and a
facsimile of real life when purporting, "Andy Warhol, silver screen—
can't tell them apart at all." Further, he suggests that Warhol might be
hung on Bowie's wall as a piece of art, encapsulating the widely held
idea (of which Warhol himself must have approved) that the artist was
himself as much a work of art as the paintings, films, and other media
he produced in his Factory.

Continuing on with acknowledging Bowie's heroes, "Andy Warhol"
gives way to "Song for Bob Dylan," a first-person address to the hero of
the sixties counterculture: "Oh hear this Robert Zimmerman—I wrote a
song for you." Adopting a Dylan-esque nasal delivery, Bowie initially
acknowledges his forebear's achievement of summarizing in song the
thoughts, desires, and attitudes of his generation, suggesting he "sat
behind a million pair of eyes and told them how they saw." Following
this, however, Bowie gives voice to his disillusionment with Dylan's
later work, clearly suggesting he has lost his voice-of-the-common-peo-
ple touch: "Then we lost your train of thought—the paintings are all
your own." A clear inference exists here, because if Bob Dylan is no
longer able to speak for youth then the way is clear for somebody else to
step in and do so. Bowie is also parodying an earlier event in popular-
music history, when, in 1962, Bob Dylan wrote a song to his own hero,
which began similarly with "Hey, hey, Woody Guthrie, I wrote you a
song."

The tributes to Bowie's heroes continue with the fourth song on side
two, the raw and edgy "Queen Bitch." This time it is an "in the style of"
song that stands out as very different from everything else on the album
courtesy of its unabashed electric aggression and complete lack of piano
or any kind of polite finesse. Dedicated on the rear cover to the Velvet
Underground, with the handwritten words "Some VU white light returned with thanks," Bowie's tribute to Lou Reed and company is so

close to the sound, song-writing style, and thematic territory of Warhol's Factory house band that it could well have been written by the famous/infamous heroes of the late-sixties New York underground scene themselves. In a tale of sordid street romance complete with curb cruisers, flamboyant queens, and sexual betrayal, as with the previous track Bowie again takes on some of the vocal mannerisms of his subject, here imitating the distinctive speak-singing style of Lou Reed. And yet the lyrics have a distinctively British flavor, with a highly contemporaneous glam rock sensibility in lines such as "She's so swishy in her satin and tat—in her frock coat and bipperty-bopperty hat." Listening to *Hunky Dory* after having experienced the *Ziggy Stardust* album, it is clear that "Queen Bitch," over all of the other songs, was the clearest portent of things to come.

Bowie writer Nicholas Pegg describes the final track on the album, "The Bewlay Brothers," as "the most cryptic, mysterious, unfathomable and downright frightening Bowie recording in existence."[1] Certainly the track is one that would baffle his audience, but while the task of identifying specific references and meanings within the lyrics may have proven beyond the majority of listeners, a general sense of alienation and otherness pervades the lyrics, thereby ensuring a sense of thematic cohesion with other examples on the album. The notion of the faker introduced in "Changes" appears again here, in "We were so turned on you thought we were fakers." The music style with which Bowie was increasingly being associated, glam rock, is obliquely noted in the reference to Max Factor makeup in the otherwise fairly incomprehensible line "the Factor Max that proved the fact is melted down."

The key to the lyrical content of the song comes when Bowie describes his brother lying on the rocks, speculating that "he could be dead he could be not." In interviews, he has admitted that the song is autobiographical and addresses his relationship with his brother, Terry. As Bowie puts it, "The Bewlay Brothers" was a "vaguely anecdotal piece about my feelings about myself and my brother." Musically complex, dark, and the complete antithesis of tracks such as "Kooks" and, well, anything else on *Hunky Dory*, "The Bewlay Brothers" almost defies adequate description in its overriding oddness.

With the arm of the turntable safely back in its cradle having completed its first full traverse of the album—the first of hundreds to come—you turn your attention back to *Hunky Dory*'s protective packaging. The thick black border at the edges of the cover lend the image a formal quality, while the lack of any words—remarkably there's no album title, no record company logo, and no artist name—contributes significantly to this impression of a formal portrait. The front cover screams *star* when you look upon the grainy, close-up picture of Bowie staring heavenward. But, rather than rock star, Bowie is presented as a movie star. His picture is highly reminiscent of publicity photographs and posters of early-twentieth-century silver-screen stars from the silent-movie age and the early talkies, famous actresses such as Greta Garbo, Lauren Bacall, Joan Crawford, and Marlene Dietrich. Now that you have heard the songs, the links between Bowie's image and the music contained on the album become clear. During "Quicksand," Bowie laments, "I'm living in a silent film," followed just a few lines later by "I'm the twisted name on Garbo's eyes." This follows hot on the heels of the scenario presented in "Life on Mars," in which "the girl with the mousy hair" seeks escape from the travails of her everyday life in her local movie theater, while elsewhere in the song the lyrics provide filmic glimpses of stereotypical scenes from Hollywood-style movies. In addition, and as previously noted, the silver screen is referenced literally in "Andy Warhol."

Hollywood actresses of the silver screen era presented themselves in highly stylized poses that were purposely pretentious and knowingly camp, adhering to a formula of loaded gestures that promoted the notion of ironic, idealized self-invention. Stardom, in their hands and in their day, was the presentation of a carefully constructed, purposely self-conscious identity incorporating a very high degree of symbolism. A clear link exists here with the foundational ethos of glam rock, most especially Bowie's version. The effect of such obvious construction was a quality of distance that suggested that while the star was physically present in all her glory in such images, at the same time she was spiritually, emotionally, and psychologically removed. Who could ever know what she was thinking deep inside, far beyond mere earthly concerns? Such a duality—the role so divorced from the person playing it—also came through in the acting style of such stars, a style that today would no doubt be considered overacting. Bowie might just as well have the back of his hand to his forehead in stylized "swoon" pose, such is his willing adoption of silver-screen acting conventions on the cover of his third album.

The picture has a high degree of artificiality that goes beyond Bowie's overtly theatrical pose, with the colors clearly hand-tinted rather than naturalistic, a feature noticeable particularly in the over-bright yellow coloring of his hair. This technique cleverly enhances the historical borrowing, as promotional postcards and posters of actresses and specific movies during the silver screen era were treated in this same way. Indeed, some of the movies themselves were similarly colorized during production, laboriously frame by frame.

The rear cover, however, shows a very different Bowie from that seen on the front. The image is once again grainy and indistinct but here the borderless black-and-white picture is informal, showing him far less obviously posed, dressed casually in mildly hippy-styled clothing with his long unkempt hair falling to his shoulders. The photograph is shot from low down, with Bowie looming tall as a result. His facial expression is serious, and he makes full eye contact with the viewer. Unlike the highly performative front-cover image, here Bowie is presented quite naturally. The suggestion of more emotional transparency on the rear cover, of open communication by the "real" David Bowie, is boosted greatly by the presence, content, and arrangement of the accompanying handwritten text—an untidy, inconsistent, but highly individualized scrawl that is shaped and contoured around his body. This taps into a centuries-held belief that handwriting "stands in" for an absent person; that a handwritten note or signature somehow carries in it an ongoing personal presence. One need only look at the value placed on autographs of famous people, or on books signed by authors, to verify this phenomenon. On the rear cover of *Hunky Dory*, Bowie makes personal contact with you in the best, most direct way he possibly can in a mass-produced work of art, by writing all details of his album in his own hand, including all of his mistakes and corrections. He even allows his writing to encroach upon his body, as if to suggest his words are drawn from his very being. Eliminating any suspicion that these might not be his own personal reflections and thoughts, he refers to himself repeatedly in the first person: "The musicians on my album are" or "Mick and I agree." In addition, he adds highly personalized dedications to some of the song titles, and also decorates some of his handwriting with, for instance, shadow lines on the words "produced" and "remixed."

The most telling moment of Bowie's personal communication on the rear of the jacket occurs when crediting Ken Scott as the producer and going on to refer to himself as "the actor" when acknowledging his own production contribution. These two words immediately bring your mind back to the front-cover image. It is Bowie's clearest, most blatant public announcement of his theatrical approach to being a rock star. For him, it is simply a role to be played.

Although *Hunky Dory* was released a mere six months before *Ziggy Stardust*, the expansive musical terrain it covers is very different from the electric guitar–based, raw rock 'n' roll of that career-establishing successor. The rapidity of such a stylistic shift is something that Bowie fans get to know only too well. We quickly learn that what might be heard on one album can never be relied upon as being indicative of what might precede or succeed it.

While still not the commercial success that Bowie, his management, and his new record company, RCA, were striving for upon its release— although the album would come to attain that status and reach number three on the UK album charts in the wake of the success of *Ziggy Stardust*—nevertheless *Hunky Dory* was a breakthrough album on several fronts. For the first time, Bowie's image, musical style, and lyrical themes melded into a largely seamless fusion that was right for his time. On the back of almost universally positive reviews, the album proved to be a powerful springboard for what was to come.

Hunky Dory might not have been what you expected as a brand-new David Bowie fan attracted by the charms of *Ziggy Stardust*, and yet it emphatically cemented your devotion further. To young and unsophisticated musical ears poised on the brink of teenage-hood and raised on color-by-numbers formulaic pop, bored with the sounds of the sixties, and completely uncomprehending of the algebraic pomposity of the in-vogue progressive rock, *Hunky Dory* was a revelation. Those who didn't "get" Bowie fell back all too quickly on accusations of gimmickry and hype. But while the sound of glam rock à la *Ziggy Stardust* and the offerings of T. Rex, Alice Cooper, et al., was not quite there, the underlying spirit of it was. In *Hunky Dory* the notion of self-betterment was an abiding theme. Ziggy's "I could make a transformation as a rock 'n' roll star" burned as brightly on *Hunky Dory* as ever. And, simply, the thematic depth of *Hunky Dory* exceeded anything you had experienced before. Who else would have dared criticize Bob Dylan and point an accusatory finger at the previous generation of "rock 'n' rollers"? Who else would have played with, poked fun at, and simultaneously raised his hat to Andy Warhol, or name-dropped Heinrich Himmler, Aleister Crowley, and Winston Churchill? And who else would have made reference to, and borrowed concepts from, Friedrich Nietzsche? In short, *Hunky Dory* inspired confidence in a new generation of popular-music fans—yourself included—that here was an artist of depth, quality, and new ideas. And most importantly of all, he was clearly a spokesperson for you and your kind.

3

MUSICAL BEGINNINGS

David Bowie, 1967

On June 1, the first day of summer in vibrant, colorful, Swinging London of 1967, twenty-year-old David Jones, aka David Bowie, must have awoken tremendously excited, and for good reason. On this day his self-titled debut album would go on sale, its fourteen tracks comprising the most emphatic artistic statement to date of a musical career barely out of first gear. It was recorded for his latest record label, Deram, and hopes were high that the disappointment of a string of unsuccessful single releases for no less than three previous labels would at last be laid to rest. The willingness with which successive record labels had been prepared to sign the unproven artist was testament to his obvious talent. And yet, lacking any sense of a clear direction or stylistic home and with his song-writing skills undeveloped and inconsistent, success by any tangible measure had proven frustratingly elusive. Still, past events had nevertheless propelled the artist as far as this debut album release, and perhaps *David Bowie* was to be the game changer: the vehicle that would launch the career he so fervently desired.

Throngs of highly excited music fans duly queued before the counters of record stores throughout London and beyond on that day. But it was not *David Bowie* that they gleefully plucked from the racks and off the shelves. The object of desire they clutched tightly and reverently to their chests as they awaited their turn at the ever-jangling tills was a very different title. June 1, 1967, was also the release date for *Sgt.*

Pepper's Lonely Hearts Club Band, the much-anticipated eighth studio album by the all-conquering Beatles. While *Sgt. Pepper's Lonely Hearts Club Band* would triumphantly cement its place in music history, spending twenty-seven weeks at the top of the UK album charts and fifteen weeks at the top of the US Billboard 200, *David Bowie* would disappear almost without a trace. For David Bowie, an artist who would himself go on to achieve Beatles-esque status as one of the greats of popular music, it was a highly inauspicious beginning.

Twenty years earlier, on January 8, 1947, the very same day that Elvis Presley turned twelve, Margaret and Haywood Jones (better known as Peggy and John) had celebrated David's birth in Brixton, South London. The Jones family household also included Peggy's first child, David's half brother, Terry Burns, who was ten years his senior. Although he moved south to the outer London suburb of Bromley in 1953, the young David would spend all of his childhood in the boroughs of England's capital city.

Music became a consuming passion very early on, with Elvis Presley the ultimate idol. Graduating from learning the recorder, he owned a record player and a guitar before reaching the age of ten, and with Britain's very own rock 'n' roll star Tommy Steele also firmly in his sights as a role model, he quickly gravitated toward forming friendships with similarly rock 'n' roll–fixated youths during his school years.

At Christmas 1961, John Jones gave his son a saxophone to encourage David's burgeoning interest in the instrument, the result of a growing fixation with Little Richard. Shortly afterward, and following the purchase of a more professional model, he commenced lessons with local jazz celebrity Ronnie Ross. Rapidly achieving a level of basic proficiency, by the middle of 1962 David became a member of the semiprofessional cover band the Konrads, fronted by his close friend George Underwood. While with the Konrads he would also take turns on lead vocals.

In 1964 the two friends formed their own rhythm and blues band, the King Bees, with David on lead vocals. Quickly coming to the attention of agent Leslie Conn, the band secured a deal with Decca to record a single, "Liza Jane," a song credited to Conn. Thus began the recording career of David Bowie, albeit still David Jones at this point, and named on the single as Davie Jones (the full band credit being "Davie Jones with the King Bees"). Despite generally positive reviews and an appearance on the television program *Ready Steady Go!* the song didn't sell well and failed to garner interest in the band, ultimately prompting David to consider joining another band, the Manish Boys. Similarly rhythm and blues oriented, David was duly welcomed into their lineup and for a short time persevered as a member of both bands before ultimately pulling out of the King Bees altogether when it became clear that "Liza Jane" would not be successful.

The beginning of 1965 saw the newly named Davie Jones and the Manish Boys record a debut single for Parlophone, a cover of the 1961 Bobby Bland hit, "I Pity the Fool." Of more historical significance, however, the B side featured David's own composition, "Take My Tip." This, then, was the first of his self-penned songs to ever be officially recorded and released. But before the record was pressed the Manish Boys objected to their singer's star billing on the record's label, and to David's dismay the release came out credited simply to "the Manish Boys." This event, coupled with other tensions within the band and a lack of gigs, created a difficult working environment. With sales of the single dismally failing to meet hopes and expectations, by mid-year David was set to move on again.

The Lower Third were a hard-hitting trio in the style of the Who, with a carefully constructed mod image. At this time they were seeking a front man and it was for that position that David successfully auditioned. This event marked something of a sea change in the budding artist's early career trajectory because, while ostensibly the Lower Third were no more visibly successful than his previous two bands, within this lineup he was clearly and undisputedly the kingpin. Not only were his lead vocals at the forefront of their sound but his song writing also quickly became a dominant feature of the band's set lists. When the Lower Third gained a contract to record a single for Parlophone, it was David's songs that featured on both the A and B sides of the release. "You've Got a Habit of Leaving" backed by "Baby Loves That Way" was released in August 1965 and, with a minor respelling of his first name, was emphatically credited to "Davy Jones and the Lower Third." The local *Kent Messenger* was enthusiastic in its review, boldly predicting, "It's a very catchy number and should reach the Top Thirty charts without any trouble at all." Ultimately, however, like its predecessors, it did no such thing. Nevertheless, particularly in terms of Bowie's development as a songwriter, this single must be seen as something of a landmark in his early development, and his confidence must have been significantly boosted as a result. The focus was clearly, in all facets, becoming centered on David rather than those with whom he performed.

It was at this point that he changed his name to David Bowie. He had come to the attention of manager Ralph Horton, and, in turn, Kenneth Pitt—for a time he was co-managed by both—and the change of name was devised in mutual agreement to avoid confusion with the up-and-coming star Davy Jones. Jones was at the time reaping much critical acclaim on Broadway as the Artful Dodger in Lionel Bart's musical *Oliver!* and soon after would go on to international stardom as lead singer of the Monkees.

As the newly titled David Bowie and the Lower Third, the band released another single, "Can't Help Thinking about Me," on Pye Records, backed by "And I Say to Myself." When this release also failed to trouble the charts, all-too-familiar tensions began to surface within the band, as the ever-growing attention being paid to the lead singer did not sit well with the other members, a situation further inflamed by media and venues alike at times referring to the act as simply David Bowie. At the end of January 1966, events came to a head and the band acrimoniously parted company with their singer. Bowie and his management immediately set out to handpick musicians that would serve unequivocally as a support vehicle for the main attraction. A new band, the Buzz, quickly took shape.

Despite the lack of success of "Can't Help Thinking about Me," Pye's interest remained intact and quickly David Bowie and the Buzz recorded their first single, "Do Anything You Say," along with "Good Morning Girl." This also did not fire in the charts, and within three months the band returned to the studio to record a new song, "I Dig Everything." However, the recording session was aborted due to a lack of preparation and problems with the instrumentalists. Tellingly, David returned to the studio for another attempt within a matter of weeks, but this time without the Buzz. On this occasion, using a variety of studio musicians, the song was successfully recorded along with a B side, "I'm Not Losing Sleep." When the single was released in August 1966, it was credited only to David Bowie, constituting the first genuine solo release of his career. However, the single was no more successful than any other had been, and after a crisis consultation with both Ralph Horton and Kenneth Pitt the decision was collectively made to sever ties with Pye.

Judged solely on his ongoing and ever-mounting recording disappointments, it might have seemed throughout all of this that David Bowie was going nowhere. However, he had been performing live concerts extensively with each of his successive ensembles, and as a result his reputation was growing increasingly strong, a fan base slowly building to the point where he even had his own official fan club. Nevertheless, it was clear to all that in order to elevate David Bowie to the level of popularity so many people thought him capable of—not least the man himself—something would have to change with regard to his recorded product. Radio airplay and record sales were unequivocally the benchmark by which popular-music talent was measured, and David Bowie had achieved little of either.

Newly freed from his record contract, David Bowie and the Buzz reentered the studio in October to record three songs, funded by Kenneth Pitt. "The London Boys," "Rubber Band," and "Please Mr. Gravedigger" duly resulted, and when Pitt presented the recordings to Decca, Bowie was signed immediately. This completed a highly circuitous cycle, with Decca having earlier been the very first record company to show interest in Bowie, releasing the King Bees' first single, "Liza Jane," two years earlier.

In November 1966, Decca's faith was such that Bowie entered its Broadhurst Gardens studio to record his debut album. The Buzz were retained for the project but on the basis that they were to be session musicians only, appearing alongside many others who were called in on an as-and-when-needed basis. In all aspects, this was to be a David Bowie solo venture.

Two singles were released by Decca on its Deram subsidiary label in advance of the album's release. The first, "Rubber Band," backed by "The London Boys," came out in December 1966, accompanied by a press statement and brief biography from the record company claiming, "David lives with his family in Kent, works hard on a cabaret act and has high hopes that 'Rubber Band' will advance his ambitions." Meanwhile, an unnamed reviewer in *Disc and Music Echo* opined,

> I do not think "Rubber Band" is a hit. What it is is an example of how David Bowie had progressed himself into being a name to reckon

with. . . . Listen to this record and then turn it over and listen to "The London Boys," which actually I think would have been a much more impressive topside. But both are worth thinking about. (Anonymous, *Disc and Music Echo*, December 1967)

A second single, released in April 1967, was the children's song "The Laughing Gnome," paired with "The Gospel according to Tony Day." Ominously, both releases fell into the familiar pattern of not reaching the charts.

And so it was following this promise-filled and yet ultimately disappointing three-year journey that David Bowie's self-titled debut album would come to sit virtually untouched upon music store shelves, thrown headlong into a hopeless battle against the juggernaut of *Sgt. Pepper's Lonely Hearts Club Band*.

DAVID BOWIE, 1967

A remarkable, creative debut album by a nineteen year old Londoner who wrote all 14 tracks and sings them with a sufficiently fresh interpretation to make quite a noise on the scene if he gets the breaks and the right singles. —Anonymous, *Disc and Music Echo*, June 1967

Completely unloved by the public and seemingly a source of total embarrassment to Bowie himself, the album is the vinyl equivalent of the madwoman in the attic. —David Buckley, *Strange Fascination: David Bowie: The Definitive Story*

Side One

1. Uncle Arthur
2. Sell Me a Coat
3. Rubber Band
4. Love You Till Tuesday
5. There Is a Happy Land
6. We Are Hungry Men
7. When I Live My Dream

Side Two

1. Little Bombardier
2. Silly Boy Blue
3. Come and Buy My Toys
4. Join the Gang
5. She's Got Medals
6. Maid of Bond Street
7. Please Mr. Gravedigger

The cover of *David Bowie* was designed to attract a hip, youthful, Swinging London audience. Looking every inch a sharp young mod-about-town in the head-and-shoulders color portrait on the front cover, Bowie stared earnestly back at anybody who might chance upon his record, making full eye contact and virtually demanding to be taken seriously. Once the record had been taken down from the shelf, a potential purchaser flipping the cover over would find Bowie pictured in black-and-white on the rear, slightly less formal in his pose but every bit as serious as on the front, his eyes once again leveled directly at the viewer's. If the eyes are indeed the much-vaunted window upon the soul, then here Bowie was most emphatically baring his soul to all and sundry. Manager Kenneth Pitt's short biography of Bowie on the rear cover, designed to introduce his little-known charge to the world, tellingly added gravitas to this impression, stating: "His line of vision is as straight and sharp as a laser beam. . . . David writes and sings of what he sees to be the truth." Together, the cover photographs and Pitt's biographical snippets worked to convey the impression of an honest, confessional-type artist who would lay bare through the art of song the truths of his society and his times, seen through "the eye of an articulate eagle."

In addition to this promise of unmitigated honesty, other messages ensured that any potential purchaser was left in little doubt that David Bowie was fully "hip" with the popular music of the day. His name on the front was written in a psychedelic, bright blue, highly stylized hand-drawn font typical of pop art of the day. The high-neck garment he wore was reminiscent of a military tunic, the large gold button with the crown insignia adding greatly to this impression. Pitt's words related that Bowie had been seen wearing a military jacket as far back as 1964, thereby creating a visual alignment with top acts of the era who had dressed similarly, including the Beatles, the Rolling Stones, the Kinks, and Jimi Hendrix.

The most emphatic clue given to the potential buyer as to what musical style might lie within the grooves of the unknown artist's debut album was Pitt's claim that Bowie's musical roots lay within rhythm and blues, with Little Richard being cited as a major influence. Emphasizing the point, he also credited Bowie with forming two of Britain's earliest rhythm and blues bands.

These visual and written elements on the cover, then, were the only available clues as to what this fresh-faced new artist on the vibrant Swinging London scene might *sound* like. How accurate would they prove to be?

With folk-styled, nasal, double-reed melody driven by handclaps in the verses, and jaunty snare beats in the sing-along chorus, the first song, "Uncle Arthur," is a vignette about a highly dependent thirty-two-year-old man who moved out of his mother's house against her wishes, having finally met a girl. Being away from home proved to be more than poor Uncle Arthur could cope with, however, and so he "packed his bags and fled back to mother." The unorthodox and defeatist subject matter set to a decidedly non-pop backing emphatically set the scene for the kind of eclecticism that would permeate the entire set of four-teen songs. Here on his debut album Bowie would explore themes that frequently had no discernable relevance to or resonance with the pop-obsessed youth of 1967 who were still tuned in to, and turned on by, countercultural notions of rebellion and power to the people. As an opener, "Uncle Arthur" could not have been more antithetical to such prevailing notions.

"Sell Me a Coat," the second song, is a poignant tale of loss, with Jack Frost accused of leading Bowie's girl away: "And when she smiles, the ice forgets to melt away. Not like before, her smile was warming yesterday." Here, the folk sensibility of the first song gives way to a more contemporary pop sound somewhat reminiscent of Peter, Paul and Mary or the Mamas and the Papas, yet dominated by a largely orchestral backing of French horns and a full string section.

Rock music might as well have not existed, such was the stylistic departure of the album's third song, "Rubber Band." The failed single release from December 1966 was rerecorded for the album, but in a very similar arrangement to its predecessor that still featured tuba as the lead instrument, supported by euphonium, cornet, French horns, and a full string section. The Decca Records media release referred to the song as "pathos set to tubas. A happening song." But despite the use of such a psychedelia-aligned buzzword, any "happening" in the song was certainly not aligned to what was actually happening outside the recording studio amid the popular culture of the day. Another song with an unhappy ending, "Rubber Band" is the nostalgic reminiscence of a young man remembering back to 1910 and the girl he met in a library garden while a band played nearby. Back then he was "so handsome and so strong—my moustache was stiffly waxed and one foot long." However, he went away to fight during World War I and found upon his return that the leader of the "Rubber Band" had married the girl he loved during his absence. His distraught parting shot, "I hope you break your baton," spoken as the song fades, is a one-liner straight out of vaudeville. But what strikes the listener about this song, even if—to use a phrase consistent with the English Victoriana the song so strongly evokes—it might not be one's cup of tea, is the undeniable skill with which Bowie creates this piece of aural theater. The song begins with a brief introduction of faux-romantic sentimentality in a style reminiscent of Gilbert and Sullivan, whereby the euphonium takes the melody only to hand it over to unmuted trumpets, before they in turn surrender it to a comedic fanfare of muted cornets. At this point the song proper begins, and Bowie starts the story off with a reiteration of the song's joke-title, making it clear from the outset that we are listening to the very Rubber Band in question. The strict 4/4 marching time; the walking bass line of the tuba that is so characteristic of a marching brass band; the long-held notes on cornet and trumpet that harmonize the melody: all such components combine to convincingly portray a marching brass band. At the point where Bowie narrates the loss of his girl, advising us in a voice breaking with highly stylized, theatrical emotion that she is now married to the leader of the band, the song's strictly maintained march time breaks down. One can almost see in one's mind's eye the bandsmen falling over one another as they miss their step and the formation falls into chaos. The music only briefly paints his mental turmoil, however, before quickly reestablishing the joke when the melody is taken up by solo tuba playing in its high register, the same kind of comedic instrumental effect one hears in works such as "Teddy Bear's Picnic," "Tubby the Tuba," or Camille Saint-Saëns's "Carnival of the Animals." The song then ends, just two minutes and seventeen seconds after it began, with an amen motif that is also typical of the way hymns conclude when performed by brass bands. Overall, the musical language is highly appropriate for the period parody Bowie has set out to create. While the song may have fallen well short of engendering any sense of relevance to the youth of the day, it is nevertheless a telling early example of the artist's talent for immersing himself completely and convincingly in a specific, albeit on this occasion extraordinarily unfashionable, musical style, and for creating theater through his music.

Military brass band timbre then gave way to the far more pop-infused "Love You Till Tuesday," which was selected as one of the single releases from the album (albeit in a rerecorded version). Here, cellos, oboe, piccolo, a string section, and a military snare drum were used to enhance rather than usurp the standard pop instrumentation that formed the song's basis. More jolly and upbeat than anything encountered so far, the song is the closest on the album to a bona fide contemporary pop sound. Curiously, Bowie employed precisely the same joke tactic at its conclusion when, playing the lad-about-town, he quipped (with implied wink), "Well I might stretch it to Wednesday." Despite garnering several of the most positive reviews of his career thus far—*Record Mirror* described it as a "stylish performance that could easily make it"—the single suffered a, by now, familiar fate.

"There is a happy land where only children live. You've had your chance and now the doors are closed sir, Mr. Grownup. Go away sir." In "There Is a Happy Land," Bowie most effectively painted a picture of generational difference. However, the division he skillfully outlined was between very young children and their parents and/or other adults rather than addressing the feelings of alienation experienced by teenagers. Therefore, set to the singularly unhip sound of celesta, cornet, and French horns, the song again offered little or no edginess such as might have attracted the ear of a discerning (and record-buying) pop demographic.

A fake news report about global population explosion, spoken in a Workingmen's Club–style comedic German accent, begins "We Are Hungry Men." Trumpets, orchestral percussion, and a dominating Hammond organ ensure that the soft tones of the album so far continue to prevail, with blunting lyrics that here present particularly hard-hitting themes including abortion, birth control, and the execution of those taking more than their fair share, as evidenced during the mid-song return of the German speaker who rants maniacally in a Hitler-esque parody: "*Achtung, achtung*, these are your orders. Anyone found guilty of consuming more than their allotted amount of air will be slaughtered and cremated." Eclectic in the extreme, it is one of the album's stranger moments.

Giants, dragons, golden horses, and castles provide the imagery in "When I Live My Dream," a slow and dreamy ballad featuring full string and woodwind sections. It is the final song on side one, and by this point it must have been clear to ears accustomed to the sounds of the Who, the Stones, et al., that while this new artist's songs were undeniably well crafted, chock-full of almost filmic imagery, and cleverly worded, their timbric presentation was, in the parlance of the day, most decidedly, square. In opposition to the accepted language of rock music of the day—its *sound* characteristics so essential for the expression of generational angst (which was the whole point)—Bowie's was a musical language steeped in yesterday. Even when the message contained in the lyrics might have stood a chance of resonating with a youth audience, the lack of electric guitars, crashing drums, and booming bass in favor of brass, woodwind, and strings meant the musical delivery was more akin to the musical tastes of their parents, from whom they were, of course, actively seeking to distance themselves.

Waltz time ushers in side two of *David Bowie*, in a dark tale of an old war veteran who befriends two children but is run out of town on suspicion of being a pedophile. "Little Bombardier" is a well-crafted song in its own right; nevertheless, the trombone, honky-tonk piano, and woodwind and string sections further the rock instrumentation snub.

The slow-paced "Silly Boy Blue" addresses Buddhist themes: "Child of Tibet, you're a gift from the sun—reincarnation of one better man." The vocal line is doubled on cello and, at times, trumpet, with a full brass section in restrained support. The effect is a vocal line with a curious floating effect, very much in keeping with the subject matter. While unique and, at times, even beautiful, the song is again anything but mainstream.

Guitar takes center stage for the first time on the album in the following song, "Come and Buy My Toys." The simplicity of the fingerstyle acoustic backing, augmented by single bass notes on the first beat of each bar, provides a Simon and Garfunkel–type accompaniment for Bowie's vivid glimpses of childhood imagery, featuring "monkeys made of gingerbread and sugar horses painted red." Further addressing the previously visited theme of division between childhood and adulthood, Bowie paints a somewhat gloomy picture of a predestined future: "You shall work your father's land, but now you shall play in the market square till you'll be a man." Once again, such fatalistic subject matter fails to espouse the themes of youth empowerment and teenage rebellion prevalent in the popular music of the time.

In "Join the Gang," Bowie then virtually bites the hand that feeds; that is, he lampoons youth subcultures and rock 'n' roll, describing their promises as illusory and false: "You won't be alone, we've all got beery grins. It's a big illusion but at least you're in." The instrumentation, energy, and overall ambiance of the song are consistent with the popular music of the time, with the sitar at the beginning drawing none-too-subtle references to the Beatles ("Norwegian Wood") and the Rolling Stones ("Paint It Black"). Jaunty honky-tonk piano prevails and a clearly evident prolonged quotation of the leading riff from "Gimme Some Lovin'" (1965), by the Spencer Davis Group, features mid-song. The nature of the lyrics, however, makes it clear that Bowie is using these contemporaneous devices to poke fun at rather than to pay any kind of homage to such acts, whose success he, ironically, surely wished to emulate. For this reason, of all the songs on the album it is perhaps this one that best sums up—perhaps unwittingly—his own dislocation from the popular-music mainstream; a dislocation that the album, in its entirety, did nothing to dispel.

Gender-based alienation comes across strongly in the next song, the up-tempo "She's Got Medals." Opening with a declamatory fanfare of flutes and oboes before settling down to a more standard accompaniment of pop instrumentation, the lyrics tell the strange story of a female soldier who had posed as a man but resumed a womanly appearance to avoid detection after deserting: "Her mother called her Mary, but she changed her name to Tommy, she's a one. She went and joined the army, passed the medical, don't ask me how it's done." Described by Peter Dogget as an "uneasy blend of West End musical, garage rock and confused sexual politics,"[1] this track, too, is one more closely aligned to a contemporary pop sound—a sound, however, that was undermined by being at odds with the obtuse subject matter.

The penultimate track, "Maid of Bond Street," saw a return to 3/4 time and full employment of the orchestral forces of a woodwind section, a string section, and a trombone, while toward the end of the song a piano accordion is brought in to emphasize the last two beats of each bar, giving the track an almost Parisian flavor. The lyrics reveal the story of a girl who "makes it" as a top fashion model in London, but while she seems to have the world at her feet, such a notion is an illusion because in gaining her status she lost the boy she loved, who left her because of his jealousy: "This boy is made of envy. He doesn't have a limousine— really wants to be a star himself." In this revisited theme of things-are-not-always-what-they-seem, it is once again easy to imagine that there exists an autobiographical aspect to the lyric, with Bowie's own attempts to "make it" having been thwarted again and again.

The final track on *David Bowie* is by far the strangest of all. "Please Mr. Gravedigger" is not so much a song as it is a radio drama, with Bowie's sung monologue not set to musical instruments but instead to sound effects of rain, church bells, and bombs exploding in the distance. Singing from the viewpoint of a child killer whose ten-year-old victim, Mary-Ann, is buried in the graveyard in which the murderer now stands, Bowie adopts a highly affected voice riddled with cold or flu, warning the gravedigger to keep his mouth shut and not inform upon him to the authorities: "No, Mr. GD, you won't tell. And just to make sure that you keep it to yourself I've started digging holes myself, and this one here's for you." The total absence of musical instruments, and thus any harmonic elements, makes for an eerily stark atmosphere, conjuring in the mind of the listener an almost Hammer Horror–like mental image.

So there it was, *David Bowie* in its entirety. For a debut album, it was extremely confusing. With the exception of just a few of the fourteen tracks, what the vinyl contained was far removed from what might reasonably have been expected on the promise of its cover. Far from offering the listener a dose of rhythm and blues, the orchestral instrumentation, song styles, lyrical themes, and Bowie's cockney-inflected vocal style were much more akin to quirky, innately British, music hall–type character songs such as those popularized by Anthony Newley or Bernard Cribbins. It's certainly true that the influence of music hall was not completely unknown within British pop music at this time, with some very big-name acts writing and recording songs in that whimsical tone, including the Kinks, Pink Floyd (in their early Syd Barrett era), and even the Beatles themselves. Indeed, *Sgt. Pepper's Lonely Hearts Club Band* contained two such examples, "When I'm Sixty-Four" and "Being for the Benefit of Mr. Kite." However, in the case of these other acts, the songs could rightly be explained as endearingly self-indulgent anomalies within much broader, already well-established musical styles and repertoires. Simply, everyone knew such songs were not indicative of the core sound or style of those acts. In Bowie's case, to fill his debut album—his industry calling card—with such offerings was highly problematic because those fourteen songs were the only context by which to assess and "pigeonhole" him. As a result, it was extraordinarily difficult to locate the work within the prevailing pop climate of the day. The songs were mostly couched in a musical style that was highly unfashionable, leading biographer David Buckley to suggest the album was "as un–rock 'n' roll as one could imagine."[2] Another well-known Bowie writer, Mark Paytress, concluded the work was "idiosyncratic to the point of self-immolation. The album . . . wasn't consistent enough to tap into any established market."[3] In 1990 Bowie gave his own candid appraisal: "Lyrically I guess it was striving to be something, the short story teller. Musically it's quite bizarre. I don't know where I was at. It seemed to have its roots all over the place, in rock and vaudeville and music hall and I don't know what. I didn't know if I was Max Miller or Elvis Presley."[4]

Nevertheless, the album stands as a testament to Bowie's innate sense of theater, clearly showing how this quality was present even in these earliest days of his career. The songs are almost all story songs that find Bowie adopting the character of a protagonist, be he a World War I soldier who lost his girl to a bandleader, a young child warding off the dull world of adults, or even a graveyard-dwelling child killer.

Because *David Bowie* was such a commercial failure, the majority of people who have come to know it did so after later success. Therefore, most people, myself included, came to experience *David Bowie* well after its release. For me it was 1973, following my *Ziggy Stardust* epiphany. As is surely the case when any fan discovers an act they admire hugely, I had decided I needed to collect everything Bowie had ever done. Accordingly I ordered the album from my local record store, and an imported copy duly traveled the twelve thousand miles across the oceans from England, arriving some three months later. Enormously excited, I, and a similarly Bowie-fixated school friend, endured a long and restless day at the chalk-face in confident anticipation of being wowed by Bowie's debut after school. No one else we knew had heard the album, of course, and the schoolyard envy was palpable. We raced back to my house as soon as the three-thirty bell rang, pausing briefly in the kitchen for the obligatory raid of fridge and pantry, and then repaired to my bedroom. I lovingly removed the record from the sleeve and placed *David Bowie* on the turntable of my stereo, each of us then settling down on the carpet on opposite sides of the room in front of a speaker, in the manner of His Master's Voice dogs. "Uncle Arthur" came and went. So did "Sell Me a Coat." After "Rubber Band" ended we exchanged glances, shrugs, and tight, nervous smiles. Quickly, consternation turned to incredulity. By the time side one had given way to side two, our incredulity had morphed into palpable disappointment. The David Bowie of *Ziggy Stardust* and *Hunky Dory* was clearly absent here. David Bowie's music had quickly become a badge of honor for us, something to be turned up loud with windows opened to the street so that everyone would know cool, hip-and-happening cats dwelled within. But this . . . *this* was music that required one turn the volume knob sharply to the left and close the windows for fear of being heard. Were there two David Bowies in the world, then?

4

MESSAGES FROM GROUND CONTROL

David Bowie (aka Space Oddity) and The Man Who Sold the World, 1969–1971

An event took place on July 11, 1969, that initially seemed unlikely to stir up any public interest. David Bowie released yet another new single. However, on this occasion it was a song that would give him a brief but enormously significant taste of the success that he, and many others, felt he was both capable of and sorely due. Despite its subject matter, "Space Oddity" did not exactly travel at the speed of a rocket, taking a leisurely two months to climb into the top ten of the UK singles chart. Once there, however, it would go on to peak at a highly impressive number five. The song rode on the crest of a wave of worldwide fervor and excitement as the drama of the Apollo 11 space mission unfolded, the first successful moon landing turning one of mankind's most enduring fantasies into a grainy, real-time, televised reality. Global fascination with space exploration had become one of the primary influences on sixties popular culture, a source of wonderment but also unease at such a giant leap into the unknown—such a fragile melding of technology and humanity. That the Bowie single had been released just nine days before the moonwalk gave rise to barbed accusations of opportunism and some critics wrote the release off as a mere novelty song, relegating its architect to the dubious status of a probable one-hit wonder. Nevertheless, "Space Oddity" launched the name "David Bowie" into public consciousness. In addition, it ensured that, right from this very first moment of widespread public attention, science fiction and alienation were claimed as foundational Bowie themes. Perfectly packaged within a catchy pop format, Bowie's "Space Oddity" was the song that fully encapsulated this dichotomy, underscoring the triumph of man's quest while all too clearly exposing the vulnerability of our species in a formidable, all too alien environment. With his name now featuring amid the upper echelons of the pop charts, David Bowie was at last a complete unknown no longer.

Just five months later, buoyed with a deserved sense of confidence, he would attempt to repeat the success of his first hit song on an even larger scale with the release of his second album.

THE SECOND ALBUM: *DAVID BOWIE*, 1969

> The lyrics are full of the grandeur of yesterday, the immediacy of today, and the futility of tomorrow. This is well worth your attention. —Anonymous, *Music Now!* November 1969

> His love reveries are dreary, self-pitying and monotonous. But when he turns his eye to the absurdities of technological society, he is razor-sharp in his observations. —Tony Palmer, *The Observer*, 1969

Side One	Side Two
1. Space Oddity	1. Janine
2. Unwashed and Somewhat Slightly Dazed	2. An Occasional Dream
3. Don't Sit Down	3. Wild Eyed Boy from Freecloud
4. Letter to Hermione	4. God Knows I'm Good
5. Cygnet Committee	5. Memory of a Free Festival

David Bowie's second album was released on November 4, 1969. In the UK it was issued on the Philips label and was, rather confusingly, again self-titled. In the US, however, it instead bore the Mercury Records stamp along with a different title, *Man of Words/Man of Music*.[1]

The front cover shows an artist very different from the earnest young mod pictured two years earlier on his debut. Bowie's disembodied head sits at the center of the picture, over which a replicating series of blue dots is superimposed, darker at the outer edges and becoming lighter toward the center, and effectively forcing him into the background despite his centrality. It is an odd effect, the artist cut off without context. His image is very naturalistic, with long, curly hair framing his face, while his eyes, as they had on the album's predecessor, bore directly into the viewer's in candid communication. The expression on his face is serious and unsmiling. With his lips slightly parted and eyes wide, he appears to be in a state of heightened alertness. Flipping the cover over, the rear side is very different, a series of fantasy drawings that relate with varying degrees of directness to the themes contained within the songs.

A credit is given inside the gatefold cover to Vernon Dewhurst for the artwork on the front, but the optical art design is actually based upon the work of Victor Vasarely. Optical art, more commonly abbreviated to op art, had grown in popularity as the 1960s progressed through its employment by pop artists. Op art is designed to deceive the eye into believing it sees movement where there is none, and Vasarely was one of the pioneers of the style. Through the mechanical repetition of line after line of dots, squares, or other geometric shapes, perceptual ambiguities may be observed as the viewer stares deeply into the image, with the possibility that parts of the image will appear to expand or contract, rotate, appear or disappear; completely new shapes may even emerge. One of the primary reasons for the style's popularity at the time was its hallucinogenic parallels with psychedelia and the associated effects of mind-altering drugs such as LSD. In the case of Bowie's cover, any such illusory effect was wholly negated by the intrusion of Bowie's head behind the op art dots, which, while surrendering the foreground, nonetheless completely destroyed the all-important mechanical repetition of the dots. Op artists such as Vasarely, however, were not concerned solely with tricking the eye of the viewer into seeing optical illusions. While that may have been the most obvious surface intention, a much deeper rationale lay at the heart of op artists. The unrelenting, mechanical repetition of geometric shapes in op art was a deliberate attempt to depict the increasing dehumanization brought about by the rapid advancement of space age technology.

The superimposition of dots over Bowie's highly individual, human, unadorned, and unmade-up face strongly infers mechanical processing, constituting encroachment by a robotic, dehumanized, automated, technological authority that triumphs over Bowie's all too fallible human presence. The image raises questions about whether the human component of space exploration, the astronaut Major Tom, is really a feeling, thinking, emotional human being like any other of his kind, or simply another collection of wave particles configured to act as just another part of the machine that conveys him. Perhaps he is not even equal to, but subservient to, the technology that surrounds him? After all, in this image—so dominated by a mechanical representation of that technology—the human presence is relegated to the background, forced to give up the foreground. And this is despite the fact that the technology is of man-made origin. Such a dichotomy lies at the thematic core of "Space Oddity."

You really don't know what to expect of *David Bowie*, which you purchased in the wake of *Ziggy Stardust*, *Hunky Dory*, and the debut album. The young Englishman has taken you on quite a ride during the course of your relationship with him thus far. But you are still hanging in there, and despite the recent let-down of his debut release, you are confident the three-month wait for delivery of its successor will be well worth it. You slip the sleek black recording out of its sleeve with a mix of excitement and trepidation . . .

Unsurprisingly, given its recent and highly significant success, the track selected to open the album is "Space Oddity." Bowie later said of his breakthrough release:

> The publicity image of a spaceman at work is an automaton rather than a human being and my Major Tom is nothing if not a human being. It comes from a feeling of sadness about this aspect of the space thing. It has been dehumanised so I wrote a song-farce about it to try and relate science and human emotion. I suppose it's an antidote to space-fever, really. (David Bowie, 1974, in Barry Miles, *David Bowie Black Book* [London: Omnibus Press, 1980])

The song begins with a superbly worked example of aural painting as the music ever so slowly drifts into the listener's consciousness from dead silence, much in the way a spaceship might slowly and gracefully slip into view from the endless black frontier of space upon a movie screen, the familiar blue-and-green sphere of Earth perhaps glowing faintly and out of reach in the far-off distance. In addition to the gripping *Apollo 11* space mission just months earlier, this was exactly the kind of image that had so awed moviegoers the world over just one year earlier when watching Stanley Kubrick's *2001: A Space Odyssey*, the source from which Bowie borrowed significantly more than just his song title. Kubrick allowed his scenes to unfold with slow and exaggerated grandeur, and here Bowie granted the introduction to his homage the kind of spaciousness almost never seen in a pop song, with a full thirty seconds of gradually loudening buildup preceding his vocals. "Space Oddity" *unfolds*. The opening chord is an F-major seventh, a harmonic flavor made mysterious by the ringing, open top pair of E strings of Bowie's twelve-string guitar. With the note E already dominant in the listener's ear, when the harmony subsequently steps down a semitone to an E-minor chord—the shortest tonal journey possible—the impression given is of minimal movement along with a feeling of disembodiment because, sonically, we are left floating, going nowhere. A snare drum also enters during the introduction but it is not used in a simple, conventional, time-keeping role. Rather, the short, sporadic, rat-a-tat rolls have military connotations, subtle reminders to the listener of the military origins of the space program. The music continues to oscillate ambiguously between two chords, allowing the listener no solid tonal ground as the volume slowly increases. It is only once the music has swelled to its peak volume that a far more declamatory C-major chord is struck, the sudden solidity of a home key coinciding perfectly with the entry of the voice of the ground control operator, who hereafter represents home. The remainder of the introduction serves to draw the listener into the lift-off, ending with the whispered countdown and an expression of the operator's touching hope, steeped in faith-based human religiosity, that God's love will be with the as-yet-silent Major Tom. Throughout this introduction, in the role of Ground Control, Bowie's vocals remain low, measured, and earthbound, but are underpinned by the most famous-ever use of the humble but highly effective Stylophone, providing cartoonish space sounds.

A dramatic musical interlude achieved with a surprising restraint of musical forces emphatically separates the introduction from the first verse, depicting the launch of Major Tom's rocket. The rendering of this event is skillful, with the slow, carefully spoken, metronomic countdown that underpins the latter part of the introduction falling away at Bowie's whispered "lift-off" to reveal the slow-building upward momentum provided by swirling guitar, strings, and woodwind. From the listener's perspective, you can almost feel as well as hear the fight that the rocket is slowly waging with gravity, the impossibly cumbersome epitome of mankind's technological skill ever accelerating into the sky. At the peak of ascension, the voice of Ground Control resumes with the beginning of verse one. Here, post-lift-off, Bowie's voice is pitched higher in jubilation. This change in pitch also provides a literal inference that Major Tom is well above us, no longer earthbound. In addition, a high harmony line privileged loud in the mix further paints the high-off-the-ground metaphor, while the doubling effect it creates with the lead vocal introduces an echo-chamber quality suggestive of the bouncing acoustics one might experience in an enclosed space surrounded by hard surfaces: the interior of a spaceship or a "tin can."

Midway through verse one Major Tom finally responds to Ground Control as he begins his spacewalk. It has been one minute and forty-eight seconds since the song began, and hearing Major Tom's voice at last comes as a welcome relief. However, Major Tom is here embarking upon an act as dangerous as the lift-off. After all, in *2001: A Space Odyssey* it was during just such a spacewalk that the onboard computer, HAL, killed Dr. Frank Poole by severing his oxygen line and set his body adrift to float forever in space. It was the stuff that nightmares were made of in the late 1960s, and Major Tom "stepping through the door" was a highly loaded, fear-inducing lyric.

The chorus, however, serves to temporarily placate such fears, beginning with Bowie's voice sitting reassuringly for a full, comforting bar on the word "here (am I)" pitched on the familiar note E (the seventh of the F-major seventh chord), revisiting the sense of floating that permeated the very beginning of the song. The lyrics, too, are peaceful as he describes sitting in stillness "far above the world."

It is the next verse that sends a shiver up the spine. The listener is alerted to trouble when Major Tom suggests that he thinks his "spaceship knows which way to go," inferring that it is moving away from him. We picture it in our mind's eye as he hangs helpless in space, able only to watch as his tin-can sanctuary moves slowly away from his reach. This dreadful conclusion is confirmed in the next line with sudden plaintiveness: "Tell my wife I love her very much—she knows," underpinned with inherent sadness by a shift from F major to F minor. At this point all of the incredible achievements of man, the space race, and the amazing advances of the technological age are put in their place, rendered effectively worthless, as Major Tom's last communication, so personal and small, brings into focus what really matters. It is the ones we love. It is human relationships.

The truncated verse quickly gives way to a highly dramatic bridge section as Ground Control realizes that something has gone tragically wrong with Major Tom's spacewalk. Up until this point Bowie has avoided using the dominant G-major chord, the second-most-powerful chord in the key of C major, but here he finally utilizes it to great effect, underscoring the fatal drama. Major Tom is lost, and the latent fear in every Cold War–era child is realized.

When the ending chorus returns in a ghostly recapitulation of his earlier reassurance that all was well, Major Tom is no longer above Earth but, rather, "far above the moon," doomed to die a cold, lonely, dark death.

As Mark Rose puts it, such a scenario within "the vast emptiness of interstellar space . . . [created a] radical sense of alienation, of unbridgeable difference between the human and the non-human worlds."[2]

It is with "Space Oddity" that, for the first time, a clear synergy can be seen between the music and the artwork of the album cover that houses it, albeit an alignment achieved with subtlety. Seeing Bowie cut off and virtually suspended amid the blue Vasarely-styled dots is analogous to Major Tom being set adrift in space, abandoned and alienated. We have no context for him, no evidence by which we might place him in any recognizable physical environment, just the unrelenting and unhuman geometric configuration of mathematically correct rows of dots. Had human beings gone too far and overreached themselves in their thirst for technological advancement? As Bowie warns in the track "Memory of a Free Festival" later on the album, "Man has pushed beyond his brain."

It is with the passing of the first song that you, the somewhat nervous purchaser of Bowie's second album, still buoyed by his more recent successes, are yourself thrust into the unknown. "Space Oddity" was familiar to you through its success as a single in 1969 and, in terms of theme if not necessarily musical style, this is clearly still the Bowie of *Ziggy Stardust* and *Hunky Dory*. However, perusal of the track titles on the rear of the album soon confirms that this is the only song you've heard before. What, then, lies ahead?

The second song begins. To a Donovan/Dylan-esque musical palette that begins with acoustic guitar before building up to a quintessential sixties-styled rock sound, "Unwashed and Somewhat Slightly Dazed" addresses themes such as equality, privilege, and class-based marginalization. The song contains at times brutal imagery underscoring the struggle between the haves and the have-nots, exemplified through its protagonist—a long-haired hippy railing against a rich banker whose pretty rich-girl daughter spurns his advances. "Don't turn your nose up!" implores Bowie. His tone is sarcastic and cutting. "I'm the cream of the great Utopia dream," he claims, "a phallus in pigtails." It is a powerful song, but in a style clearly dated compared to the electric flash of *Ziggy Stardust*. While clearly more hip than the offerings of the first album, the sound is right out of the flower-power decade so loved by your older sisters, brothers, and cousins. This was the sound of the sixties—the very era that you looked to Bowie to lead you away from; the very thing that *Ziggy Stardust* achieved so completely.

"Don't sit down," implores Bowie in the title line of the following fragment of a song, a joke track that comes and goes within a mere forty seconds. A Beatles-esque throwaway parody, its only other lyrics are "yeah" and "baby." The song implodes upon itself before it really gets going, breaking up in comic disarray as the musicians find their joke too much to bear. Its self-indulgence and unimportance would be evidenced by its omission from the subsequent, post–*Ziggy Stardust* rerelease of the album. However, in hindsight, "Don't Sit Down" stands as a telling early example of Bowie's irreverent attitude to rock music and his obvious "at home" attitude to the recording process.

The fourth track is an intimate communication to his former girlfriend, Hermione Farthingale. "I'm not quite sure what I'm supposed to do, so I'll just write some love to you," implores Bowie in "Letter to Hermione." Biographers agree that Hermione's decision to split with Bowie affected him deeply, and his public plea that they make up fully bears this out. Again, it is difficult to avoid drawing comparisons to Donovan given the song's acoustic simplicity and heart-on-sleeve sincerity. It may be that this is the most overtly plain and honest song of Bowie's entire recording history, the clarity with which he expresses himself underscored by simple, unencumbered musical backing that mirrors the subject matter impeccably. Certainly, it is again a world away from the musical and lyrical style he would become known for.

The lyrics of the following song, "Cygnet Committee," could not be more different from the disarming intimacy of "Letter to Hermione." Here, through the passage of more than nine and a half minutes, Bowie paints a frightening view of a technologically driven future conflict, where technology gone wrong decimates the human population: "The silent guns of love will blast the sky . . . I see a child slain on the ground as a love machine lumbers through desolation rows plowing down man, woman." At the same time he acknowledges the failure of the very human-centric and idealistic raison d'être of the counterculture, name-dropping the Beatles as he does so: "[We] stoned the poor on slogans such as 'Love Is All We Need.'" Highly fragmented and impressionistic, "Cygnet Committee" is an accusatory song addressing multiple betrayals, Bowie aiming his arrows at politicians and an apathetic public, while lamenting what might have been. Over a folk sound now becoming firmly established as the album progresses, "Cygnet Committee" is, as musicologist James E. Perone suggests with tongue positioned firmly in cheek, "quite a lot to take in and digest."[3]

Side two begins with "Janine," initially a seemingly conventional song about a girlfriend, performed in the familiar sixties folk-rock style. However, Bowie's lyrics sit in contrast to the jaunty music. While he accuses the song's subject of being "too intense," it is he who comes across as the dangerously complex one, with admissions such as "I've got to keep my veil on my face," and "I've got things inside my head that even I can't face." And when he suggests, "But if you take an axe to me you'll kill another man, not me at all," it becomes evident that this song is not quite what it seems. Psychological subversion exists beneath the sing-along surface, and critics frequently point to this song as early evidence of Bowie's penchant for role-playing.

"An Occasional Dream" further advances the acoustic folk-like vibe of the album. The subject is once again Bowie's failed relationship with Hermione Farthingale, but the message contained in the lyrics is not the intensely personal appeal of the earlier "Letter to Hermione." Rather, here Bowie is contemplative and reflective, almost self-pitying as he regrets wasted time. A breathy free-form flute is used to convey the dreamlike state implied in the song title, with rather mixed results.

Looking back on his career, Bowie would claim to have helped wipe out the sixties. Here, on the next track, "Wild Eyed Boy from Freecloud," the third song of just his second album, he portrays the ultimate

failure of the counterculture through a detailed medieval fantasy scenario of which Jethro Tull would have been proud. When Bowie sings,
"And the missionary mystic of peace/love stumbled to cry among the
clouds," it is Bob Dylan who immediately comes to mind as that wild-
eyed boy with the message of hope that would, ultimately, fail. "Space
Oddity" aside, it is "Wild Eyed Boy from Freecloud" that is the standout song on the album, with its lush orchestral arrangement underpinning the fantasy story line and a melody that shows off Bowie's voice to
maximum effect. This is musical theater—a virtual mini rock opera—
and an early indication of what Bowie was capable of.

The following "God Knows I'm Good" recalls the character vignettes
of the first album as Bowie tells a story, with the detachedness of an
onlooker rather than a participant, of a hapless woman caught shoplift-
ing. Similarly remote from any pop sensibility to the songs on that debut
album, the track once again has an obvious Dylan-esque quality, Bowie
borrowing a voice rather than speaking with his own.

The final track, "Memory of a Free Festival," acts as a highly effective summation of the album. While not devoid of affection for the
decade in which he grew up, he nevertheless nails the lid on the coffin
of the sixties. "The children of the summer's end gathered in the damp-
ened grass," Bowie begins, setting up the denim-and-headband imagery. Although drawing the listener to the Woodstock ideal—the hippy
music festival as the epitome of the countercultural desire for peace,
love, and freedom—the song is drawn from Bowie's personal experience of performing in the Beckenham Free Festival in August 1969,
with London confirmed in the first verse as the geographical location.
Another lengthy offering at over seven minutes, it is constructed around
two approximately equal parts. The first three and a half minutes describe the innocent idealism of the scene: "It was ragged and naïve—it
was Heaven," to an appropriately simplistic accompaniment of a solo
organ. The concluding half consists of a chant by massed voices that
becomes almost Hare Krishna–like in its cyclic repetition. "The sun
machine is coming down and we're gonna have a party," sing Bowie and
friends to what is now a band accompaniment, everyone seemingly high
on the "bliss" that had been passed among the festival-goers as they
"walked back to the road, unchained" at the festival's end.

For those who experienced this album after *Ziggy Stardust* and
Hunky Dory—the vast majority of Bowie's fans—to hear the work for

the first time in 1972 or later via the retitled RCA rerelease was to hear it out of its rightful time. While the debut album had eschewed any kind of youth cultural stylistic categorization or relevance—and so hearing it out of its time was probably no less confusing as it would have been hearing it in its time—in contrast, much of this second album could be situated easily within a Donovan/Dylan-esque mid- to late-sixties vibe. It could hardly be said to be groundbreaking; at least, not in the way his works of just a few years later would come to be regarded. "Space Oddity" aside, there was little about the album that truly sounded original, presented as it was within a, by then, well-worn musical style. Indeed even Bowie's manager at the time, Kenneth Pitt, admitted that he "had some misgivings about the album's over-all Dylan flavour."[4] Nick Stevenson correctly suggests that "until the end of the sixties, Bowie was still searching for his own voice."[5]

Although it was another commercial failure despite the presence of his solitary hit single, the album did attract some positive reactions. Commenting in *Music Now!* in December 1969, Kate Simpson opined with quite some prescience, "He's always changing. The David Bowie of today will not be the David Bowie of tomorrow. He doesn't know which way he's going—but he doesn't care. He lives from feeling to feeling. Today he is full of ideas—tomorrow they may be completely different. He's growing up. Try and get to see him."

Indeed, Bowie's fortunes were trending upward, but still at a frustratingly slow pace. For fans turned on to Bowie through *Hunky Dory* and *Ziggy Stardust*, who had subsequently puzzled their way through *David Bowie* #1 and then #2, only one further album now remained to be explored from his back catalog.

THE THIRD ALBUM: *THE MAN WHO SOLD THE WORLD*, 1970 (US)/1971 (UK)

> This remarkable young man (who poses in feminine attire in the sleeve picture) has, as usual, written all his own material for this nine-track album. The lyrics mostly mirror the current unrest of the world. —Allen Evans, *New Musical Express*, April 1971

Bowie's music offers an experience that is as intriguing as it is chilling, but only to the listener sufficiently together to withstand its schizophrenia. —John Mendelsohn, *Rolling Stone*, February 1971

Side One

1. The Width of a Circle
2. All the Madmen
3. Black Country Rock
4. After All

Side Two

1. Running Gun Blues
2. Saviour Machine
3. She Shook Me Cold
4. The Man Who Sold the World
5. The Supermen

More than simply a bookend marking a new decade, the shift from 1969 into the seventies was something of an axis point within popular culture, and nowhere was this reflected more than in rock music. The positivity and sense of youth solidarity—related either directly or indirectly to the counterculture—that had so marked the 1960s had largely dissolved by 1970/1971. This state of affairs was graphically punctuated by the, at times, vitriolic and protracted breakup of the Beatles and also by the deaths in 1970 of two preeminent heroes of the counterculture, Jimi Hendrix and Janis Joplin. As Philip Auslander suggests, "rock music could no longer serve as the soundtrack of the Vietnam era hippie counterculture. . . . After 1970, rock would have to proceed on different economic, political, social and cultural bases."[6] Meanwhile, Barney Hoskyns, regarding himself as a typical example of post-sixties British youth, describes a cultural climate in which a new youth audience was "screaming for a new musical wave . . . to rival the one with which our older brothers and sisters and cousins had been blessed in that vanished swinging world."[7] Indeed, the history of popular music throughout the 1970s is characterized by the development of stylistic fragmentation, with Frank Moriarty suggesting, "As the new decade began, the rock world was on the brink, about to tumble into ten long years of furious invention and reinvention."[8] During the seventies, many distinct popular-music styles, including punk rock, new wave, disco, reggae, ska, and gothic rock, all found audiences within the wider popular-music marketplace, while established styles such as the monolith that was progressive rock continued to flourish and develop their own derivations. In addition, crucially, glam rock (termed "glitter rock" in the United

States) became established, and this was the emergent style with which Bowie would soon become intrinsically associated.

The disappointment experienced by the newly emergent, ardent, "seventies-kid" Bowie fans upon retrospectively discovering the artist's first two albums in the decade following that in which they were released was not due to the fact that the albums were necessarily bad in and of themselves. It was simply that they had so very little in common with the superb new pop sensibilities of *Hunky Dory* or *Ziggy Stardust*, the two works that were so completely in tune with the early-seventies era in which they were produced, and that had turned your generation on to an artist who exhibited a clearly tangible and significant point of difference from the surrounding herd. *David Bowie* #1 and #2 might as well have been created by a completely different artist (or, indeed, two different artists) from the red-mulleted, mascara-sporting, sparkling and posturing glam rock star who now looked down from the many fan-magazine posters plastered upon your bedroom walls amid the company of T. Rex, Slade, and Sweet. *David Bowie* versions #1 and #2 were just, well . . . kind of irrelevant.

April 1971: *The Man Who Sold the World* is released in the UK a mere eight months before *Hunky Dory* and fifteen months before *Ziggy Stardust*. Compared to what has gone before, the highly theatrical and stylized album cover is a radical departure for Bowie.[9] Certainly, in his recordings prior to *The Man Who Sold the World* he played roles within his music. The first two albums, and most particularly the debut, are full of such examples, albeit confined to individual songs. Bowie's theatrical cameo appearances in these songs portrayed disparate characters all played in the first person. But nothing resembling a commitment to playing a role in a visual sense was evident before. On *David Bowie* #1 and #2 he visually presented himself as himself, as frankly and honestly as he could, whereas on *Hunky Dory* and *Ziggy Stardust* you saw him present himself as, respectively, a movie star parody and a futuristic rock star hero. On *The Man Who Sold the World*, it is immediately obvious to the viewer that he is here too consciously, purposefully, presenting an archetype. On this occasion he imbues his work with visual imagery borrowed from an influence well outside the norm for popular music of the time: art history and, specifically, Pre-Raphaelite art. Thematic linkage to both latter albums is further evident even before a note of the album is heard, because the implications of androgyny on both the front and rear covers, while of a quite different nature from Bowie's glam-era work, tap into the Lauren Bacall silver-screen-star gender ambiguity of the *Hunky Dory* cover and the he/she conundrum of "Lady Stardust" and other material on the *Ziggy Stardust* album. In short, even on first appraisal of the cover of *The Man Who Sold the World*, the Bowie you have come to know—or, at least, something approximating him—is in the house. [10]

Unique both in its time and since, the cover warrants close inspection, as Bowie lies back upon a couch or chaise longue draped with a light-blue covering made from shiny fabric, perhaps silk. He is positioned on his right side facing the viewer, his right arm and shoulder supporting him as he leans on the covered arm of the couch. Stretched out to his left, his leg is visible from just below the knee, with his right one tucked in behind it. He wears a silver dress made from shiny, shimmery material, perhaps silk or satin, with blue floral designs upon it, and the garment extends down to below his knees. The design is close-fitting to the waist and then balloons out considerably below this. It is held together by two fastenings at the chest; a gap of skin is visible from his neck down to almost his navel. He wears long black boots that seemingly reach as high as his knees. In his right hand he holds a playing card between his fingers, his wrist cocked and his hand angled toward the floor, which is strewn with numerous other playing cards lying both faceup and facedown, scattered seemingly at random. His left arm is held above his head, angled at the elbow, and his fingers touch the crown of his head in what seems a contemplative, absent-minded and unconscious gesture. He wears a silver metal bangle on this arm, positioned at the forearm midway between wrist and elbow. His hair is long and brown, and falls in curls to either side of his face and down below his neck with a fringe swept over the right eye. With his eyes open and staring straight at the viewer, the expression on his face is serious, studied, and he is evidently deep in thought.

Bowie has suggested his image on the cover was a parody of the work of Pre-Raphaelite artist Gabriel Rossetti. An obvious inference in this claim is that Bowie used a painting or sketch by Dante Gabriel Rossetti (1828–1882) as his model, and certainly this is where numerous critics have attributed the inspiration for the parody, although none have pinpointed a specific work. While the generalized femme fatale qualities of Bowie's picture are certainly in alignment with Pre-Raphaelite art and certainly Rossetti's works, such as *Lady Lilith* (1866–1868), perhaps there was no specific work parodied at all. Much of what can be observed in Bowie's cover can, however, be far more candidly discerned in a poem by Rossetti titled "The Card Dealer" (1852). Rossetti's references in this poem to "her woven golden hair" and particularly the description of the playing cards lying scattered on the floor, each one falling from his female subject's hand in turn, are elements clearly evident in Bowie's cover. Equally, three of the four colors that Rossetti names in the poem, "blood-red and purple, green and blue," predominate in the cover: the red curtaining framing the upper left and right corners of the image, the purple and blue shiny silk/satin look of the material upon which Bowie lies, and the blue floral designs upon his dress. One can also claim significant association between poem and album cover in the fact that the card Bowie holds is identical to the final card that Rossetti describes in his poem. Identified in the last line, "And know she calls it Death," the card in question is the King of Diamonds, also known through history as "the death card."

An inherent quality of the femme fatale as represented in Pre-Raphaelite art was her emotional distance. That is, the subject was pictured emotionally removed or alienated from her immediate physical surroundings, distracted, contemplative, and clearly thinking about something to which the viewer is given no clue. Often she would be posed absent-mindedly combing or touching her hair, which was usually long and flowing, symbolizing a veil of entrapment for potential suitors. While there may have been no precise model for the parody, in Bowie's picture, he too touches his hair, and although he looks directly at the viewer, no glimpse into his mood or his private thoughts is given. It is an inherently alienating image that borrows much from the historically loaded Pre-Raphaelite influence.

While precise art-historical details such as these were unlikely to have been apparent to the average early/pre-teenager in the early 1970s, neither did the observer of the cover need such insights to glean the unsettling aspects of the work. Rock stars were, simply, never pictured like this at that time. And turning the cover over to observe the rear side only complicated things more. Here, the black-and-white photograph is a close-up, featuring only Bowie's upper body and head. He is clad once again in clothing that markedly feminizes him, with the collarless jacket or top he wears having noticeably padded shoulders and a zipped V neck. He wears a dark beret cocked toward his right eye, beneath which his long hair frames his downward-looking face. It is a pose of studious repose or contemplation, with just the faintest hint of a smile playing around his mouth as if secretly amused at something once again denied to the viewer. Unlike on the front cover, here there is no direct engagement with the viewer. Bowie's eyes are open but averted from our gaze.

This rear-cover image largely supports the gender play set up by the front, but with one very important difference. Unlike on the front cover there are no further props visible within the picture and therefore we are provided with no wider setting in which to contextualize the image. The front cover, if disturbing for its sheer unexpectedness at the very least, is nevertheless clearly—even to anyone not schooled in art history—a parody or a reconstruction of a historical scene. Therefore, Bowie has a reason, or excuse, to be pictured wearing a dress and in a pose and setting historically reserved for women. This quality, which has been so carefully constructed on the front, is no longer evident on the rear, however. This abandonment of the staged context is supported both by the shift from color to black-and-white and by the change of costume.

Here, then, Bowie is engaging in gender play without the borrowed context of the art-historical parody, effectively casting off both the distancing device and the justification that it provided. Without this factor, the gender signification in the picture has considerably more resonance because there is a sense that we are seeing the artist more as he really is; a feeling that we are seeing the "true" hand behind the fantasy scenario presented on the front.

The purpose of an album cover is to stimulate interest in the contents within, and the cover of *The Man Who Sold the World* achieves this. Still, with the bewilderment of the last two albums fresh in your mind, you can't help wondering just what the record might deliver.

It's crunch time. You firmly shut your bedroom door and then switch on your stereo. Within seconds, twelve inches of brand-new black vinyl with the distinctive black Mercury label at its center is spinning seductively upon your turntable at thirty-three revolutions per minute, and the warm preemptive crackle-hum of needle upon record brings your speakers to readiness. You lie back upon your bed, still perusing the album cover at elbow length as you wait for side one to begin.

"The Width of a Circle" is first up, and it's an eight-minute cracker. Beginning quietly and calmly with a hypnotic descending four-bar melodic phrase that is repeated four times, it slowly builds its instrumental power with each repetition until finally featuring a full band accompaniment heavily saturated with booming bass, drums, and electric guitar. The introduction then gives way to a thickly textured riff-based rock feel carried by a fast and virtuosic bass line as the opening lyrics situate the action in the past tense. References to "the master" and to prayers immediately establish an indeterminate religious thematic undertone. While it is hard to penetrate the lyrics with any more exactitude, at the conclusion of the first verse Bowie sings a rhyming couplet that immediately attracts your attention: "Then I ran across a monster who was sleeping by a tree. And I looked and frowned and the monster was me." Hooray! Bowie is playing with identity once again, his real self and his hidden self placed there on the same page before you. And just as occurred on *Hunky Dory*, you "can't tell them apart at all." It's the duality of Ziggy Stardust/David Bowie, performance and performer, Bowie playing "the wild mutation as a rock 'n' roll star." The musical underpinning of "The Width of a Circle" is heavier than what he has offered before and demands to be turned up loud. This is music to *feel* and engage with on a physical level, no mere tinkling melody performed by a denim-clad troubadour designed to accompany the act of sitting back in a beanbag, wrapping one's poncho around oneself while pondering Vietnam with joint in hand. With melodic lines uncomplicated by the whimsy of the previous albums sitting easily atop the unrelenting rhythmic intensity of the electric guitar, bass, and drums, the song, simply, rocks along. At four minutes and forty-three seconds, however, a sparse, swirling, atmospheric, repeating section begins. Initially instrumental, the melody is a reworking of the descending motifs of the song's introduction. When this is then passed over into group vocals the effect is that of a heavenly choir, adding strength to the quasi-religious connotations of earlier lyrics. At its zenith, at five minutes and thirty-three seconds, the choir succumbs to a fast, fat, full-band blues shuffle worthy of early Deep Purple or Black Sabbath, quite unexpectedly upping the ante further when you might well have thought the song could not rock any harder. With the midsection having acted as a buffer, the song has effectively been split in two. This new development gives the song an intensely sleazy feel and texture that would become a mainstay of glam rock as exemplified in the future by songs such as Alice Cooper's "School's Out," Suzi Quatro's "Can the Can," Sweet's "Blockbuster," and Bowie's own "The Jean Genie." Here, pre-glam, the sound is extraordinarily exciting, carrying with ease the homoerotic and somewhat violent shift in the lyrics that also occurs at this point: "His nebulous body swayed above—his tongue swollen with devil's love. The snake and I, a venom high. I said 'Do it again, do it again.'" While God was name-dropped earlier in the composition, here amid this prototype glam-rock wash of dirty rhythm and blues it is Satan who controls the events, described vividly as a "spitting sentry horned and tailed waiting for you."

Bowie's delivery, sneering and confrontational, marks out this opening song as a considerable departure from his previous work in terms of performance style. Heavier in texture than the soon-to-transpire Ziggy Stardust–era quintessential glam rock, and addressing subject matter perhaps too sophisticated for the teen and preteen audience who would shortly come to constitute Bowie's main body of fans, nevertheless, in "The Width of a Circle" one can plainly hear the future.

The similarly textured "All the Madmen" is tasked with the difficult job of following the album's emphatic opener. Much has been made of this track, too, by Bowie biographers, journalists, and academics over many years, who frequently align the contents of the lyrics to the artist's relationship with his psychologically troubled older half brother, Terry Burns. While this extremely personal issue surely did contribute, the most remarkable aspect for the listener lies in the clear empathy displayed for the underdogs of society, here represented in the form of the mentally ill. "'Cause I'd rather stay here with all the madmen than perish with the sad men roaming free," sings Bowie. More than simply empathizing with those whom society deems mad, Bowie completely breaks down the them-and-us societal barriers, by clearly stating that the sane and the (supposed) insane are identical: "'Cause I'm quite content they're all as sane as me." This is the most powerful early example of Bowie writing about such extreme alienation, a topic that would go on to become a thematic cornerstone.

"Pack a packhorse and rest up here," sings Bowie in the opening line of the following song, "Black Country Rock." Demanding considerably less of the listener than the album's opening tracks, the lyrics consist of just four lines that are repeated throughout, presented within alternating two-line verses, the simplest of musical structures. A heavy electric blues reminiscent of early Led Zeppelin, in "Black Country Rock" Bowie analogously provides the listener with exactly the opportunity to "rest up" that was promised in the opening line. "You never know, you might find it here," he sings later, but exactly what "it" is, is never revealed. Unusually for a Bowie song, here the power of the musical groove provides the focus rather than the lyrics or melody.

In unexpected medium-slow waltz time, the fourth and concluding song of side one provides the strangest four minutes of *The Man Who Sold the World*. In what biographer David Buckley regards as the album's "hidden gem,"[11] "After All," Bowie abandons the heavy rock ambiance of what has gone before—and, indeed, of what will follow—to present a spooky, spacious, ethereal, Lewis Carroll–esque tune that addresses the notion of adults never growing up, because "they're just older children, that's all." A clear glam rock sensibility exists, for those discovering the album post-Ziggy, in the line "We're painting our faces and dressing in thoughts from the skies, from paradise." It is a strange conclusion to the first side.

You flip the record over and settle back down to listen, the strangeness of "After All" still ringing in your head. But side two's opener, "Running Gun Blues," comes as a shock. The song starts with strummed acoustic guitar, recalling the signature sound of the previous album in opposition to the prototype heavy-metal offerings of side one, and this thin, folkish texture sustains throughout the first verse. When Bowie begins to sing, however, it is in a manner quite different from anything heard on side one. He adopts a fey vocal styling made all the more remarkable because it sits in total contrast to the song's uncharacteristically violent and direct lyrics, which tell the story of a deranged Vietnam veteran who runs amok, killing indiscriminately in order to satisfy his bloodlust. He is clearly resentful of the protest movement, lamenting, "It seems the peacefuls stopped the war—left generals squashed and stifled. But I'll slip out again tonight 'cause they haven't taken back my rifle." The aggression of the music and the lyrics when juxtaposed against the light, fey vocal style is most unsettling.

The start of the following "Saviour Machine" quickly restores the sonic territory of side one, fading in from silence in an almost filmic manner reminiscent of the technique used two years earlier in "Space Oddity." The lyrical theme of "Saviour Machine" also sits close to that earlier song, a hard-hitting and bleak warning about the dangers of unchecked technological advancement; of man overreaching himself. Just as control of the spaceship was given over to the onboard computer, HAL, in Kubrick's *Space Odyssey*, here in "Saviour Machine" the population of Earth has gifted control of the planet to a supercomputer named the Prayer, which promises Utopia but eventually malfunctions due to boredom, pleading of its creators, "Please don't believe in me, please disagree with me. Life is too easy. A plague seems quite feasible now, or maybe a war, or I may kill you all."

The heavy blues rock of Cream is a clear stylistic influence on the riff-heavy guitar virtuosity of "She Shook Me Cold," while the sexually violent lyrics—albeit heterosexually themed on this occasion—provide a link to the opening song, "The Width of a Circle." Adopting a straightforward rock vocal style, Bowie sings callously, "I had no time to spare, I grabbed her golden hair and threw her to the ground," elsewhere proudly announcing, "I was very smart, broke the gentle hearts of many young virgins." Nicholas Pegg describes the song's lyrics as "little more than a swaggering rock 'n' roll boast," and this is a description hard to argue against. Certainly, "She Shook Me Cold" is one of the album's lesser moments.

The penultimate placement on the album is reserved for the title track. In terms of its instrumentation and overall musical vibe, "The Man Who Sold the World" stands out as being very different from the others on the record, with none of the nascent heavy-metal hallmarks for which the album has become revered. With chord organ as the predominant accompanying instrument throughout the verses, a highly prominent guiro leading the percussion, a heavily phased and understated vocal track, and a repeating, hypnotic guitar hook, the song has a quirky pop flavor and is by far the most obviously commercial track. The catchy chorus is cleverly set up by the paired words "Oh no. Not me," or, subsequently, "Who knows? Not me." These pairs of single-syllable words are set to the highest-pitched notes to be found anywhere within the song's melody—an oft-used songwriter's trick that ensures a chorus will stand out—and the first note of each pair is pitched higher than the second, resulting in a distinctive rise-and-fall motif that paints an image in the listener's mind of hands raised in the air and an accompanying shoulder shrug, such as one might give when one is asked a question but doesn't have a ready answer. In song-writing parlance, it is fine word-painting. "Who knows? Not me."

In addition to the blunting of his voice by the heavy use of phasing on the vocal track, Bowie contributes further to the strange sense of distance evident in his delivery by singing with a minimum of effort. It's as if he is in second gear, unwilling to commit more energy and meekly following rather than leading the musical accompaniment.

While the song has said all it has to say within three minutes, verses and choruses expended, a lengthy coda of layered vocal "oohs" then ensues, extending the track out to four minutes and furthering its spacious, floating, and almost timeless essence.

Lyrically, the song is extraordinarily hard to pin down. After passing a mystery man on the stairs, Bowie opines, "Although I wasn't there, he said I was his friend." While difficult to fathom, some kind of identity struggle seems evident within the mostly obscure story line, with what seems to be a current version of the song's protagonist meeting an earlier version, and noting with surprise, "I thought you died alone a long, long time ago."[12]

Quirky pop simplicity gives way to a return to heavy textures in the final track, "The Supermen." The first lyric lines set the mythological scene: "When all the world was very young and mountain magic heavy hung, the supermen would walk in file. Guardians of a loveless isle." Bowie's response to Friedrich Nietzsche's concept of the Overman, as expressed in Nietzsche's four-part book *Thus Spake Zarathustra* (1883–1885), the song is, quite literally, heavy going for the listener. Bowie's vocal line is notable for its high degree of affectation, a strong cockney inflection to the fore that thus lends a pretentious, theatrical quality to the conclusion of the album.

So there it was. You had just listened to David Bowie's third album, *The Man Who Sold the World*, in its entirety. The two albums that had been released in the 1960s had been, frankly, and not discounting some shining moments, disappointing, tossed about as they were in the considerable wake of *Ziggy Stardust* and *Hunky Dory*. As the artist's first album of the 1970s, how did *The Man Who Sold the World* stack up against the two enormously different pairs of albums that sat on either side of it? Simply, to this day the work sits as a clear bridge between those early, stylistically tired and at times derivative works and those that followed, in which Bowie so clearly found his own voice and a newly established confidence. *The Man Who Sold the World* might have lacked the infectious three-minute pop sensibilities and directness of lyric to be heard on its successors *Hunky Dory* and *Ziggy Stardust*, and yet it was easily the most pleasing of David Bowie's back-catalog albums that you had worked your way through since he burst into your consciousness. Thicker and sometimes impenetrable, the heavy-metal-esque sound nevertheless sat significantly closer to the glam rock of *Ziggy Stardust* than the music hall of the debut album or the acoustic confessional singer-songwriter musings of the second album.

More than a bridge between 1960s Bowie and 1970s Bowie, however, *The Man Who Sold the World* sits today as a litmus test for the passage of rock music between the two turbulent but hugely different decades of the 1960s and the 1970s.

5

IRRESISTIBLE DECADENCE

Aladdin Sane, Pin Ups, and *Diamond Dogs,* 1973–1974

By 1973 David Bowie was a major international star. While he himself had been no overnight success, his glam rock creation, Ziggy Stardust, was, and it was with delicious irony that life therefore imitated art. By channeling himself through the persona of Ziggy, he'd become a real star in the real world. Launching a new phenomenon within rock music—the fake star who openly *admitted* to being so—Bowie completely polarized the popular-music audience and critics alike. He was intensely unsettling to the purists, and unprecedentedly exciting to his legions of young fans delighted to have something to call their own instead of riding on the worn-out coattails of the swinging sixties. In a telling 1973 essay, rock critic Simon Frith, later to become one of the world's leading musicologists, nicely summarized the situation:

> Bowie constructs his music around an image rather than a sound or a style and it's this that disturbs rock purists. I mean, what a cheek, deciding to be a star before he'd even got a fan. But it isn't a con trick. Ziggy Stardust is the loving creation of a genuine rock addict and the purpose of the Bowie show isn't to give pop a falsely glamorous glow but to point up the reality of the continuing star/audience relationship. Since 1967 and peace and love, rock has been faking a community, as if Jimmy Page, by being scruffy, became a man of the people. But smoking dope together in a field doesn't turn an audience into a society and it's this pretence that Bowie rips apart.

I'd welcome Bowie to rock if only because his live act (down to the flaunted bisexuality) makes explicit aspects of pop usually ignored. But it's equally fascinating to follow his attempts to create a musical style to support the theatrics. His aim is to combine a tone of voice (world-weary narcissistic), an instrumental urgency (Mick Ronson's aggressive and melodic riffs) and a lyrical mythology (science fiction plus New York depravity). It doesn't always work but when it does the result is a gripping rock statement. (Simon Frith, *Let It Rock*, June 1973)

A contrasting view of Bowie's worth was provided by another now-iconic rock journalist, Nick Kent, in his review of a Bowie concert just one month after the launch of the *Aladdin Sane* album:

And there he was: the little man in the red spaceman suit exhorting his aficionados to "Give me your hands." It was beautifully symbolic in a way, because that gig was a formidable batch of nails set in the potential coffin for which the whole Bowie mystique will soon be placed and solemnly laid to rest. And all the costume-changes and mime-poses in the world won't compensate for that, sweetheart. (Nick Kent, *New Musical Express*, May 19, 1973)

Simply, by now nobody was ambivalent. You were either for Bowie or against. But while this was a conundrum for the public, the artist had an issue of his own to grapple with. *Hunky Dory* had thrived on the album charts in the wake of the success of *Ziggy Stardust* and kept an army of new fans temporarily appeased in the process. But Bowie now faced the difficult task of following up a breakthrough album with another. When *Aladdin Sane* was released on April 13, 1973, to an eager audience, more than one hundred thousand of whom had preordered the album in the UK alone, for the first time in his career all eyes were on him. What would Bowie—or was it Ziggy?—deliver?

Ziggy Stardust was written from the perspective of an aspiring star guessing at the likely effects of fame; an album written from the outside looking in. However, *Aladdin Sane* was written by an artist in the act of experiencing fame; an album written from the inside looking out. And it is precisely this split between the pre-star man and the star he had become that permeates the album, giving it a split, schizophrenic undertone and a kind of urgent, somewhat out-of-control desperation. Nevertheless, the core musical qualities present at the heart of the

Ziggy Stardust album remain evident, a highly important linkage due in no small measure to the signature efforts of the Spiders from Mars (Mick Ronson, Woody Woodmansey, and Trevor Bolder), retained by Bowie as the foundation of his band. However, there are also significant differences. The addition of virtuosic American keyboard player Mike Garson to the ensemble ensured a vastly expanded palette of piano and keyboard possibilities far and above the far more perfunctory pianistic contributions to the former album by Mick Ronson and also Bowie himself. In terms of *Aladdin Sane*'s instrumental flavor, Garson's contribution is a distinctive one that includes mellotrons, a Moog synthesizer, and highly avant-garde in-the-moment acoustic piano stylings frequently at the forefront of the mix. Also markedly different from *Ziggy Stardust* was the drum sound achieved by producer Ken Scott, which was considerably more live than before, imbuing the album with a raw element that, in conjunction with Bowie's less quintessentially pop-like songs, created a darker ambiance.

Bowie did not play it safe; although thematically and musically comparable to its famous predecessor, *Aladdin Sane* was anything but a dish of *Ziggy Stardust* reheated.

ALADDIN SANE, 1973

> Firstly, the cover, which will be a definite asset to any chic home. You'll see it strewn on Axminster carpets in expensive colour supplement stereo ads, and carried with token attempts at unobtrusiveness under the arms of the fashionable. —Charles Shaar Murray, *New Musical Express*, April 1973

> David Bowie was last year's Ziggy Stardust, this year's Aladdin Sane and probably next year's Pinocchio. —Nick Kent, *New Musical Express*, April 1973

Side One

1. Watch That Man

2. Aladdin Sane
(1913–1938–197?)

Side Two

1. Time

2. The Prettiest Star

3. Drive-In Saturday   3. Let's Spend the Night Together
                                        (Jagger/Richards)

4. Panic in Detroit   4. The Jean Genie

5. Cracked Actor   5. Lady Grinning Soul

You numbered among the many thousands who preordered Bowie's
sixth album. Here it is—the day of release, and there are queues at the
checkouts. Bright-red Bowie rooster haircuts, makeup, sequins, Lurex,
and satin feature prominently in the uniform of the excited throng. You
have new purple platforms—what a golden opportunity to show them
off! Unlike today's non-tactile, digital-download-in-the-privacy-of-your-
bedroom world, in the era of the vinyl LP there was nothing—*nothing!*—more exciting than receiving into your hands a new album by one
of your rock heroes. A big-name release, such that Bowie's *Aladdin
Sane* was, brought forth a whole community of like-minded youth to the
cultural shrine of the record shop. Sure, there were long-haired hippies
flicking through the record racks elsewhere in the shop who eyed you
with clear distaste (you could smell 'em, couldn't you? That whole "getting back to nature" thing had its drawbacks), but those in front of and
behind you in the queue knew where it was at and you simply stared
back, empowered by the knowledge that *you* were now one of the cool
kids. Their day was done. You and your fellow outcasts finally had your
own in crowd to belong to, and "No Tie-Dye or Facial Hair" was emphatically emblazoned above the clubhouse door.

   You hand over your money. A twelve-inch-by-twelve-inch cardboard
square is pulled from a box, placed in a paper bag, Sellotaped, and
passed across the counter to you. The prize you have long anticipated is
yours. Before you've moved three steps from the counter you've ripped
the bag open, and you just can't stop looking at it. *Aladdin Sane* is the
most startling cover of Bowie's career. Before a note of music is heard
the cover communicates loudly its tribal affiliation, and even the act of
carrying it home from the shop affords a thrill in itself. A glam rock
masterpiece of design, it is in complete visual synergy with the music
contained inside.

   In a heavily manipulated photographic portrait Bowie is pictured
with long orange hair, red lipstick on his slightly parted lips, red eye
shadow, no eyebrows, and long black eyelashes. Dominating and split-
ting his face is a red, black, and blue lightning flash symbol. His face is

unnaturally pink and his high cheekbones are heavily accentuated. Contrasted against these bright colors is the metallic gray of his upper shoulders and neck, which then blends to an overexposed, brilliant white for the remainder of his visible torso. Bowie casts no shadow, creating a lack of context. It is as if he is floating in nothingness; a vacuum. With his eyes closed and therefore eliminating direct communication with the viewer, he has a neutrality of expression. Inexplicably, a pool of liquid lies at his left collarbone, defying gravity. As Nick Stevenson puts it, "it is as if the image is asking you to guess where the 'real' Bowie begins and where the fabricated image ends."[1]

The closed eyes are problematic. It is not for nothing that the eyes are known as the windows to the soul, and here, with access emphatically denied, the viewer is left unable to detect the slightest flicker of human emotion. Bowie is alienated from us, and we from him. It is not even clear whether Bowie—in this new guise of Aladdin Sane (or a lad insane)—is alive or dead. Certainly, the pure white skin of his torso suggests he has no blood in his veins. Overall, he appears so unreal that he might not even be a human being at all but a mannequin or dummy. Or even, particularly given the science fiction allusions in his previous work, a cyborg; a kind of human/machine hybrid. Such a possibility recapitulates upon the essence of "Space Oddity" and his attempt to juxtapose the all-too-human astronaut with the science that took him into such an alien environment.

Beyond the impression of alienation and artificiality, the dominant feature is the lightning flash symbol. Historically, the symbol has carried multiple meanings, all of which align to Bowie's appropriation. It is a worldwide symbol for danger, particularly designating electrical danger. Similarly, it evokes memories of World War II, when it was used as the insignia of the Nazi Storm Troopers. Because it descends from the heavens in a flash, lightning has also been used extensively as a metaphor for divine inspiration or sudden comprehension—by Friedrich Nietzsche, for instance, but also by many other philosophers, inventors, artists, musicians, and writers.

The split face is also a long-established symbol of schizophrenia; of split personality. Artist Paul Klee, for instance, used the lightning flash to divide the face of his subject in his painting *Physiognomic Flash* (1927).

Listening to *Aladdin Sane*, psychological disturbance quickly becomes evident as the preeminent theme, supporting the front-cover image. Bowie has spoken of the duality of the character, including saying, "Aladdin Sane was a schizophrenic."[2] More specifically, he has claimed that the album reflected a point in his career where the boundaries between his private and performative lives were difficult to discern, resulting in "this kind of schizophrenia that I was going through."[3]

Some critics have attributed Bowie's interest in schizophrenia to the psychological disorders in his family history. Most crucially, his older half brother, Terry, was diagnosed with the condition and committed to a psychiatric hospital, from which he would ultimately escape and commit suicide. Beyond this personal motivation for the exploration of mental illness, however, a wider significance exists when one considers the presentation of psychological disorder within the wider context of Bowie's most frequently visited of thematic topics: alienation. The mentally disturbed are, by nature, alienated from society.

Having completed your perusal of the cover, it is now time to check out the record. While you have become familiar with Bowie's eclectic back catalog during the last few months, this will be the first new music you've heard from him since *Ziggy Stardust*, and the prospect is nerve-wracking. You want to *love* it, but this anticipation is tempered by having been bitten twice.

The heavily distorted, fanfare-like opening guitar chords of the first song, "Watch That Man," instantly reassure you. A mood-setter for the album and one of the most up-tempo tracks, "Watch That Man" displays the sleazy rawness that will permeate the album. This is glam rock with an extra serving of world-weary decadence. Bowie's image-laden lyrics describe scenes at a party that "Shakey" has thrown. Vignettes of partygoers paint a picture in the listener's mind in much the same way that "Five Years" did on the previous album. The party guests are desperate in their revelry, and one imagines them drinking and dancing like there is no tomorrow over Ronson's rough-edged Keith Richards–style guitar lines and Garson's honky-tonk-esque piano. It is a 1973 version of a danse macabre—a dance of death—and a thick air of live-for-today-for-tomorrow-we-may-die fatalism prevails.

The title track, "Aladdin Sane (1913–1938–197?)," appears second, and the bracketed dates that accompany it in the track listing give clear clues not only to the song's lyrical essence but also to understanding more fully the track that preceded it. The first two dates reference the years immediately preceding the first two world wars, with the third an obvious speculation upon a third. The desperation of the partygoers in "Watch That Man" is, we learn, fueled by a sense of impending doom that manifests in a drink-up-before-it's-too-late, pre-cataclysmic fatalism. "Battle cries and champagne—just in time for sunrise," confirms Bowie in "Aladdin Sane." Dominated by the piano virtuosity of Mike Garson, the style draws more from cabaret than rock 'n' roll, and an air of resigned decadence worthy of the Weimar Republic permeates. "Passionate bright young things. Takes him away to war," continues Bowie, further declaiming the thematic territory. The extended solo that occurs over two endlessly repeating chords—the simplest of harmonic platforms—finds Garson given complete creative license to do whatever he feels, a rare luxury accepted with evident relish. Initially Bowie's saxophone joins the discordant melee, but it quickly gives way to the supremacy of the piano. The many moments of disharmony between the improvised piano melody and the underlying, highly stable, two-chord backing underpin the alienation of the song's character, as the question is repeatedly posed, "Who will love Aladdin Sane?" The question remains unanswered, and the song ends with an unexpected touch of humor as Garson is left alone to execute a rapid, unsupported, music hall–style plinkety-plonk passage.

A similar air of nostalgia exists in the following "Drive-In Saturday"; however, this time the musical association is with 1950s American doo-wop. With Bowie's saxophone at the fore, the lyrics are disjunct and random, perhaps evidence of Bowie here employing the cut-up method of writing favored by beat poet William Burroughs, a technique he was becoming increasingly interested in. "Pour me out another phone—I'll ring and see if your friends are home," sings Bowie. Futuristic imagery makes it clear that while the musical style may be dated, the setting is not, as Bowie tells of "strange ones" living in a dome. A glimpse of nuclear conflict comes later in the song, evidence that the fears raised in the first two songs are now being realized: "It's hard enough to keep formation amid this fall-out saturation."

Images of violent conflict, survivalism, and loneliness dominate track four, "Panic in Detroit." Over a dense backing that includes bongo drums highly reminiscent of "Sympathy for the Devil" by the Rolling Stones, Bowie name-drops Che Guevara while singing of "the only survivor of the National People's Gang" amid descriptions of police sirens and reprisals, an armed struggle at the culmination of which "a trickle of strangers were all that were left alive." Although not made clear, this is surely the conflict inferred in the opening two tracks of the album.

Over a stomping and sleazy shuffle beat led by blues-style guitar and Bowie's wailing harmonica, the last track on side one, "Cracked Actor," is one of the album's rockiest. The story is told from the first-person perspective of another societal outcast, a washed-up fifty-year-old "has-been" Hollywood actor who finds solace in drugs while receiving oral sex from a prostitute. "Forget that I'm fifty 'cause you just got paid," he exhorts. With both protagonists highly alienated from society—in addition to a prostitute, the song describes the woman as a porcupine, inferring frequent use of needles—the song critiques the transient nature of celebrity while exposing the futility of such transient escape mechanisms.

"Time" begins side two of the album, and overt theatricality is set up in the opening line, "Time—he's waiting in the wings." Here, the cabaret inferences evident earlier in the title track receive a full-blown cabaretic treatment, with Garson again at the fore. Bowie adopts the German sing-speak style of vocal delivery known as *Sprechstimme* during the verses, the lyrics of which critique the inability of man to influence time. Escapist diversions such as the use of "quaaludes and red wine" are shown as ineffective, while even glam rock itself is unable to withstand time's demands, with the death of New York Dolls drummer Billy Murcia memorably referenced in the line "demanding Billy Dolls and other friends of mine." In concert, Bowie would play up the cabaret qualities of the song, donning a feather boa and revisiting the Greta Garbo/Marlene Dietrich silver-screen gestural nuances he had employed on the cover of *Hunky Dory.*

On "The Prettiest Star," the lightest song on the album in terms of lyric content and set to an easy-paced, loping, toe-tapping musical backing, Bowie returns to a nostalgic doo-wop style, with saxophone and harmonized backing vocals at the fore. Star worship is the theme, but with his vocal delivery fey and understated, the notion is presented somewhat sadly, as if the object of his affection has already fallen from his/her show-business peak: "Staying back in your memory are the movies in the past."

Somewhat surprisingly, a cover song features next, with the Stones' "Let's Spend the Night Together" given a frenetic treatment that remains largely faithful to the original. At the end of the song, the fastest on the album, the band fades out, leaving Garson to once again dominate with stab-like virtuosic piano phrases interspersed with saxophone utterances. Here Bowie speaks new lyrics that were not part of the original song, beginning with a line that exhibits again his now-familiar advocacy for youth: "They said we were too young—our kind of love was no fun." In so doing, he claims the song for his generation of fans. He further exhorts, "Do it! Let's make love."

The most successful single release off the album occupies the penultimate position. With the title a play on the name of controversial French writer Jean Genet, "The Jean Genie" is a straight-out simplistic but stomping blues song, again with distorted sleazy glam edge. Image heavy, with pictures painted in the mind of the listener through every line of lyric delivered, the song's central character is, as James E. Perone puts it, "the ultimate outsider."[4] With no recourse to narrative, unrelated snippets of behavior and personality relating to the song's (anti)hero are presented: he "bites on a neon—sleeps in a capsule" and "keeps all your dead hair for making up underwear." Once again, Bowie's harmonica plays a large role, while Mick Ronson remains the dominant force within the instrumental mix.

"Lady Grinning Soul" completes *Aladdin Sane* and is a surprise. It is a beautiful love song with an appropriately fashioned melody that effortlessly matches the sentiment of Bowie's sincere words of love and gratitude to the lady, whoever she might be. Torch-singer styled, the song is also the final outing for the ten-finger-and-forelock piano adventures of Mike Garson, who, as elsewhere on the album, seizes his opportunity. Ronson too is given the chance to shine in an unexpected role, with a flamenco-style solo that features call-and-response phrases with Garson as well as some exquisite unison playing. "Touch the fullness of her breast—feel the love of her caress," sings Bowie in the album's most virtuosic vocal performance. The track serves as a salve to the extreme tension and desperate alienation that has preceded it, leaving the listener with an unexpected assurance that all may, in fact, be well after all; that love *may* conquer in the end. It is *Aladdin Sane*'s version of "Give me your hands," the salvation offered at the end of "Rock 'n' Roll Suicide" on the *Ziggy Stardust* album.

The rear cover of *Aladdin Sane*, often overlooked in appraisals of the album, is in its own way as startling as the front, consisting of a thinly outlined silhouette of the front-cover photograph. Bowie's head is outlined in red, while his torso is rendered in blue. Background and foreground are now seamlessly merged. All of Bowie's facial features are absent and the viewer is confronted by what is effectively a faceless, empty shell, a bare framework completely devoid of all personal characteristics. As Stevenson puts it, "Bowie has evaporated."[5] In terms of the schizophrenic tension between Bowie the performer (presented in the role of Aladdin Sane) and Bowie the man, it is clear that the former has won out. The rear sides of all of his previous album covers have featured a photograph of Bowie that has been less staged and performative than on the front, as if showing the actor out of role and claiming authorship of the work much in the manner that authors' portraits appear on the rear covers of books. Here, however, there remains only the actor on the front cover and nothing on the rear except the outline of where he had been: the album-cover equivalent of the magician vanishing in a puff of smoke.

In summation, *Aladdin Sane* knocked your socks off; a killer of an album. *Ziggy Stardust* might have had more conceptual coherence and "ta-dah—look what I invented!" surprise about it, but *Aladdin Sane*, dripping with glorious hands-on-hips pretension and multiple manifestations of alienation, epitomized glam rock in every facet. You could hear Bowie posing in every line and on every note, pretension writ large throughout. And for the first time in rock music, this was OK. Desirable, in fact, depending on to whom you spoke. Considering *Aladdin Sane* within the wider context of glam rock, simply, no other artist associated with the style could possibly have come up with such a work, proof positive that although the association with the style served Bowie well, his craft often surpassed the style's frequently simplistic musical and lyrical parameters.

With six albums of original songs now behind him and each one a surprise package, what would Bowie do next in order to keep up with the overwhelming attention surrounding his every move?

PIN UPS, 1973

> Although many of the tracks are excellent, none stands up to the originals. —Greg Shaw, *Rolling Stone*, December 1973

> *Pin-Ups* slowly, but surely, dies a death . . . [It] fails to live up to its promise. —Ian MacDonald, *New Musical Express*, 1973

Side One	**Side Two**
1. Rosalyn (Duncan/Farley)	1. Friday on My Mind (Young/Vanda)
2. Here Comes the Night (Berns)	2. Sorrow (Feldman/Goldstein/Gottehrer)
3. I Wish You Would (Arnold)	3. Don't Bring Me Down (Dee)
4. See Emily Play (Barrett)	4. Shapes of Things (Samwell-Smith/McCarty/Relf)
5. Everything's Alright (Crouch/Konrad/Stavely/James/Karlson)	5. Anyway, Anyhow, Anywhere (Townshend/Daltrey)
6. I Can't Explain (Townshend)	6. Where Have All the Good Times Gone (Davies)

Pin Ups, an album of cover versions of songs from the sixties, is often seen as troublesome within the Bowie canon. Some critics have regarded it as mere treading water between *Aladdin Sane* and *Diamond Dogs*, two albums unequivocally perceived as iconic. But for an artist so full of surprises and changes of direction even by this still relatively early stage of his career, was it really so surprising? That Bowie was not averse to playing the songs of others was quite evident in the fact that *Hunky Dory*, *Ziggy Stardust*, and *Aladdin Sane* had each contained a cover version.

To a fully committed thirteen-year-old Bowie fan, securing another new Bowie album just six months after *Aladdin Sane* had been released was heaven on earth. You'd heard the pre-publicity and knew it was an album of cover versions of Bowie's favorite songs. Had that fazed you in any way? No. You'd preordered again, and were back at the record store on the appointed day with your heart beating fast as you stared down the hippies. In the *New Musical Express* you'd seen the advertisement featuring the front cover, and this image fueled your confidence further. This was the disturbing Bowie you wanted.

For the first time on one of his covers Bowie is not alone. The pairing with sixties supermodel Twiggy is strange and intriguing. Both naked and showing head and shoulders, Bowie's body is pale next to the tanned Twiggy. The heavy makeup each wears gives the impression that they are wearing masks, an impression enhanced by the dark borders at the outer extremities. However, because Bowie's face is darker while Twiggy's is lighter, there is the suggestion that these masks are interchangeable; that they could be swapped from one torso to the other. An underlying message that gender itself may be a kind of mask can be gleaned from this interplay.

In addition to Twiggy's mask being lighter than Bowie's, other small differences between the two are evident, primarily around the eyes. Bowie has no eyebrows, an alien feature retained from the previous album cover, while Twiggy's are thin and immaculately manicured. Bowie's eye shadow is a soft brown color, matching his hair, while Twiggy's is a shiny metallic blue, closely approximating her eyes and the tight-fitting blue cap she wears. Lastly, the difference in both size and color of Bowie's irises is clearly evident, far more so than has been the case on any previous album cover and a feature that adds significantly to the unreal, alien quality. But Bowie's image is not as overtly alien as was the case on *Aladdin Sane*. Although the disparities discussed play a part in distancing him from a normal human appearance, the predominance of natural skin tones renders him far removed from the overt cyborg-like artificiality of *Aladdin Sane*. On *Pin Ups*, the viewer sees a human being wearing a mask more than an absence of humanness altogether.

Aside from the implied interchangeability of the two subjects, the most unsettling aspect of the picture is the contrasting expressions they bear. Bowie, eyes wide and mouth slightly open, gives the appearance of experiencing anxiety, the kind of alarm or shock that evinces a fight-or-flight state. His body language, shoulders thrust back as he holds himself erect and tense, supports this notion. With his pupils two different sizes and the obvious disparity in his eye colorings, as noted, his face overall is a site of tension. Twiggy's countenance is in contrast to Bowie's heightened sense of anxiety. Her mouth is closed, eyelids heavy and partially covering her pupils, and her head is relaxed upon Bowie's neck. She is oddly absent, bored or tired, in comparison to her very present partner. In relation to the album title, while both Bowie and Twiggy are established pop and fashion pinups in their own right, their appearance together on the cover of *Pin Ups* shows them completely at odds with the usual kind of poses and expressions normally found on such celebrity pinups.

There is no evident explanation for the contrasting emotions the subjects convey, with the plain, unbroken, pale-blue background offering the viewer no context. Tom Fraser and Adam Banks, in their belief that the perception of color is often loaded by our experience of natural phenomena, posit that any expanse of light blue, such as that seen here, engenders a universally held invocation of the sky and associations with freedom, introspection, wisdom, solitude, space, truth, beauty, and serenity.[6] In this regard, then, Twiggy's calmer expression seems more consistent with the genial ambiance set up by the background. Bowie's evidently alarmed, disturbed facial expression, however, seems totally at odds with any such inference. The combined message is a mixed one, a disturbing juxtaposition of opposites.

Having featured in "Drive-In Saturday" on the *Aladdin Sane* album in the line "She'd sigh like Twig the Wonder Kid and turn her face away," Twiggy's inclusion on the *Pin Ups* cover is very significant. Certainly, her presence serves the retro vibe of the album, as her fame was at its peak during the Swinging London years from which the songs were selected. However, there is more to her involvement than meets the eye. Twiggy, like Ziggy Stardust; like Aladdin Sane; like Bowie himself, was a construction. In keeping with Bowie's own ideas on the malleability and constructedness of stardom and celebrity—notions firmly established on the albums that preceded *Pin Ups*—Twiggy was widely seen as an everyday girl *playing* the role of a fashion celebrity. Twiggy's real name was Lesley Hornby, a cockney born in a poor area of North London who had a working-class upbringing. Much credit for her success was attributed to her boyfriend, photographer Justin de Villeneuve, who shot the *Pin Ups* cover photograph. Villeneuve, in turn, was the invented alter ego of Nigel Davies, also a cockney, who assumed several different names during his career. Twiggy gave frequent credit to Davies for her reinvention and elevation to the status of supermodel, suggesting, "Twiggy isn't just me, it's me and Justin. Honestly, sometimes I think Justin invented me."[7] Such critiques on the nature of stardom would clearly have resonated with Bowie. Twiggy is, then, in a sense, a female version of Bowie's performance persona: androgynous, constructed, supremely image-conscious, and media-savvy.

The cover is, therefore, a continuation of Bowie's critique of the mechanisms of stardom and celebrity, an exploration of the idea that those who are considered worthy of being *Pin Ups*—those elevated persons vaunted and revered by media and general public alike—are not divinely chosen but may be constructed to *appear* starlike.

Like Bowie, Twiggy was androgynous, her body thin and boyish and her hair frequently cut short and styled with a parting like a man's. A 1967 headline from *Look* magazine encapsulated this quality as it posed the question, "Is it a girl? Is it a boy? No, it's Twiggy!" With Bowie having firmly established androgyny as a central part of his own style, it is clear that he would have valued the same quality in Twiggy.

Turning the cover over, on the rear side, in a message handwritten in pink fluorescent ink, Bowie explains that the songs he has selected are important to him on a personal level, describing them as "among my favourites from the '64–67' period of London." Naming three iconic music locations synonymous with the London music scene of the day, he further goes on to name the original artists, including the Pretty Things, Them, Pink Floyd, the Kinks, the Easybeats, the Who, the Yardbirds, the Mojos, and the Merseys. By paying homage to his past, *Pin Ups* is, therefore, autobiographical. The use of handwriting is highly pertinent to this, suggesting—as was the case on the earlier *Hunky Dory*—intimacy, even down to similar messily corrected errors. As befits such an intimate, firsthand message, he signs off with "Love-on ya!"—a highly informal sentiment such as one might use to a close friend, family member, or lover. Finally, he autographs his work with a heavily stylized "Bowie," underlined and featuring a heart shape instead of a dot above the "i." This is the first time he has omitted his first name and referred to himself simply as "Bowie," a tactic mirrored on the front side, although he remains David Bowie on the cover's spine. Tellingly, he is here, for the first time ever, presenting himself as a totally ficti-tious artist and thereby subtly undermining the highly personalized message above. The absence of his given name, David, in favor of his unofficially adopted surname, Bowie, alone represents a further step forward in terms of his ever-developing artificiality.

The pink fluorescent ink of Bowie's handwriting helps further the nostalgic resonance of the work, as such vibrant color harks back to the late-sixties era of psychedelia, most especially in the hallucinatory effect it causes whereby the words seemingly lift off the page in an illusory trick.

The cover of *Pin Ups* furthered Bowie's reputation for producing the most startling album covers of the glam rock era, and you stare at it for a long time, creating your own meanings and nuances. But what of the music it houses?

From the moment Bowie begins singing the first track, the Pretty Things' "Rosalyn," it is clear that he is in fine, strong vocal form and relishing the freedom from song-writing duties. He is celebratory in his acknowledgment of his musical roots, and the enjoyment and, at times, humor he experiences in recording such classic songs is evident in his voice throughout the album. But it would be inaccurate to suggest he simply sings the songs on *Pin Ups*. Rather, he reinterprets them, bringing a unique 1970s glam sensibility while, ever respectfully, not losing the original raw essence. In this first track, for instance, note the affectation—the glam braggadocio—he places upon the last word of the line "Do you love me *true?*" You can almost *see* the accompanying foot stamp, hands on hips and chin high, behind this musical moment.

The opening track lasts just two minutes and twenty-one seconds before a guitar power slide segues into Them's "Here Comes the Night." It is a slick and theatrical moment indicative of the album as a whole.

With so many albums to consider, I have taken the decision to not visit each and every song on *Pin Ups*. But in so doing I do not join the ranks of the many who undervalue this album. In terms of its contribution to Bowie's iconographical legacy alone, it simply must not be ignored. And isn't this where Bowie must be acknowledged as a most extraordinary interdisciplinary artist? The cover of *Pin Ups* belongs as much within the fields of gender studies and fashion as it does in music.

Many critics have regarded Bowie's versions as inferior to the originals—predominantly those who grew up hearing those originals, no doubt—but for young Bowie fans eagerly plucking *Pin Ups* out of the record rack during October 1973, the album was anything but a disappointment, and its commercial success was a testament to that. The Spiders from Mars remained at the album's heart, minus Woody Woodmansey, whom Bowie replaced with Aynsley Dunbar, and therefore the core *Ziggy Stardust/Aladdin Sane* glam-era Bowie sound remained intact. For this reason, and as Perone correctly suggests, "a song such as the Yardbirds' 'Shapes of Things,' for example, sounds as much like a 'Spiders from Mars' song as a mid-1960s classic, due to the setting and Bowie's vocal style."[8] This observation holds true for the entire album, and never more so than on the album's hit single, "Sorrow," formerly recorded by both the McCoys and the Merseys, which reached number three on the UK singles chart.

What should also not be overlooked is that, for younger Bowie fans, in particular, who had started listening to music in the early seventies and were not familiar with most, or even all, of the songs on the album from when they were popular the first time around, it was these covers by David Bowie that quickly became the preeminent versions. As had happened with "Let's Spend the Night Together" on *Aladdin Sane*, Bowie had once again gifted to a new audience recontextualized classic music from the past that stood up well to its new treatment. (I count myself among the beneficiaries of this phenomenon. To this day, the originals sound less appealing to my ears, so used did I become to Bowie's interpretations.)

Pin Ups found Bowie effectively creating a glam rock album from preexisting, found objects. While the glam rock uniform adopted by musicians and fans alike utilized adaptations of the baubles of a bygone era—the glitzy show-biz trappings of original fifties rock 'n' roll—here, then, was Bowie doing the same thing with music by purloining songs from the past and dressing them up in his own glam sound and image, affording them new meaning and a new, willing audience.

In a sense, and despite the usually lesser regard in which it is held, the album is as important to the study of the glam rock phenomenon as many other glam artists' original music albums are. While Pegg has termed it an "underrated throwaway,"[9] and Stevenson an "interim album . . . [that] kept the fans interested until Bowie's next big project,"[10] in truth *Pin Ups* really is far more worthy than that.

And you, as a fan, were well pleased with it in every regard. Not that Bowie's next work was not already looming large on your horizon as well, of course. Bowie had been consistently releasing albums at a rapid rate in the last two years, and you were well aware that the next, *Diamond Dogs*, was due for release in just another six months. These were boom times on the David Bowie/glam rock fronts, indeed.

DIAMOND DOGS, 1974

> Once more into the apocalypse. . . . The "mood" is the ultimate in punk SF post-atomic doom—where "after dark" is forever, rock 'n' roll mutants are real mutants, and the glitter won't come off your face because it is your face. —Ian McDonald, *New Musical Express*, May 1974

> D-d-d-*dec*adence, that's what this album is all about, thematically and conceptually. . . . [He] pretentiously likes to think of himself as the prescient chronicler of a planet falling to pieces, so this is again a quasi-Orwellian concept album about a future world where the clockwork orangutans skulk like dogs in the street while the politicians etc. and blah blah blah . . . I'm getting a bit tired of his broken-larynxed vocals; they're so queasily sincere they reek of some horrible burlesque, some sterilely distasteful artifice. It's the same old theatrical delivery of pretentious lyrics. —Lester Bangs, *Creem*, August 1974

Side One

1. Future Legend
2. Diamond Dogs
3. Sweet Thing
4. Candidate
5. Sweet Thing (Reprise)
6. Rebel Rebel

Side Two

1. Rock 'n' Roll with Me (Bowie/ Peace)
2. We Are the Dead
3. 1984
4. Big Brother
5. Chant of the Ever-Circling Skeletal Family

Your speakers emit a threatening fanfare of howling dogs as the needle plows the first grooves of Bowie's eighth album, his last of the glam rock era. Taking the listener by surprise, this canine opening to "Future Legend" morphs into a spoken poem. The howl of the Diamond Dogs fades, and discordant strings and dissonant synthesizers take over to provide the backdrop to Bowie's equally disturbing opening line: "And in the death, as the last few corpses lay rotting on the slimy thoroughfare . . ." Setting a chilling, image-laden scene, the protagonists of the album's title, the Diamond Dogs, take a threatening center-stage position from the outset, mirroring the centrality of Bowie's own highly disturbing mutant canine form on the front cover in a perfect marriage of sound and vision.

Devoid of any sense of human emotion, Bowie delivers his one-minute-and-eight-second introductory tale of a hellish post-apocalyptic world, identified as Hunger City. So strong is the imagery, the effect is filmic, as if we have a camera up to our eye and are nervously panning around the ruins of an urban environment ravaged by nuclear war. The track's special effects support this notion, as we hear the obscene sound of the "fleas the size of rats" as they suck on "rats the size of cats," and the chilling "Love me" calls of the mutant prostitutes plying their trade on Love Me Avenue.

This startling beginning is a comprehensive scene-setter for what follows, drawing together with stark clarity the themes of loneliness and alienation evident in Bowie's earlier work, and once again tapping directly into the very real fear of a nuclear Armageddon that was held by a generation. The as-yet-nameless narrator, wandering the broken, dangerous city streets while being watched by unseen eyes from the tops of the windowless skyscrapers, is as isolated and threatened as was Major Tom of "Space Oddity," alone and adrift in space with no way to return to his wife on Earth; as lost as Ziggy Stardust, washed up and coked out in "Rock 'n' Roll Suicide"; as estranged as the schizophrenic "Cracked Actor" of *Aladdin Sane*; as marginalized as the subject of "Please Mr. Gravedigger" of the debut album eight years earlier. He is George Orwell's Winston Smith of *1984* brought to life in a rock 'n' roll dystopia. This is no accident, as Bowie's original intention was to create an entire musical version of Orwell's novel; however, he was unable to secure the rights to do so from the deceased author's estate. Nevertheless, *Diamond Dogs* is peppered with references, both obvious and subtle, from this uncompleted work. Our tour through the ruins of Hunger City completed, "Future Legend" ends with an anguished cry: "This ain't rock 'n' roll—this is genocide!"

Just as the title track of *Aladdin Sane* followed the scene-setting "Watch That Man," so too "Diamond Dogs" appears via segue from "Future Legend." Almost six minutes long, the title track furthers the danger of the album's opener in an unrelenting rock 'n' roll epic set to the screams and applause of a fake audience of apocalypse survivors. Though Bowie had dispensed with all of the Spiders from Mars except

Mick Ronson, listening to "Diamond Dogs" assuages the fear that the glam rock magic of his core sound had been compromised. To the contrary, the glam rock sleaze is here present in bucketloads. Musically conventional in song form and instrumentation, the sound is reminiscent of the Rolling Stones; however, Jagger and Richards would never have approached such subject matter. The character of Halloween Jack is introduced in the song, an alter ego never as well formed nor as fleshed out as Ziggy Stardust, but "a real cool cat" nevertheless, who gains access to the street Tarzan-style by swinging down on a rope. A heroic figure in this inner-city wasteland, he "meets his little hussy," whose "face is sans feature but she wears a Dali brooch." The characters are all outsiders, freaks, and non-heroic survivors, some seen crawling on hands and knees. Tod Browning's controversial 1932 film *Freaks*, starring actual carnival freak show exhibits, is name-dropped, aligning music to album cover image emphatically.

"Sweet Thing" then slows the pace considerably, while enhancing the doomsday mood that has been crafted by the album's opening tracks. Bleak in the extreme, Bowie's vocals begin as low and solemn as they have ever been as he assures us, "It's safe in the city to love in a doorway," before opining, "Isn't it neat—putting pain in a stranger?" The chorus is sung from the perspective of a burned-out, emotionless prostitute, enticing her clients with, "Boys, boys, it's a sweet thing . . . If you want it, boys, get it here, then. For hope, boys, is a cheap thing, cheap thing."

Another segue occurs, this time over military-sounding snare drum rolls joined initially by mournful saxophone lines, later doubled by distorted guitar and ultimately kicking into the up-tempo "Candidate." The theme of illicit and risky sex continues, as Bowie offers to "caress you on the ground while shaking in fright," before admitting, "Well, on the street where you live I could not hold up my head for I gave all I have in another bed. On another floor, in the back of a car; in the cellar of a church with the door ajar." The song is rampant with the unnamed protagonist's desperation for hope and relief, and, with none forthcoming, even suicide is contemplated as a solution: "We'll buy some drugs and watch a band, then jump in the river holding hands."

Subsequently, "Sweet Thing (Reprise)" occurs via another effortless segue, acting as a recapitulation to end side one's mini-trilogy. Here, the prostitute returns, suggesting acceptance of the new world order is the only viable option; that one should let go of hope and accept survival and life on the street for what it is: "Then let it be, it's all I ever wanted. It's a street with a deal. It's got taste. It's got claws. It's got me, it's got you."

Coming at a time when the domination of glam rock in the popular music of the UK was beginning to show the first signs of waning, "Rebel Rebel" is glam's anthem. Released two months before the album and reaching number five on the singles chart, the last song on side one announces itself rudely and with garage-band brashness when a Keith Richards–esque fanfare riff as memorable as the opening of "(I Can't Get No) Satisfaction" kicks in on guitar over simple 1, 2, 3, 4 clicks from the drummer's sticks. The drums enter fully at the fifth bar with the snare played on every beat, Motown-fashion, and with cymbal crashes creating an aggressive wash of sound. Bass, rhythm guitar, and vocals join for a further eight bars from bar nine, with Bowie's falling "doo doo doos" decorating one of the most angst-ridden yet infectiously catchy introductions imaginable. (In the year of its release, at fourteen years of age and on the occasion of my sister's wedding, I witnessed the ability of this song to fill a dance floor within the first few seconds, a phenomenon that endures to this day.) Sixteen bars in, Bowie begins the first verse with a line that could not better sum up glam rock's hallmark quality of parent-worrying androgyny: "You've got your mother in a whirl—she's not sure if you're a boy or a girl." As the verse frenetically continues, the lyrics paint a clear picture of youthful exuberance, of a passion for bands and dancing, and, most importantly, of acceptance— "Hey babe—your hair's alright"—in the face of rejection by others, because "they put you down—they say I'm wrong." Possessing none of the underlying threat to be found in the rest of *Diamond Dogs*, "Rebel Rebel" instead offers a fist-raising celebration of *being* a rebel; of not fitting in. In addition to becoming an anthem for glam rock, therefore, the song stands as an anthem to Bowie's own performative ethos and raison d'être as champion of the alienated. Masterful yet restrained word-setting of the song title in the chorus, "Re-bel, Re-bel," whereby the two syllables of each word form consecutive pairs that descend in pitch, the second word beginning on the last note of the first, renders the beginning of the chorus a declamation, proud and empowering. In true anthemic fashion the song also features a declamatory sing-along line, "Hot tramp! I love you so."

"Rebel Rebel" has played all of its cards by the end of the first chorus, with verse two following in an almost exact repeat of the first. But the middle-finger-raised-to-the-world power of the song sustains throughout, not letting up even in the outro, which lasts for over a minute.

Side two begins relatively quietly after the tumult of "Rebel Rebel," with the power ballad "Rock 'n' Roll with Me." Co-written with his childhood friend Geoffrey MacCormack (aka Warren Peace), now one of Bowie's backing singers, the track has a smooth and highly soulful feel in opposition to the abrasive sonic territory of side one. Piano and saxophone are at the forefront, while the intense pressure of Ziggy Stardust's global success is vividly recalled: "Tens of thousands found me in demand," sings Bowie. However, "when you rock 'n' roll with me," everything is all right.

Just as "Sweet Thing," "Candidate," and "Sweet Thing (Reprise)" worked as a trilogy on side one, track two of side two, "We Are the Dead," begins a three-song subgroup. Here, the link is George Orwell's novel *1984*, the surviving song of that uncompleted former project. Winston, the protagonist of Orwell's novel, uttered these exact words to his partner, Julia, knowing that their actions in defying Big Brother would likely result in death. In Bowie's post-apocalyptic environment of Hunger City, survival has simply meant a stay of execution and a live-for-the-moment lifestyle in which the protagonists might just as well be dead. For the main character, escape can only be found through sex: "Heaven's on the pillow." Amid the wretched scenes described in the lyrics, the survivors live a life of paranoia: "For I hear them on the stairs," Bowie sings, echoing just such a scene in Orwell's story. Crying out for humanity, he beseeches, "Now I'm hoping some one will care. Living on the breath of a hope to be shared." But there is no hope. The song paints its theme most expressively, its changing form and tonality meandering in a nonstandard format that allows no sense of home or safety. And Bowie's voice has effects layered upon it that sound eerie and ethereal, joined in the choruses by massed backing vocals that sound like a choir of lost souls.

The third song of side two, and second in the Orwell trilogy, is the unequivocally titled "1984." Fast in tempo, the song is one of Bowie's most compelling juxtapositions of opposites in terms of lyrical content versus musical style. Rock 'n' roll takes a backseat as disco melds with soul and funk, with a clear stylistic similarity to Isaac Hayes's 1971 hit "Theme from Shaft." Despite the feel-good dance vibe of the music, however, the lyrics serve only to further the dystopian flavor of the album at large, with all hope for humanity lost in the reign of Big Brother, and pleasure to be found only in fleeting addictions: "They'll split your pretty cranium, and fill it full of air . . . You'll be shooting up on anything, tomorrow's never there." With wah-wah guitar at the fore and an elaborate string section giving a convincing evocation of Philadelphia soul, the song's roots lie emphatically on the other side of the Atlantic, a very long way from Bowie's Swinging London beginnings.

Last in the trilogy is Orwell's master villain, "Big Brother." A commentary on those who meekly acquiesce and surrender self-determination by willingly, blindly placing their faith in others, and therefore closely aligned to the earlier "Saviour Machine," here the central subject has given up all hope and beseeches Big Brother to lead the populace, caring not whether it is a trick. Simply, he wants "someone to claim us, someone to follow. Someone to shame us, some brave Apollo. Someone to fool us, someone like you. We want you Big Brother." Such a triumph of totalitarianism lays bare the ultimate nightmare of *Diamond Dogs*, and parallels can easily be drawn from history, for instance with Adolf Hitler, whose genocidal reign had ended less than three decades earlier. The instrumental beginning is characterized by starkness, a lonely trumpet providing a mournful fanfare over massed voices that recall the choir of lost souls heard earlier on "We Are the Dead." The sense of loneliness, abandonment, and extreme alienation is palpable, and we experience the moment where the unnamed protagonist gives up all hope and looks to Big Brother to save him. His opening lines are delivered without emotion, dead and cold, but when he begins to plead for Big Brother to take him the voice becomes an emotion-filled cry for help and you can almost see him on his knees, head thrown back, hands aloft. In a last, lucid aside during the song's brief bridge section, he describes the only other choice left to him beyond complete compliance: "Lord, I'd take an overdose." At this point the pleading chorus resumes, as self-determination in the form of suicide is now taken from him too.

A further segue moves the action into the final track, "Chant of the Ever-Circling Skeletal Family." It is literally a chant; aside from its rock instrumentation its closest referents lie in Hindustani music, the classical music of eastern Pakistan and northern India. The instrumental contributions and vocal utterances repeat phrases of uneven, disparate length that leave the listener on highly unstable ground throughout the track's two-minute duration. Here, in a dramatic finale, all order has broken down, humanity has been subsumed, and technology reigns victorious. The album's final seconds feature a fragmentary tape loop repeating the first syllable of the word "brother" before fading slowly to silence: "Bro bro bro bro bro . . ." It is a very ominous moment, as if the new order is already breaking down, evoking once again images of HAL, the malfunctioning onboard computer in Kubrick's *2001: A Space Odyssey*. This abrupt end leaves no room for doubt about the album's central theme. It is one Bowie has visited often and this is his most fully realized version of the concept. It is doomsday. It is bleak. But it is magnificent.

While the album has been playing you have been turning the cover over and over, opening it up to its full gatefold length and taking in every detail. Bowie's skill in aligning sound with vision is obvious, as the music of *Diamond Dogs* is fully reflected in the cover. Bowie lies propped up on his elbows on a wooden floor, a stage or boardwalk perhaps, partially concealing a billboard situated immediately behind him. He is visible from the waist up on the front cover, his head positioned to the center left of the picture, his face front-on and his eyes wide, staring straight at the viewer. The muscles and sinews of his naked body are highly accentuated by shadowing, and his hands are crossed on the floor in front of him with fingers splayed like claws. When the cover is opened to reveal his body in its entirety, it is clear that the lower part of his body is that of a dog, a transformation so complete that Bowie no longer has human feet but, rather, canine paws. A gold bangle adorns the wrist of his left arm, while a large, round gold earring hangs from his left earlobe and long red hair hangs down over his shoulders. A carefully back-combed crown of hair also sweeps back from the center front of his head. His face is heavily made up, with dark eye shadow, bright-red lipstick, and rouge on his cheeks. Although his pose is relaxed, the expression on Bowie's face is one of hyperawareness. Watchful and alert, his eyes are wide and focused and his head is erect, giving the impression that he could easily spring into action at any moment.

Behind Bowie, the billboard features two highly anthropomorphic female cartoon figures who have paws instead of hands, flaming red hair, silver/gray flesh, and red lipstick on their smiling mouths. Each has a small remnant of green clothing, consisting of a strip around the waist of the one on the left, and a narrow strip across the breasts of the one on the right. The hair on the righthand figure is teased straight up, while that of the figure on the left hangs down. Behind them, to the top left of the cover, lies the dark silhouette of a city skyline beneath a dark gray cloudy sky. The buildings are gray and featureless with no light emanating from the windows. A couple of trees can be seen, leafless and dead. The impression is that of a bleak, uninviting, urban landscape. It is Hunger City.

Bowie captures startlingly the essence of his recorded work on his album cover by once again utilizing sources borrowed from well beyond the realm of rock music. The caricatures of the two barely clad, grinning anthropomorphic women-dogs pictured on the billboard behind Bowie's own man-dog form are based upon real people, freak show exhibits from the days when human abnormalities were highly marketable and acceptable entertainment for the masses. Alzoria Lewis and Johanna Dickens were staples in the Coney Island freak shows from the 1930s to the 1950s, and in re-creating their images, complete with a freak show banner that crosses the gatefold sleeve declaring them "The Strangest Living Curiosities," Bowie could not have more convincingly drawn our attention to the notion of an existence well outside of mainstream human society. It is a perfect image of the "other"—an alienated state of being.

The cover was painted by Belgian artist Guy Peellaert, under Bowie's commission. Peellaert was an artist very much riding the crest of a wave of popularity at the time of the album's release, due to the extraordinary international success of his 1973 book of fantasy paintings of top rock artists, including Bowie, titled *Rock Dreams*. The book was aptly named, as all of the subjects were pictured in totally fictitious situations and locations drawn from Peellaert's own imagination, to which rock journalist Nik Cohn added a short and equally fictitious written commentary. Peellaert's style was photorealism, a specific style of painting that used photography as its starting point and that was at the peak of its popularity during the mid-1970s, having originated within the pop art movement of the 1960s. Interestingly, Peellaert had used freak show imagery in his work prior to working with Bowie. One of the pictures in his book *Rock Dreams*, for instance, featured Jim Morrison, Brian Jones, Janis Joplin, and Jimi Hendrix caught in anguished poses above the entrance to a freak show–styled sideshow exhibit titled *The Greatest Show on Earth*. A white-singleted ticket collector sits in his booth ready to admit the curious, while the text written to the viewer's upper right of the stage proclaims, "Congress of the World's Strangest Curiosities."

The message is clear: the rock star is the modern-day equivalent of a carnival freak show exhibit—a veritable clown for the world to boo and hiss at, or cheer and champion, according to their whim.

In *Aladdin Sane*, *Pin Ups*, and *Diamond Dogs*, Bowie's obvious otherness is at the fore. It is strongly present in the music of *Aladdin Sane* and *Diamond Dogs* but, beyond a generalized, borrowed, youth angst already existing in the cover songs, not so in *Pin Ups*. However, on all three album covers the artist's overt freakishness could not have been more explicitly rendered, and this iconography acted as a beacon to those who felt similarly marginalized, whether by age, ethnicity, gender, physical appearance, psychological state, or any other means of social division. In a simple explanation for the confirmation of his superstardom during the immediate post-Ziggy period addressed in this chapter, when he became *the* preeminent rock star of the era, what teenager does *not* feel different?

Just as the Beatles had done for the generation before you, and, similarly, Elvis Presley before him, in David Bowie you had found a spokesperson who expressed the concerns of your generation in a new and exciting manner that was, crucially, not approved of by parents and older siblings.

"Oi, Chapman!" came the aggressive yell. Oh no! I'd ventured too close to the rugby pavilion on my way out of school. When would I *ever* learn! Feigning having not heard a thing—extremely unlikely though that clearly was—I put my head down and increased my walking speed. "Chapman!" came another call, more aggressive than the first. "You'd better stop, or else!" With a mental sigh, I stopped. Experience had told me that outrunning rugby players was not my forte. Next minute, there they were. Three Neanderthals were crowding around me, smirking as they circled. Knuckle-draggers. Zeppelin fans, for sure. And there I was, with no bananas in my bag that I could toss into a nearby bush while I made my getaway. Now don't get me wrong, I had nothing against Led Zeppelin. In fact I liked them a lot. But in my high school the battle lines were drawn very clearly and if you were an overt Bowie fan like myself, with rooster cut and all, the twain could never meet. The heavy rock boys would make sure of that.

What would it be this time? A bit of a smack around? A knee in the nuts? The tired old ritual of opening my bag, strewing its contents around, and then throwing my books or my lunchbox onto the pavilion roof?

"What's that?" one of them demanded, pointing at the badge pinned to my schoolbag with a finger the size of a sausage. Actually, it may have been a sausage.

"Nothing," I mumbled, eyes down.

"It doesn't look like nothing to me," he responded, which was fair enough under the circumstances because it *was* something, clearly.

I pulled my schoolbag close to me. Big mistake. The next minute, six hairy-knuckled hands were ripping it from my scrawny frame. I fought back momentarily but pointlessly, and quickly found myself on my back on the ground. While one primate held my bag, another roughly pulled the badge from it and held it before his ugly, squinty eyes.

Now, I should point out that in New Zealand in 1973 you could not buy rock 'n' roll badges from just anywhere—in fact you'd be hard-pressed to buy them *anywhere*—and so I had sent off to England a mail-order form via airmail, reverently clipped out of the back pages of an *NME* magazine. To my great excitement, three Bowie badges had duly arrived in our letterbox three months later. One was a picture of Bowie performing live as Ziggy Stardust, the second was the reissued black-and-white front cover of *The Man Who Sold the World*, and the third, my favorite, featured the *Aladdin Sane* album cover. It was *Aladdin Sane* that the missing link was now holding aloft in his furry hand.

"David *Bowie!*" he shrieked, putting on a mincing, taunting voice on Bowie's surname. "What a bloody poofter he is! What have you got *him* on your bag for?"

I said nothing, hoping with all my being that a sudden unexpected surge of evolution would wipe the three of them off the face of the earth before my eyes. The thing is, though, they never liked it when I wouldn't answer their stupid questions.

"Well?" he demanded.

"What are ya?" another of them growled, getting right up in my face, to the point where I could smell on his breath the small animals he'd eaten earlier in the day.

"Why don't you listen to *real* music?" said the third, with a sneer, obviously keen to not be left out of the fun.

That was it! *"Bowie* is *real music!"* I shouted in a voice that must have been heard over the whole school. My nostrils flared, the red mist descended, my small fists bunched and I bared my teeth, momentarily becoming just like them.

They loved that, of course. Like three cats tormenting a mouse they easily held me at bay while I windmilled furiously. But then . . . calamity! The one who held my badge had come up with a nasty plan that must have used all of his brain cell. "This is what I think of David bloody Bowie," he said, pulling his arm back and throwing my precious badge with rugby-player accuracy onto nearby Peachgrove Road. It's a very busy road, is Peachgrove Road; the main thoroughfare through the town.

"No!" I yelled in pure anguish as I watched my precious badge skitter for a few feet and then come to a stop in the middle of the southbound lane. This couldn't be happening! "No!" I yelled again.

They held me down, the three of them. Bastards. I pleaded and I struggled but it was no good. They held me there until, sure enough, an obliging bus ran over David, squishing him flatter than a pancake. Only then was I allowed to get up, and I ran straight to the road. Prizing David from the chip seal as I fought back tears, I wondered at the sheer unfairness of the world.

Such was the vehemence of ill feeling held against David Bowie in certain quarters of the rock 'n' roll trenches at my school. But did it make me curb my enthusiasm? Oh no. It did the opposite, making me even more devoted to the cause. I was now more isolated and alienated than ever—a veritable Bowie martyr. We couldn't have been closer than we were at this moment, David and I.

PLASTIC SOUL AND THE BIRTH OF THE EUROPEAN CANON

Young Americans and *Station to Station,* 1975–1976

By 1975 David Bowie was the world's greatest glam rock star. In the space of just under two and a half years he had compiled a five-album set, spanning *Hunky Dory* to *Diamond Dogs*, that defined the style and eclipsed the efforts of every other glam exponent. However, glam rock's status as the preeminent popular-music style of the day in the UK and Europe began to wane through 1975. Early front-runner Marc Bolan, Bowie's friend and rival, saw his fortunes plummet with each successive release, and in the best transient tradition of pop music, the turn-of-the-decade preteens and early teens that had comprised glam rock's primary audience were now in their mid- to late teens and ready for a new "next big thing." Nobody, however, expected the quantum about-face that David Bowie was about to deliver.

YOUNG AMERICANS, 1975

> The main item on the menu is none other than ye olde Loneliness Of
> The Long-Distance Superstar—an odd one for Bowie considering he
> built a sizeable proportion of his reputation on exploring his divorce
> from stardom, being outside looking in on fame . . . it sounds virtually

nothing like the Bowie we've all come to love or loathe. —Ian Mac-Donald, *New Musical Express*, March 1975

It's the phoniest R & B I've ever heard. . . . If I ever would have got my hands on that record when I was growing up, I would have cracked it over my knee. —David Bowie in David Buckley, *Strange Fascination*

I was speechless! [But] . . . with all teenage fashions, how it worked was that you could pick up and put down the likes of Bolan, Gary Glitter and Sweet, as and when the whim took you, but where Bowie led you simply had to follow. —Philip Cato, *Crash Course for the Ravers: A Glam Odyssey*

Bowie has just changed his props . . . this tour it's black folk. —Lester Bangs, *Creem*, 1975

Side One

1. Young Americans
2. Win
3. Fascination (Bowie/Vandross)
4. Right

Side Two

1. Somebody Up There Likes Me
2. Across the Universe (Lennon/McCartney)
3. Can You Hear Me?
4. Fame (Bowie/Lennon/Alomar)

Young Americans proved to be a pivotal album for Bowie in that it finally launched him as a superstar in the United States. Prior to this, his status as a preeminent artist in the UK, Europe, and other countries throughout the world, including New Zealand and Australia, had never been matched in that biggest of popular-music marketplaces. Most particularly, success on the singles chart had always eluded him. The *Young Americans* album duly reached number nine on the US Billboard album charts and number two in the UK, but crucially, "Fame," the single co-written with John Lennon and Carlos Alomar, gave Bowie his first US number-one hit.

The cover of *Young Americans* telegraphs Bowie's radical change of direction emphatically. On an album on which he performs in a wholly borrowed style, describing his work as "plastic soul," he visually presents himself to his audience with similar faux honesty. In a heavily airbrushed photograph, Bowie catches the gaze of the viewer in an open, intimate manner. The image oozes self-confidence, the relaxed mood and posture painting a portrait of an artist fully at ease with both who he is and what he has to offer, his soul laid bare. The gaze is so direct it borders perhaps on arrogance, with no hint of the masking or other theatrical affectations that formed so much a part of his glam rock–era work. And yet the picture remains highly stylized and obviously constructed, the careful backlighting providing an almost halo-like effect, the smoke from his cigarette trailing upward perfectly, while careful frontlighting creates a perfectly placed sparkle on his silver bangle. He is dressed in a muted gray/blue plaid shirt—the very antithesis of his glam iconography—and his hair is nonchalantly yet carefully coiffured.

There is no preemptive scene-setter first up on *Young Americans* as there was on the glam-era albums. Instead, the title track is right there at the beginning of side one, setting its own scene of a young couple questioning what it is to be American in post-Vietnam, post-Watergate 1975. Even before Bowie begins to sing, soulful saxophone lines performed by the then up-and-coming David Sanborn sway sensuously above a percussion-driven Latin rhythm, immediately serving to locate the sound in Philadelphia, a very far cry from the post-apocalyptic London of *Diamond Dogs*. While some critics rightly point to the soul aspects of "1984" from the *Diamond Dogs* album as a clear precursor, such nuances were present only in the music of the song, with the doom-laden lyrics residing a whole world away from the thematic material addressed in typical soul music.

"Scanning life through the picture window," Bowie's young Americans yearn for the American Dream but fall well short, the brief sexual encounter of the first verse setting up a story of unfulfillment in the shadow of an America that exists only *in* their dreams. "He kissed her then and there. She took his ring, took his babies. It took him minutes, took her nowhere." The backing music to this drama is authentic soul, and as Bowie's band was made up of genuine, handpicked soul musicians, any plasticity is Bowie's alone.

It is a strange experience listening to the title track of *Young Americans* for the first time as a young and committed David Bowie fan. You identified fully with the glitter monster that had been Ziggy Stardust/Aladdin Sane/Halloween Jack, those invaluable touchstone personas upon whom you had hung your own sense of alienation. Yet, as

Peter Doggett suggests, "'Young Americans' presented a Bowie who had never been heard on record before, catching almost everyone who had followed him by surprise."[1] You couldn't help but admire the accuracy and depth of his ruse with this new soul sound. Hearing him singing high in his register, particularly in the latter parts of the title song, you could hear the strain and effort involved; he might as well have been screaming, "Listen to that—I *do* have a soul!" Nevertheless, after the five minutes and fifteen seconds that it took for "Young Americans" to run its course, your first reaction was to want the old Bowie back. You'd fallen in love with a glam rock star, not an American soul boy. The disappointment you experienced at hearing *David Bowie* #1 and #2 began to prickle again at the back of your mind.

Track two, a sensuous ballad titled "Win," is expansively arranged, with shimmering strings and saxophone providing a dreamscape above which Bowie's voice carries the significant depth and gravitas of a soul singer. However, the lyrics exhibit cynicism similar to that of the first track, as Bowie rails against those who expect success to be handed to them on a plate and who regard winning as everything that matters: "Now your smile is spreading thin. Seems you're trying not to lose. Since I'm not supposed to grin. All you've got to do is win."

In the following "Fascination," co-written with Luther Vandross in a reworking of his existing composition titled "Funky Music (Is a Part of Me)," Bowie allows his backing singers to take the lead while he sings responses, a bona fide soul music technique that is here very well utilized. Based upon a simple and repetitive infectious funk groove, this is one of the more up-tempo dance tracks of the album, with a lyrical theme that conversationally (trading parts with his backing vocalists) explores his fascination with a sexual partner: "(I can't help it) I can't help it (I've got to use her) got to use her (every time, ooh) Fascination comes around."

While it couldn't be said that this was what you were used to nor what you particularly wanted from Bowie, by this stage of your listening experience you were full of admiration at the chutzpah of the man. And, undeniably, your foot was tapping on the floor to the album's infectious rhythms.

The fourth and final track on side one, "Right," is completely groove-based, with minimal lyrics and harmonic progression over a percussion- and bass-heavy musical platform. Once again the backing vocalists are given as much prominence as Bowie himself, an antiphonal technique common to soul. The lyrics are simply a nonspecific evocation of the song's title, open to numerous interpretations: "Taking it all the right way. Never no turning back. Never need, no. Never no turning back." A uniformly positive song, this is perhaps the most authentically soulful moment of the album thus far, with no hidden Bowie-esque irony, barb, or angst anywhere in evidence. And you liked it.

"Somebody Up There Likes Me," claims Bowie in the first track of side two, the longest song on the album at six minutes and thirty-five seconds. With an extended cool saxophone introduction that further cements the album's emphasis on groove, it is over a minute before Bowie enters. When he does it is to address a topic familiar to Bowie fans, that of the dangers of fame and undeserved media-hyped adulation. The subject in his sights might be a politician or a rock star or indeed any other kind of public figure, because "he's everybody's token, on everybody's wall. Blessing all the papers, thanking one and all. Hugging all the babies, kissing all the ladies." Bowie himself seems to have had politics in mind when writing the song, suggesting, "Really, I'm a one-track person. What I've said for years under various guises is, 'Watch out, the West is going to have a Hitler!' I've said it in a thousand different ways. That song is yet another one."[2] While the message may be serious, "Somebody Up There Likes Me" is smooth and sophisticated, blunting the barbs significantly. Humorous, high-pitched, periodic "woo-hoo" utterances from the backing vocalists do nothing to diminish the otherwise almost celebratory mood of the music, and this overall vibe is even further enhanced by gospel-style handclaps.

The introduction to the second song of side two, "Across the Universe," is immediately familiar despite the sparseness of its acoustic guitar and vocal treatment. A Lennon and McCartney song from the 1970 album *Let It Be*, here Lennon is a guest on the recording. In Bowie's hands, and despite the understated beginning, once it develops the song is given significantly more instrumental and rhythmic punch than the Beatles' version, something Lennon was reportedly very pleased about (but apparently this was not so for many Beatles fans). A lengthy "Hey Jude"–style coda extends the song and Bowie takes the opportunity over the repeated mantra of the title line to give full vent to his newfound gravelly soul vocal tricks, these vocal calisthenics extending the track out to almost a minute longer than the Beatles' version.

The penultimate song of *Young Americans*, "Can You Hear Me?" is termed by James E. Perone as "the closest thing to a prototypical soulful love song that David Bowie has ever written . . . [and] one of the most autobiographical-sounding songs he has ever recorded."[3] This accurately describes a lyric in which he confesses to his lover his many affairs while touring: "There's been many others—so many times. Sixty new cities, and what do I, what do I? What do I find? I want love so badly, I want you most of all." It is the most personal lyric since "Letter to Hermione" from the second album, and the soul style upon which the album is predicated suits the subject matter here to perfection. Backing vocalists, call-and-response saxophone, and luscious strings all play their part in one of *Young Americans'* absolute highlights, while an unexpected a capella coda ensures this most personal of songs on the album ends with the most personal musical touch possible, that of unaccompanied voice making a direct plea to his lover to "take it in right to your heart."

The final song completely cemented the success of *Young Americans* and underlined the perfection with which Bowie had been able to adopt a totally new style and win for himself a whole new fan base in the process. "Fame," co-written with Carlos Alomar and John Lennon, reached number one on the US Billboard singles chart in September 1975 and gave Bowie the elusive success in America that British artists had always striven for. Almost none of the UK artists with whom Bowie had so recently been aligned during the glam rock era had managed to make any significant impression across the Atlantic, including heavyweights such as Marc Bolan and T. Rex, Slade, and Sweet. Yet here was Bowie on top of the world with a new look, a new band, a new sound, and a number-one hit.

From the opening bars of "Fame," it is clear that Bowie has completely mastered the art of the soul groove. After a quick fade-in, another example of a favorite technique, the groove is established immediately. Heard elsewhere on the album in various guises, here it is fat and infectious with open hi-hat swishes, a minimalist but declamatory bass line, synth stabs, and jingly guitar all combining in a sparse but very rhythm-heavy and mostly unchanging musical platform above which Bowie is able to play with a repetitive melody. Each lyric line in the first half of the song is founded on the title word being uttered and then instantly repeated in a higher register in another example of antiphony, the call-and-response technique used with much impact on the album. The lyrics once again address the nature of stardom and celebrity, with Bowie's ongoing critique in this instance rendered in plain language with a directness that previous incarnations lacked. "Fame, makes a man take things over. Fame, lets him loose, hard to swallow. Fame, puts you there where things are hollow." The trappings of fame are laid bare throughout, and the warning that fame confines you, robbing you of both your freedom and your future, is made candidly clear: "Fame, what you like is in the limo. Fame, what you get is no tomorrow." The theme of the song was also reportedly a topic close to Lennon's heart, and Nicholas Pegg correctly suggests, "'Fame' is an immaculately produced slice of bump-and-grind funk that cuts to the quick of Bowie's (and indeed Lennon's) very immediate disaffection with the trappings of stardom: money-grabbing managers, mindless adulation, unwanted entourages and the meaningless vacuity of the limousine lifestyle."[4]

While the musical underpinning remains mostly unchanging in order to maintain the groove, above this Bowie has the freedom to literally play with his voice, at times using falsetto, and at times delivering lines that have their own syllabic pulse: "Bu-lly-for-you. Su-gar-for-me." At three minutes and thirty-six seconds studio magic allows for a string of twenty-four repeats of the title word, "Fame," starting impossibly high and moving downward in stepwise motion to impossibly low at a strict one utterance per beat. It is a highly effective trick that adds considerable interest to the latter stages of the track. The freedom with which Bowie approaches his vocal task on "Fame" is a quality not heard before, at least nowhere near to this extent, and introduces a playful quality that adds much to the track's allure.

For an artist whose performative palette features change as a primary component, *Young Americans* is one of the most extreme stylistic changes he has ever undertaken. After all, as the dangerous glam-monster "Halloween Jack," he had been prowling the sterile skyscrapers of the Hunger City stage set only months earlier while touring to support the *Diamond Dogs* album. And now here he was, a Plastic Soul Man whose image suggested glam had never existed. Although a very successful album in commercial terms, *Young Americans* remains one of the artist's most controversial works. As Pegg attests, "to this day *Young Americans* splits Bowie fans down the middle."[5]

While stylistically the album is undeniably a quantum shift from its predecessors, an air of continuity nevertheless exists in the two recurring ideas of the nature of fame and celebrity, and also alienation, felt here both in his own (and Lennon's) isolation, as expressed so clearly in "Fame," but also most particularly in the disillusioned young American couple of the title track.

Despite your early misgivings, following the first few back-to-back plays you quickly grew to love *Young Americans*, and it spurred you on to begin seeking out more soul music in order to find out what Bowie had been listening to that had inspired him so. In a sense, Bowie was also now your music teacher. With Bowie, part of the deal was that you would never know what was coming next.

STATION TO STATION, 1976

> DAVID BOWIE, never one to maintain continuity in his work or in his life, has become more elusive than ever in the past year. . . . Will the Philly bump 'n' hustle which he rightly calculated as his springboard to American chart success remain his stock-in-trade a while longer, leaving his staunch Ziggy-era fans alienated through another release? With *Station to Station* (the RCA album's original title was *Golden Years*), Bowie answers the question with an emphatic "No."
> —Richard Cromelin, *Circus*, March 1976

> *Young Americans* was a successful experiment, but rather than creating another entrapping persona, he had simply created an audience for his work that was apart and very different from his *Ziggy* army. So his task became not the creation of yet another persona, but the unification of an audience he'd divided by success. That's where the new album, *Station to Station*, fits in. —Ben Edmonds, *Phonograph Record*, January 1976

Side One

1. Station to Station
2. Golden Years
3. Word on a Wing

Side Two

1. TVC15
2. Stay
3. Wild Is the Wind (Tiomkin/ Washington)

Recorded in Los Angeles in 1975 and released in 1976, *Station to Station* was another considerable commercial success. Reaching number three on the US album chart, thereby eclipsing *Young Americans* and consolidating Bowie's newfound status there, it also achieved a placing of number five in the UK. The first single, "Golden Years," also performed well, reaching number eight in the UK and number ten in the US.

The cover is a stark, black-and-white still frame taken from Nicolas Roeg's movie *The Man Who Fell to Earth*, released two months after *Station to Station* and in which Bowie played the leading role. The movie has a science fiction theme, with an alien named Thomas Jerome Newton (Bowie) becoming stranded on Earth unable to return to his doomed, far-off planet to save his wife and child, who are dying of dehydration. The still frame shows Bowie/Newton entering his spaceship.

Pegg suggests that the broad white border surrounding the photograph symbolically cuts Bowie off from his surroundings, alienating and separating him from contact with the outside world by confining him to "a soundproof chamber, whose walls eliminate extraneous and ambient sound, leaving only heartbeat and electrical brain activity audible."[6] Such a reading of the image, implying sensory deprivation, has some credence in that the cone-shaped objects on the walls resemble the sound baffles found on recording studio walls, surfaces designed to reduce the transmission of sound waves and create an environment of "dead" air. While a viewer of the cover might not have projected to the extent that Pegg suggests, nevertheless an air of aural sterility pervades.

The three words that comprise the album's title are run together followed by the artist's name, all written in capitals, with none of the words separated from each other. This unbroken lettering has a dehumanizing effect. It is as if the words are being issued by a robot, possessing neither the requirement to draw breath nor the knowledge of syntax and phrasing inherent to human language.

Bowie has suggested that the stark imagery was appropriate to the music he was creating at the time, affirming that he wanted to convey "a kind of Expressionist German-film look . . . a black-and-white movies look, but with an intensity that was sort of aggressive."[7]

Having ascertained the alienating nature of the cover—the personable warmth of the *Young Americans* cover is in complete absence—it is time to listen to where the Plastic Soul Man has now gone in a musical sense.

As on the previous album Bowie opens with the title track, and at over ten minutes it is the longest song he has ever recorded. Organized in four disparate sections, "Station to Station" merges musical styles and lyrical perspectives. In the first section the listener hears the sound of a train fading in from complete silence. Then, quite literally, you hear it travel from the left speaker of your stereo system across to the right, simulating physical movement right there in your room. The train, which remains alone in the soundscape throughout the entire first minute, picks up considerable speed as it travels. With just over a minute gone it is joined tentatively by Earl Slick's heavily effected electric guitar mimicking the octave leap of a train's whistle, and then other instruments join in to create a plodding, slow pulse as the train sounds slowly fade. This pulse is the beginning of the second section and is allowed to very slowly build in intensity, accompanied by a core motif in the form of a repeating two-note piano figure. Strange textures and sounds come and go randomly while the track develops, creating a spacious, hypnotic, and strangely timeless experience for the listener.

Bowie does not enter the song until a full three minutes and seventeen seconds has passed, an introduction longer than the entire span of many pop songs. The music stops briefly and dramatically at the entry of his voice before resuming the pulse. His opening lyric introduces a new character, the Thin White Duke. Somewhat cryptically, he introduces himself in this new guise with the line "The *return* of the thin white duke." It is well documented that this line was originally intended to also be the album title before *Station to Station* was chosen. The lyrics concern Bowie's imagined spiritual journey from the "modern" world of contemporary America to the "traditional" world of Europe: "There are you. You drive like a demon from station to station." The analogy is drawn with taking a transcontinental train trip, Bowie proclaiming repeatedly, "The European canon is here," thereby firmly divorcing himself from the American focus of his last work. Even the instrumentation mirrors this journey closely, as he eschews the guitar, bass, and drums sonic platform of glam rock and the brass soulfulness of *Young Americans* to explore the keyboard-driven textures of Kraftwerk. The title, "Station to Station," clearly confirms this notion of travel, and as Hugo Wilcken suggests, "those train sounds herald the theme of restless travel as a spiritual metaphor. . . . Sonically, *Station to Station* is a voyage in itself, journeying from the mid-seventies funk of the New York disco scene to the pulsing motorik beat of experimental German bands such as Neu!, Can or Kraftwerk."[8]

The significance of lyrics such as "the magical movement from Kether to Malkuth" would largely have gone unheeded by the majority of Bowie fans—and I include myself in this category—unlikely to comprehend the depth of meaning in the words. The line refers to *The Tree of Life*, an ancient Kabbalistic treatise in which Bowie had developed a keen interest. Photographs taken during the recording show Bowie drawing the diagram that accompanies the treatise upon the studio floor. Bowie has himself retrospectively suggested, "I had this more-than-passing interest in Egyptology, mysticism, the Kabbalah, all this stuff that is inherently misleading in life."[9]

This exemplifies one important element frequently evident in Bowie's work; that is, he provides multileveled meanings for the listener. Whether this is always intentional or not is a moot point; the fact is that his offerings are often nonspecific enough for consumers to take what they will from them—what they see as pertinent to themselves at whatever level that might be—and potentially make their own meaning from it. Certainly, in the case of the album's title track, "Station to Station," the notion of travel comes through loud and clear, but it may be either geographical, spiritual, or both to the listener.

At four minutes and forty-two seconds the train sounds return briefly and the instrumental pulse drops away, leaving Bowie to repeat his opening lyric introducing the Thin White Duke as the second section of the song ends. Then, at five minutes and eighteen seconds, a far more up-tempo funk feel begins section three, over which Bowie begins a highly personal and nostalgic introspection: "Once there were mountains on mountains and once there were sun birds to soar with. And once I could never be down. Got to keep searching and searching. Oh, what will I be believing and who will connect me with love?" It is here that we learn why Bowie is traveling and what he is looking for. It is a very universal want expressed here, and there is much for listeners to apply to their own lives. This section lasts less than a minute before the lengthy fourth and final part of the song begins at six minutes and two seconds, sustaining through until the track ends more than four minutes later. Here the rhythm changes midstream to a frenetic, almost celebra-

tory disco feel as Bowie promises, "It's not the side-effects of the cocaine. I'm thinking that it must be love." Bowie tells us that his salvation
lies in the form of good old-fashioned romantic love for an (unnamed)
woman: "I must be only one in a million. I won't let the day pass
without her." Yet this is immediately tempered with the disquieting
"It's too late to be grateful," ensuring that ambiguity exists throughout
the remainder of the track as Bowie's lyrics trade with guitar solos until
the track's end.

Biographers almost universally regard the *Station to Station* period
of Bowie's career as the time during which he developed a heavy cocaine addiction, Wilcken summarizing the situation thus: "By this stage,
Bowie had practically stopped eating and was subsisting on a diet of
milk, cocaine and four packets of Gitanes a day . . . [He] could go five or
six days without sleep, the point at which reality and imagination become irretrievably blurred."[10] Claims such as this have been supported
on many occasions by Bowie: "I can't even remember the studio. I know
it was in LA because I've read it was."[11] Bowie further admitted, "By
the end of each week my whole life would be transformed into this
bizarre nihilistic fantasy world of oncoming doom, mythological characters and imminent totalitarianism."[12]

"Station to Station" is as epic as the subject matter tackled, and with
its stylistically contrasting sections, as an album opener it is hard to
compare to the work of any other artist. In terms of showcasing the
songwriter's craft and also in terms of its scene-setting qualities for the
remainder of the album, "Station to Station" is jaw-dropping—one of
Bowie's most audacious songs.

The successful single, "Golden Years," follows the title track. Unlike
its predecessor, a clear musical link is immediately evident with the
Young Americans album as soul, funk, and disco influences effortlessly
combine in an ultrasmooth groove-based track, with minimal harmonic
movement allowing the focus to fall upon the dance beat while giving
Bowie much freedom to play with his melody line. Just as he did on
"Fame," on "Golden Years" he explores the full extent of his range from
very low right up to highest falsetto. Thematic linkage exists with the
preceding title track as the lyrics of this love song easily follow on from
the revelation of finding romantic love. Here, he expresses his desire to
grow old with his partner, professing, "I'll stick with you baby for a
thousand years. Nothing's gonna touch you in these golden years." De-

spite the positive nature of the lyrics, nevertheless Bowie again unsettles things toward the end with the unexplained instruction to "run for the shadows."

While the first two songs on *Station to Station* promised fulfillment and actualization through earthbound, human romantic love, on the third and closing track of side one Bowie is found looking further afield. In what is virtually an open prayer, he seeks divine guidance from God: "Lord, I kneel and offer you my word on a wing . . . Lord, my prayer flies like a word on the wing. I don't stand in my own light . . . I walk beside you, I'm alive in you." Never before had such obvious religiosity featured in a Bowie song, and here this unabashed soul-baring is clear from the opening bars, where a simple single-note piano line sits highly exposed with a thin, haunting string section beneath. One can imagine Bowie on his knees here, looking heavenward with his hands clasped together, such is the effectiveness of the painting of the song's mood. The first verse of the song finds the melody set low in Bowie's register and he delivers his lines with humble, unforced simplicity. This choice of melodic pitching serves an additional purpose, however, as it allows him to keep in reserve the upper extensions of his vocal range so that when he does actually sing of being on his knees his voice takes on an imploring tone filled with emotional strain. And when an extended version of the first verse repeats later in the song, Bowie remains a full octave higher than where he began, further heightening the emotive qualities in his words. The pure unadulterated sounds of piano dominate the backing of this song, as a constant accompaniment but also trading melodic phrases with Bowie. It is another long song, at over six minutes, and he offers no darker or subversive lyric line late in the piece, the prayer allowed its full due.

The opening track of side two is the upbeat, science fiction–oriented, and even oddly humorous "TVC15," the album's second single release. The lyrics tell the story of Bowie's electronic friend, a television set, whom he watches every night: "He's quadraphonic . . . he's got more channels. So hologramic, oh, my TVC15." Over a honky-tonk piano accompaniment—completely unexpected given the nature of the musical offerings of side one—Bowie relates how he brings a girlfriend home one night only to see the TVC15 swallow her: "I brought my baby home . . . she sat around forlorn. She saw my TVC15, and then baby's gone. She crawled right in, oh my." A clear relationship to *The Man Who Fell to Earth* exists here, as, in one of the most memorable scenes from the movie, Bowie/Newton is seen transfixed by an entire wall of television sets, mentally lost inside their glowing, flickering screens. The climb between verse and chorus repeats the words "transmission" and "transition," both highly loaded words in the context of Bowie's past work, and thematically, the song revisits this territory. On the *Ziggy Stardust* album, for instance, television sets were featured in "Five Years"; Ziggy's communication to the youth of Earth came through the television set in "Starman"; the "electric eye" of "Moonage Daydream" was a television set; and of course there was the "wall-to-wall" television that calls to Ziggy in the album's finale, "Rock 'n' Roll Suicide." Equally, the blurring of human and machine—the very idea of being swallowed up by technology—even literally—is entirely consistent with Bowie's raison d'être.

"Stay," the second-longest track on *Station to Station*, is next up, and given that there are only six songs on the album—the smallest number ever on a Bowie recording—it is the penultimate track. An unsettling hybrid of soul, funk, and hard rock, the song cracks along at a fast tempo, with the groove allowed plenty of time to establish the mood due to another lengthy introduction that delays the entry of the vocals for over a minute. The fusion of styles allied to the pace of the song ensures synergy with the ambiguity and uncertainty felt by the song's protagonist, who wants his lover to stay but has much difficulty in saying so. "Stay—that's what I meant to say or do, something. But what I never say is stay this time." Bowie sounds torn and uncertain, far from the conclusiveness of the romantic love revelations of "Station to Station," the surety of love's longevity heard in "Golden Years," or the confident religiosity of "Word on a Wing." The melody of "Stay" is the most complex and difficult on the album and a challenge to sing, further testament to the scattered emotions of the subject matter. If his current lover won't stay, perhaps he will go out and find another? "Heart wrecker, heart wrecker, make me delight. Right is so vague when it brings someone new. This time tomorrow I'll know what to do."

Perhaps the biggest surprise on *Station to Station* is the final song, a cover version of the Ned Washington and Dimitri Tiomkin song "Wild Is the Wind." Originally recorded by Johnny Mathis as the theme song for the 1957 movie of the same name, the song had also been covered by Nina Simone as the title track of her 1964 album. While turning it into a rock ballad, it is the Simone version that Bowie mirrors, to the extent of frequently mimicking her phrasing and intonation. The intensity of Bowie's personal plea to God in "Word on a Wing" is here matched by an equally direct plea to his lover: "Love me, love me, love me, love me, say you do. Let me fly away with you." Softly intense yet restrained in his vocal styling during the early part of the song, Bowie describes the impact that such perfect romantic love has upon him: "You touch me, I hear the sound of mandolins. You kiss me, with your kiss my life begins." As the song progresses through its six-minute duration, the emotional intensity of his vocal performance incrementally increases to the point where, by the song's conclusion, he is, as Doggett puts it, "on the verge of hysterical despair."[13]

The *Station to Station* album juxtaposes musical representations of cold and clinical technological dominance against heart-on-sleeve human emotion and feeling. This is clearly demonstrated if one compares the first track, "Station to Station," to the last, "Wild Is the Wind." In the former the rhythm is set up by purely mechanical means, the steel-and-steam sonic imagery of the train ushering in the album and then mimicked by Bowie's band. Throughout this title track, the human element, Bowie, is found subservient to the all-dominating pulse of the music. On "Wild Is the Wind," however, Bowie's all-too-human flesh-and-blood frailty—as represented by his voice as much as the song's words—is constantly at the forefront, the backing charged only with supporting and serving him. This battle—on "TVC15" it is rendered quite literally—is firmly established as a Bowie hallmark, and while it was not as central a theme on the previous album, *Young Americans*, *Station to Station*, in its thematic entirety, strongly recalls the subject matter of early-career songs such as "Saviour Machine" and "Space Oddity," again espousing the underlying threat that existed in the *Ziggy Stardust*, *Aladdin Sane*, and *Diamond Dogs* albums in particular.

Your reaction to *Station to Station* was a very positive one. Bowie's return to a more rock-based musical style rather than the soul/funk offerings of *Young Americans*, enormously well-rendered though it was, was met with widespread approval. The cover, with its obvious science fiction allusion, also appeared much more within the Bowie sphere of "normal" operations as they were understood by most fans. *Station to Station* found David Bowie at his creative best.

7

THE SOUNDS OF EUROPE

Low, "Heroes," and *Lodger, 1977–1979*

Early evening, January 1977. Midsummer in New Zealand, and you're just a few days away from turning seventeen. School will soon be a thing of the past. You should have a career in mind but in truth you haven't a clue what to do. Being a musician would be good, but you never put the work in to learn to play your long-discarded guitar. Enveloped by your giant purple beanbag, you are sitting in your bedroom with the door closed and the blinds drawn against the tar-melting sun. Down the hall your parents are having a cup of tea and a biscuit while watching *Coronation Street*. You'll never understand that, will you? How could the fictional doings of a bunch of down-in-the-mouth Mancunians possibly be of interest to anyone? Outside it's twenty-five degrees Celsius and very humid, but it's even hotter in your room. Though your legs stick to the vinyl of your beanbag your windows remain firmly closed, denying the existence of the outside world. There's a rugby game at the park down the road but your headphones ensure you remain blissfully unaware, except during the silence between album tracks when sounds of cheering break through. The lava lamp on your dresser pulses but has lost the battle for your attention as you remain deep inside your teenage gloom. No one understands you. No one. In your hands you hold your just-purchased copy of *Low*. Five minutes into the album, and you are confused. The first track, "Speed of Life," sounded like part of an unfinished song. Bowie's a singer, right? But where were his vocals? And

what about track two! Less than two minutes long, it was a mere fragment. The style of music is like nothing you've ever heard before.
Where's the soul of *Young Americans* or the rock/funk of *Station to
Station*? Then, "What in the World" begins . . . and suddenly, right
there in your headphones, Bowie sings, "So deep in your room, hiding
in your room." It hits you then that this is *you* he is talking about! In this
moment you understand what is going on. You are not alone, after all.
Just like Bowie promised as the glittering androgyne Ziggy Stardust,
"Oh no love, you're not alone." And you realize, regardless of the fact
that this new music is the strangest thing you've ever heard, that Bowie
is *still* your champion.

LOW, 1977

[*Low* consists of] . . . music and sounds so synthetic and depersonal-
ized as to imply that the instruments did the playing after the band
had gone home." —Charles Shaar Murray, *New Musical Express*,
January 1977

At a time when punk rock was noisily reclaiming the three-minute
pop song in a show of public defiance, Bowie almost completely
abandoned traditional rock instrumentation and embarked on a kind
of introverted musical therapy. —David Buckley, *David Bowie: The
Complete Guide to His Music*

Bowie has gone right out on a limb with this album. He'll probably
lose a bunch of fans, but I admire him for having the courage to put
it out. He could have cruised on churning out *Ziggy Stardust Part 22*
forever, instead, he battles on, donning new styles and guises, widen-
ing his scope and improving all the time. And that's part of the
reason he's so exciting . . . you never know what he'll get up to next
but can rest assured he won't stay trapped in the same bag, regardless of how successful it may be. —Kris Needs, *ZigZag*, February
1977

Side One	**Side Two**
1. Speed of Life	1. Warszawa (Bowie/Eno)

2. Breaking Glass (Bowie/Davis/ Murray)

2. Art Decade

3. What in the World

3. Weeping Wall

4. Sound and Vision

4. Subterraneans

5. Always Crashing in the Same Car

6. Be My Wife

7. A New Career in a New Town

In January 1977, Bowie released the most controversial album of his career. Although a commercial success in the UK, reaching number two, *Low* did not match the heights of *Young Americans* or *Station to Station* in the US, reaching only number eleven. Of the eleven tracks, only two, "Sound and Vision" and "Be My Wife," were released as singles, the former reaching number three in the UK.

Low was released when Bowie was seeking to free himself from his cocaine addiction and when punk rock was hitting its peak of popularity. The Sex Pistols, the Clash, Elvis Costello, and the Damned all released seminal works, while in the US, Blondie, Television, and the Dead Boys released their debut albums. With so much focus on this new "next big thing" (punk rock and its close though poorly defined cousin, new wave), just how an established artist like David Bowie might react was anyone's guess.

Although most of the *Low* album was recorded at the Château d'Hérouville near Paris, by August 1976 Bowie was living a reclusive life in Berlin and this influence is very evident. Indeed, in the popular press and many scholarly works, *Low* and the two albums that followed it, *"Heroes"* and *Lodger*, have come to be known as the Berlin Trilogy. Bowie had long been fascinated by Berlin for, as Lorne Murdoch believes, "its cultural reputation and interdisciplinary possibilities."[1] Nicholas Pegg's view is that "in a sense Berlin was the very pattern of the post-apocalyptic urban landscape David had already envisaged in *Ziggy Stardust* and *Diamond Dogs*."[2]

Bowie himself has often spoken candidly about the influences that drew him to Berlin:

Since my teenage years I had obsessed on the angst ridden, emotional work of the expressionists, both artists and film makers, and Berlin had been their spiritual home. This was the nub of Die Brücke movement, Max Reinhardt, Brecht and where Metropolis and Caligari had originated. It was an art form that mirrored life not by event but by mood. This was where I felt my work was going. My attention had been swung back to Europe with the release of Kraftwerk's *Autobahn* in 1974. The preponderance of electronic instruments convinced me that this was an area that I had to investigate a little further.[3]

Following the *Low* recording sessions in Paris, the remainder of the recording and all of the mixing was carried out at the Hansa-by-the-Wall studio in Berlin. Located only thirty meters from the Berlin Wall, rolls of barbed wire, armed guards, and gun turrets were clearly visible from the studio windows. Bowie had recorded there before on Iggy Pop's album *The Idiot*, and was enthused by the edge this environment gave to the recording experience.

From silence "Speed of Life" swoops rapidly into the listener's consciousness—Bowie's favorite trick employed here once again—with a sudden overpowering synth-wave of buzzing, crackling electricity. Just two minutes and forty-seven seconds long, *Low*'s opening track is a short burst of energy complete with strong melodies, a driving beat, and continual momentum that draws the listener ever forward. And then . . . it is gone as quickly as it came. It's a track that promises more will happen than ever does, and a common question in the minds of excited purchasers of *Low* upon giving the album its first listening was, "When is he going to start singing?" Patience in such matters had been taught to Bowie fans, to an extent, via *Station to Station*'s title track, in which the entry of Bowie's vocals was delayed for more than three minutes. But in "Speed of Life" Bowie never does start singing because it is his first-ever full instrumental. How unexpected even for David Bowie, by now firmly established as rock's master of the unpredictable. Every success that had come his way had featured his voice as his signature, his trademark. He *is* a singer, after all. While highly extolled as a songwriter too, he has always, *always*, sung the songs he has written. Would Elvis have ever begun one of his albums with an instrumental? Would Rod Stewart have done so? While Elton John had begun his *Goodbye Yellow Brick Road* (1973) with the instrumental "Funeral for a Friend," it never sounded like a stand-alone track because of the way it seamlessly segued into the following "Love Lies Bleeding," thereby making the opener appear to be simply an extended introduction. "Speed of Life" throughout sounds like it is about to introduce Bowie, but doesn't. This seeming lack of completion—the impression that something is missing—is a portent.

Normality seemingly resumes at the onset of track two, "Breaking Glass," with the familiar strains of Bowie's voice entering after a short introduction of drums and electric guitar. The track settles here into a funky, twisted, dance/disco rhythm complete with open hi-hats on the offbeats. But there is something inherently wrong with the equation. "Baby I've been breaking glass in your room again" is the disquieting opening vocal line to both the song and, thereby, the album, as aggressive synthesizer lines engage Bowie in call-and-response passages. Immediately following, a warning that Bowie has drawn something "awful" on the carpet completes the lyric couplet of a highly minimalist first verse. A chorus follows directly, its opening line, "You're such a wonderful person, but you've got problems," confirming dysfunction. Unexpectedly, only one more lyric line remains in the entire song, with Bowie assuring the unknown protagonist that he will never touch them, presumably because of the unspecified problems mentioned moments earlier. After this declaration, all that remains is thirty seconds of outro, including fade-out, occurring over the revisited verse chords. "Breaking Glass" has been a mere fragment: a two-line verse, a two-line chorus, a glimpse of emotional trouble, and then gone.

"What in the World" begins in frenetic style. Fast-paced and with loud, abrasive drums, an irritating bubbling synthesizer line dominates while an ascending angular three-note lead guitar motif destabilizes proceedings, played in 3/4 time repeatedly over the track's 4/4 rhythm. Bowie's vocals appear early but the intensity of the instrumental backing continues unabated and makes no space for him, breaching convention in terms of the sanctity of vocals in popular music and forcing him to elbow his way into the melee. Strangely emotionless in his delivery, he introduces the subject, "a little girl with gray eyes," straightaway, going on as the verse progresses to inform us that she is silent and fearful of crowds. At the onset of the chorus we learn that she is also damagingly reclusive, with Bowie accusing, "So deep in your room, you never leave your room." Bowie's vocal melody emphatically paints the lyric, with the second half of the line a mirror of the first, and therefore going nowhere. It is another mere fragment of a song, at just two minutes and twenty-three seconds, and the most telling lyrics are left for the strangely monotonal closing lines, where Bowie ponders the question as to what this girl might say, do, or be, to "the real me." Clearly, his ongoing critique of identity remains at the fore.

Track four brings a sense of order and familiarity to the listening experience, and it is unsurprising that "Sound and Vision" was selected by a nervous RCA Records as *Low*'s primary single. While largely retaining the abrasive drum sound and angular, aggressive sonority that characterized the preceding tracks, here Bowie provides a rather more accessible three-minute pop song that possesses a faint harking back to a fifties doo-wop influence previously visited at times during his glam period. And yet in truth the track is only rendered more accessible than the earlier ones by virtue of the greater extent of their deviance. Convention is still roundly flouted in "Sound and Vision," with Bowie's vocals not appearing until fully half of the song has passed, precedence in the track once again given to mechanical-sounding instrumentation while the human element of Bowie himself is relegated to an afterthought role. The lyrics inform us that this is because he has nothing to offer, with "pale blinds drawn all day—nothing to do, nothing to say." Bowie appears impotent and beaten, "drifting into my solitude, over my head," content to wait for sound and vision (television again?) to appear and relieve his tedium. His vocals, both in the lifeless delivery and the nature of the lyrics he sings, contrast with the doo-wop female backing that nostalgically suggests better times.

"Always Crashing in the Same Car" continues exploring Bowie's inability to move forward with its inferences of circularity of behavior; of repeating mistakes and being unable to progress and improve one's lot in life. Its scenario of "going round and round the hotel garage" is a very far cry from *Ziggy Stardust*'s infectious and empowering positivity of 1972, with its proffered notion that one could seize control of one's own destiny, perhaps making "a transformation as a rock 'n' roll star." Here there is no hope of transformation. Bowie's voice is torpid and completely uninspired, as if lacking the most basic motivation to even engage with the act of singing. Pegg's description of the song as "a beautifully crafted and spine-chilling slice of self-doubt and paranoia"[4] is very apt.

Given the precursive gloom and alienation of the preceding songs, the sixth song, "Be My Wife," appears a logical, if desperate, measure to stop the slippage into complete isolation. "I've lived all over the world— I've left every place," Bowie sings, restless and unfulfilled. As far as his proposal of marriage goes, the song is devoid of love for whomever he is addressing, the lyrics instead appearing completely self-serving; the offer of marriage reduced to a one-sided tactic designed to arrest the solitude of "Sound and Vision," because "sometimes you get so lonely— sometimes you get nowhere."

The title of the seventh and final track on side one suggests an alternative proactive solution to alienation and withdrawal. "A New Career in a New Town" has no lyrics; however, the album's second instrumental is a bookend to the opening "Speed of Life." The track is built upon two very different sections juxtaposed against each other and repeated. The first is a smooth, soft, reflective piece of electronica that is stylistically similar to Kraftwerk, while the second is almost honky-tonk in nature, with piano and harmonica at the fore. It is as if two quite separate ideas—one robotic, one organic—have been forced together, and yet the tangible senses of tension (part one) and release (part two) complement each other perfectly, resulting in a song that works well in its own right.

If fans baffled by the new Bowie appearing on side one of *Low* were hoping for a return to a more familiar listening experience on side two, they were in for anything but. The psychological withdrawal evident in the lyrics and the resignedly understated style of singing of side one are here taken to their logical conclusion, as Bowie abstains from singing any discernable lyrics at all for the rest of the album. When his voice *is* heard, it is used almost exclusively as a color or texture. Eschewing language altogether, his sparse vocal contributions become another instrument at times on a par with—but never elevated above—the strings, percussion, and other instruments. But most especially they are subservient to the dominating synthesizers of Brian Eno. Here, in the four instrumental tracks of side two, technology wins. Portrayed in many guises through Bowie's career to this point, the technological threat has become literal. And the battle is lost.

"Warszawa" sets the tone for complete unconventionality and experimentation throughout side two. Although the longest song on the album at six minutes and twenty-four seconds, it goes on a full four minutes before Bowie is heard. When he does enter he is positioned deep within the mix, a part of the backing. Immediately following this entry he does come to the forefront to sing a melody, but it is a strange, wordless chant evoking images of ancient religious ritual. Slow-paced, sparse, almost funereal, the vocal and instrumental themes of the track, supported by the unhurried and ever-changing electronic backing, paint the bleakness of the Polish landscape from which the song derives its title. "Warszawa" is allowed to organically unfold.

The total absence of human voice on the following "Art Decade" reinforces the demotion of the traditional rock-singer role on *Low*. Highly minimalist and again eschewing the standard building blocks of popular music—fixed chord sequences, tonal melody and harmony, and rigid bar structures—this track too is allowed rare space to unravel, despite lasting only three minutes and forty-seven seconds. Like the earlier "A New Career in a New Town," the track is organized around the repetition of two contrasting sections that undergo extensive dynamic variation. A four-note descending melody of non-stable pitches is the glue that holds the piece together. However, this motif gradually decays, becoming halved to just two notes and then, finally, one. It may be that this subtly paints the song title's obvious pun, "art decayed," as Bowie has commented that the song reflects his view of West Berlin as a deteriorating city estranged from its own culture and art.

The album's penultimate track, "Weeping Wall," is Bowie's emotive critique of the misery of the Berlin Wall, and features a heavily repeated melody recognizable as a derivation of the opening line of the traditional English folk ballad "Scarborough Fair," made popular worldwide by Simon and Garfunkel in 1968. Whether Bowie intended a discernable association or not, this modification of such a well-known melody, performed here by robotic synthesizer and set to ambient, cold, and minimalist backing, is one of the most disturbing moments on *Low*. When the melody is repeated in a higher register it sounds despairing, a wailing cry that mourns the passing of the simple idealism of the flowers-in-your-hair 1960s counterculture. The alienation saturating *Low* is thus presented in yet another way, as such hippy idealism, wonderfully and intrinsically human, if ultimately proven hopelessly idealistic, is coldly dispatched by music far removed from such old-fashioned, faith-driven, romantic hope. The 3/4 pulse upon which the track depends is unrelenting until the final moments, yet frequent destabilization is created by the erratic entry of instruments, the broadly ranging tone colors, and seemingly haphazard pitch choices. Bowie contributes voice-as-instrument moments, his vocals often heard in a drone-like low register providing support to the automaton-like atmosphere rather than leading. The only instrument to challenge the supremacy of the synthesizer is the ever-present vibraphone that opens the song and continues unabated until its conclusion.

"Subterraneans" brings *Low* to an end in mostly summative fashion. This second-longest track, at five minutes and thirty-eight seconds, is Bowie's tribute to East Berliners trapped behind the Berlin Wall, the soulful strains of his saxophone providing a purposeful and emotive specter of prewar jazz. The song meanders gently throughout its first three minutes, highly abstract yet held together loosely by a repeating five-note bass line that serves as a virtual flashlight in the dark amid dominating washes of synthesizers and strings. Here and there, Bowie's voice appears in the now-familiar subdued role of simply adding color to other instrumentation. However, three minutes and fifty seconds into "Subterraneans"—fashionably late yet again, one might jest—we finally hear Bowie's voice granted a solitary privileged moment on side two. Although once again there are no true lyrics involved, nevertheless Bowie's voice, during this four-line passage, reclaims its status as lead instrument. As was the case earlier in "Warszawa," the words here are of no known language, seemingly assembled for their phonetic and emotive qualities. Despite this, here the combination of vowels and consonants within the contrived language sounds more familiar to a Western ear than the monk-like chant of that previous song. This eleventh-hour return of Bowie's highly recognizable voice in a sense imbues the final track with an element of hope because, as well as the familiarity of sound, here he sings with something approaching passion and enthusiasm, a quality markedly lacking elsewhere, even on side one, in the more traditional popular-music song formulas. The respite is brief, however, and once the moment has passed the track resumes its course. Bowie returns to anonymity until ultimately the track simply self-destructs mid-phrase, without any semblance of a proper conclusion. One moment it is there, the next it has collapsed in upon itself, unresolved and interrupted.

The overriding bleakness of *Low* is represented in abundance on the album cover. The side-on view of Bowie shows him gaunt and unsmiling, eyes focused on some far-off scene. His dark, thick, bulky clothing appears to be a robe such as a traveling monk might use, the roll-neck sweater pulled up to offer protection, while his hood hangs back ready to be donned in the face of dust storms, acid rain, or whatever else might transpire. He gives the impression that he is traveling across some vast distance, a desert perhaps, given the featureless landscape all around him. The expression on his face is not one of fear; rather, it is one of focused concentration or deliberation, or perhaps complete resignation. The latter hypothesis supports the feeling conveyed by the music that technology has triumphed over humanity; that traditional forms of narrative-based communication have given way to electronic ones, and that the human condition is forever altered. The overall ambiance of the image suggests bleak survival, but at the cost of individuality, self-expression, and human-style interaction. The cover, like the music within, offers a featureless, barren existence.

Frank Moriarty suggests, "Even the album cover was intimidating; the front depicting a gaunt Bowie in profile against a sky of flame-colored clouds, while the back was simply an expanse of orange, broken only by record label logo and catalog number."[5] The image is a post-apocalyptic one that carries the implication of recent cataclysm. It therefore fits easily within the Bowie canon following the science fiction threads of "Space Oddity" and *Ziggy Stardust*, the pre-world-war chaos of *Aladdin Sane*, and the post-apocalyptic vision of *Diamond Dogs*. The angry, orange sky gives every impression of a world in flames, and this is also reflected in Bowie's hair. Even the lettering of the album title is orange, while the artist's name is rendered in yellow.

The absence of lyrics on side two forces the listener to draw deep upon his/her own imagination in an attempt to make sense of the proceedings. Images are cleverly painted with aural textures, but nothing is served up conveniently on a plate. Never before had a popular-music artist demanded so much of his audience, and it was in this inherent requirement of effort on the part of the consumer that the album's highly divisive popular and critical reaction lay. *Low* was loved and hated in equal measure.

In the rock trenches of the schoolyard, however, *Low* didn't make things particularly easy for Bowie fans. The heavily in-fashion spiky-haired brigade were not a problem, because punks were society's new outcasts with a degree of inherent respect for Bowie as the previous holder of the ultimate outsider award. Besides, many of them had cut their teeth on *Ziggy Stardust*, learning invaluable lessons about fashion as they did so. (To poorly paraphrase "Rock 'n' roll Suicide," they were the kids who'd killed the man before he broke up the band.) The chin-scratching proggies weren't an issue either, as all of them (well, *both* of them) were too busy trying to decipher meaning in *Animals*, Pink Floyd's latest feel-good brow-furrower. No, it was the chest-beaters who were the problem. The new heroes of the hirsute, AC/DC, re-leased *Let There Be Rock* within weeks of *Low*. For those who liked their meat raw, there was nothing better than Bon Scott wrapping his chainsaw-on-steel vocals around "Let there be drums—there was drums. Let there be guitar," and so on. Yes, rock 'n' roll in its most primitive form was alive and well. And who better than a bunch of croc wrestlers (Australians) to serve it up? This was a good thing—rock de-served to be kept alive. But, with such an anthem to the old way still ringing in their ears, the knuckle-dragging enforcers who roamed the schoolyard struggled with the concept of a thin, pale Englishman trem-ulously warbling, "Car-line car-line briding me shelly shelly shelly om," for no evident reason. Typical of the kind of unsolicited advice that would come a Bowie fan's way: "It doesn't even make fucking sense! You should listen to some *real* music!" Well, thank you, King Kong . . . but Bowie is still fine by me.

"HEROES," 1977

What to make of " *Heroes*" I dunno. I never know what to make of Bowie albums. I just absorb them, they're hateful to analyse. —Tim Lott, *Record Mirror*, October 1977

That's it then, a strange, cold sometimes impenetrable album, but Bowie makes all these unlikely ingredients work. Bits fail but so what? He could live in luxury for the rest of his days and just churn out another *Ziggy* every year. Instead he's on the move, going places he ain't gone before. Good for Bowie. —Kris Needs, *ZigZag*, October 1977

David Bowie is the most inconsistently appealing genius in rock. With his chameleon ability to change from disco to space-rock to

romantic ballads to astringent mechanomusic, Bowie has demonstrated that he can master and present music any way he cares to. —
Ira Robbins, *Crawdaddy!* January 1978

Side One	Side Two
1. Beauty and the Beast	1. V-2 Schneider
2. Joe the Lion	2. Sense of Doubt
3. "Heroes" (Bowie/Eno)	3. Moss Garden (Bowie/Eno)
4. Sons of the Silent Age	4. Neuköln (Bowie/Eno)
5. Blackout	5. The Secret Life of Arabia (Bowie/Eno/Alomar)

"Heroes" was released in October 1977. Although a considerable commercial success in the UK, reaching number three, the album failed in
the US, where it peaked at a lowly thirty-five. Only the title track met
success as a single, reaching number twenty-four on the UK singles
chart. A second single, "Beauty and the Beast," reached number thirty-
nine in the UK, but neither charted in the US.

"There's Old Wave, there's New Wave, and there's David Bowie,"
pronounced RCA in the advertising campaign for *"Heroes."* These ten
words capture how Bowie had by this time set himself apart from the
rock mainstream. Categorizing Bowie in 1977 must have been a PR
person's nightmare, as no box he had ever been placed in had ever held
him.

In 1975 the *Young Americans* album was a quantum leap from what
he had done before, but the following *Station to Station* had brought
Bowie back to something more akin to a middle ground, with soul/funk
influences still in evidence but the rock element acting as a recapitulation toward his rock-oriented past. In the same way, *"Heroes"* would act
to temper the stylistic shock of *Low* by offering, at least on side one,
more traditionally structured songs and fuller lyrics, while retaining an
electronic experimental foundation.

"Heroes" was recorded in Berlin in the number-two studio at Hansa,
which was located slightly farther away from the Berlin Wall than studio
one, where *Low* had been finished. Nevertheless, the window still com-
manded a full, unobstructed view of the wall, as producer Tony Visconti
recalls:

> Russian Red Guards [were] looking at us with binoculars, with their
> Sten guns over their shoulders, and the barbed wire, and I knew that
> there were mines buried in that wall, and that atmosphere was so
> provocative and so stimulating and so frightening that the band
> played with so much energy. (In Nicholas Pegg, *The Complete David
> Bowie* [London: Reynolds & Hearn, 2002], 266)

The album cover features a black-and-white photograph of Bowie
shown from the chest up. He wears a shiny, zipped black leather jacket
and his hair is swept back. His right hand is placed across his chest in a
kind of hand-on-my-heart gesture, thumb splayed upward toward his
throat. His left arm is extended upward before him, palm toward his
face, fingers locked together and thumb splayed out in a highly stylized
gesture that could almost be a salute of some strange kind. The expression on his face is a very focused one, wide-eyed and unsmiling, conveying an interested, surprised—perhaps even bemused—look to the viewer.

Bowie's appearance, with his black leather biker-like jacket and his
swept-back, James Dean–like D.A. hairstyle, resembles that of a sixties
rocker. He could be Gene Vincent, Eddie Cochran, or any one of a
number of rocker icons—even Elvis Presley. Any attendant "tough guy"
insinuations that come with that iconography, however, are totally undone by Bowie's pose.

The album title is rendered in double quotation marks, thereby ironically suggesting that, whoever the heroes are that he speaks of, they are
not real heroes but merely stand-ins. He is presenting an image of the
traditional rock 'n' roll hero but subverting this in a way that suggests
such *"Heroes"* are nothing of the kind. They are constructions. This
reading of the cover fits in neatly with his ongoing critiquing of stardom. This is a thematic thread that, as has been discussed, has been
present from his earliest works, coming to widest attention during the
Ziggy Stardust era when the concept became both blatant and, arguably, the main thrust of his artistic credo.

While living in Berlin, Bowie spent much time with his friend Iggy
Pop, whose album *The Idiot*, co-written and co-produced by Bowie,
had been released just six months earlier. The two men reportedly
spent many hours at the Brücke-Museum, which houses many works by
artist Erich Heckel, whose extremely angular style was concerned with
the expression of inner turmoil or sickness. Among these was the paint-

ing *Roquairol* (1917), which provided the inspiration for the covers of both albums.

Side one of *"Heroes"* begins in emphatic fashion with the up-tempo "Beauty and the Beast." The fragmented stop-start introduction is passed around between percussion, piano, synthesizer, and guitar until, after twenty-five seconds, Bowie's vocals join in with a protracted upward swoop. After a scene-setting, seemingly innocent opening line, "Weaving down a byroad, singing the song," the lyric harks back to the dangerous schizophrenia of *Aladdin Sane*: "There's slaughter in the air, protest on the wind. Someone else inside me, someone could get skinned." Such duality permeates the track, "something in the night, something in the day," and reflects the division of East Berlin from West Berlin that was clearly observable from right outside the studio window. The high-pitched backing vocal cries of "my, my" act in a call-and-response role, responding to Bowie's often highly impressionistic lyrics and providing a sense of inner dialogue.

The notion of more than one personality dwelling within is explored further in the second song, "Joe the Lion." Here the protagonist, Joe, seeks to break out of everyday humdrum and becomes emboldened after "a couple of drinks on the house," becoming "a fortune teller." The song has at its core the real-life events of 1974 when, in California, performance artist Chris Burden had himself nailed to the roof of his Volkswagen Beetle. "Nail me to my car and I'll tell you who you are," sings Bowie. The extremes of the violence of crucifixion and the mundanity of everyday life are represented candidly in the music, with tumult represented by instrumental busyness and complexity in the mix giving way in an instant to a sudden clearing of the sonic palette at the beginning of verse two, as Bowie sings the party-killing line "It's Monday," in a droll, bored monotone that sits in complete contrast to his agitated and frenetic delivery just moments before.

The album's title track, co-written with Brian Eno, features next. Many consider "'Heroes'" to be David Bowie's finest moment. It is a song that has seemingly become more highly regarded in the decades following its release than it was at the time. Certainly, the aural picture he created of two lovers kissing under the shadow of the Berlin Wall is one of the strongest visual images he has ever conjured up. Biographer David Buckley correctly describes "'Heroes'" as "a huge wall of sound; a droning, repetitive, oncoming, unstoppable, mechanical block of sound."[6] From the moment the song begins, all of the elements are present in the mix at full impact, with no cumulative building of an introduction or preparation. Rather, the listener is plunged straight into the maelstrom provided by a combination of loud and abrasive drums, synthesizer, and guitar, which show no dynamic sensibility and just continue on and on with a robotic-like consistency. Similarly, with chord variations kept to a minimum, the harmonic simplicity upon which the song is built is not sufficient to relieve the onslaught. This very full musical palette is maintained relentlessly throughout the more than six minutes of the track.

The lyrics themselves are set up most carefully, with the central tenet of ordinary people dreaming of better lives and overcoming extreme adversity clearly espoused in the opening lines of the first verse: "I, I will be king. And you, you will be queen . . . We can be heroes, just for one day." In the succeeding lines the two protagonists are identified as being all-too-fallible human beings just like you and me: "You, you can be mean. And I, I'll drink all the time." Despite the admission of such common faults, it is their love that overcomes all. "'Cause we're lovers and that is that." These emphatic last three words carry remarkable strength.

Despite the steamroller-like body of sound that Buckley so accurately describes, "'Heroes'" nevertheless has a strong sense of development when, just over halfway through, at three minutes and seventeen seconds, Bowie begins to sing an octave higher than he did during the first half, unleashing all of the power and passion he can muster. The sense of anguish and desperation that this adds to the song's message is immense, creating a potent poignancy that reflects the lyrics with a tangible synergy. Having used the first half of the song to build the characters and convey to the listener their intimate yet universal hopes and desires, it is here, amid this heightened sense of climactic tension, that Bowie delivers the pivotal scene described above, where "the guns shot above our heads and we kissed as though nothing could fall." Love may, indeed, conquer all.

Many of Bowie's songs before "'Heroes'" had in various ways critiqued the power of simple human love in the face of overwhelming odds, most frequently set against the dark forces of technology or totalitarianism. The enormous feat of erecting a city-wide wall and the draconian control wielded by those in charge offered a potent and real set, upon which Bowie could construct his most direct exploration of this theme. And, of course, Bowie's joke is that the two lovers are not real heroes at all; they are just ordinary people doing the best they can to live their lives to the fullest under oppressive circumstances—hence the irony-loaded quotation marks around the song title. It is very hard to fault "'Heroes'" in any way and it remains one of Bowie's finest moments.

The sustained intensity of the album's title track dissipates quickly with the following "Sons of the Silent Age." In an oddly brooding track, the musical underpinning of the verses evokes imagery of 5 a.m. in a small basement jazz club where a small experimental jazz ensemble with a bored singer and a tired saxophonist see out their contracted hours. The choruses, in comparison, come to life with vocal energy, helped by a melody pitched significantly higher and expansive backing vocals. Lyrically, the verses and chorus are similarly distanced. The verses describe the lifestyle of the strange group of men introduced in the song's title: "Sons of the silent age stand on platforms blank looks and note books. Sit in back rows of city limits. Lay in bed coming and going on easy terms." The choruses, in contrast, are a heartfelt pledge of fidelity by the protagonist, sung in first-person perspective, to an unnamed lover: "Baby, I'll never let you go . . . Baby, baby, I'll never let you down." Simply, "Sons of the Silent Age" is Bowie at his most impenetrable.

The concluding song of side one of "Heroes" is the bleakest on the album, with even the title, "Blackout," telegraphing this quality. While it is a far more up-tempo song than its predecessor, the structure mirrors that of "Sons of the Silent Age" in the contrasting verses and choruses. Here, however, it is the verses that are energized and frenetic, both vocally and instrumentally, while the choruses are understated. Once again the verses describe action, and here it is dangerous and edgy: "The weather's grim, ice on the cages. Me, I'm Robin Hood and I puff on my cigarette. Panthers are steaming, stalking, screaming." The choruses, meanwhile, are once again a direct plea to an unnamed lover: "If you don't stay tonight I will take that plane tonight. I've nothing to lose, nothing to gain." As the last track of side one, "Blackout" provides an intensity and experimental flair that is as satisfying as it is confusing. As the arm returns to its cradle, you look forward to side two but with little clue of what to expect.

Side two of *"Heroes"* begins with a military flavor, the title of the opening song, "V-2 Schneider," clearly alluding to Germany's deadly V-2 rockets of World War II, the world's first long-range ballistic missiles. In Bowie's hands the reference becomes symbolic of the potential for technological advancement to threaten humankind; for it to be used against its makers. The introduction to the song none too subtly underlines this inference, beginning with a high-pitched synthesizer line that fades from silence into the listener's consciousness. While at first it sounds like an air-raid siren, a phasing effect implies movement and it sounds more like the far-off, yet rapidly nearing, approach of a missile. Joined by a bass guitar that also fades in, ten seconds into the track this is followed by the loud rattle of a snare drum playing a succession of five-stroke rolls, a parade-ground rudiment. Once the song proper gets going, it is revealed as an instrumental except for the heavily effected song title repeated by Bowie again and again. The lead instrument is saxophone, which at times plays out of step with the beat, creating a tension relieved only when it comes back into synch. The second part of the song's title finds Bowie tipping his hat to Florian Schneider, founding member of Kraftwerk, and the song's stylistic debt to these electronic masters is clear.

The bleak musical soundscapes of side two of *Low* are recalled in the following "Sense of Doubt." In what is not so much a song as an atmosphere, the opening four-note descending piano motif returns throughout the track as the brooding, threatening core of a musical experience that otherwise lacks any sense of a clear pulse. Above this, other various and seemingly random textures come and go, pitched both high and low, but never overshadowing the central motif, which sweeps all before its menacing presence. At times, washes of synthesizers recall the soundtrack of Stanley Kubrick's *A Clockwork Orange* by Walter Carlos, music that created a similarly threatening ambiance. "Sense of Doubt" convincingly brings to musical life the very essence of its title.

The Japanese koto takes center stage on the third song of side two, the instrumental "Moss Garden." In this, another atmospheric piece, swirling synthesizer-generated sounds provide a slowly evolving, subdued, and understated platform above which the koto is heard, heavily foregrounded at the front of the mix. Earlier, in "Blackout," Bowie rather inexplicably sang "I'm under Japanese influence," and here, three songs later, that pronouncement is felt keenly. Such influence does not come completely out of the blue when one takes Bowie's career to date into account, because much of his costuming during the glam rock years had paid clear homage to the fashions of Japan. However, to hear it here as a dominating force in his music is a new development. As was the case with the tracks on the second side of *Low* and those that preceded "Moss Garden," Bowie's musical choices and unexpected juxtapositions create powerful imagery, and a picture of a quiet, serene, and elegant Japanese garden is easily brought to the mind's eye of the listener. "Moss Garden" is another of Bowie's Berlin-era songs that is granted the time and space to gently evolve rather than being "played" in the manner of a conventional song.

Neuköln is a district within Berlin that is heavily populated by Turkish people, and here in the penultimate track of *"Heroes,"* which bears its name, Bowie highlights the isolation and struggle faced by the populace, living as aliens within a foreign land. Bleak in the extreme, the slow three-note descending motif around which the mostly ambient piece is constructed sounds cold, lonely, and hopeless. Bowie's saxophone stands in as the voice of the Turkish people, and never has his playing been so authentically avant-garde, virtuosic, and assured in its free-form stylings. Highly evocative and moving, this quality is most evident at the end, when the ambient backing drops away to nothing and the saxophone is left on its own, desperate and beseeching in its closing drawn-out wails.

Unlike on *Low*, where instrumental tracks closed out the album, on *"Heroes"* Bowie returns to a vocal song to conclude. Surprisingly, "The Secret Life of Arabia" is the most vocally lush of the entire album, with Bowie's voice multitracked while extensive backing vocals ensure, for the only time in the entire work, that the instrumental backing is relegated to an obvious accompaniment role. The feel is funky, a harking back to *Young Americans*, while hand claps add to the human touch. Bowie's vocal melody gives full vent to the extremes of his range and he sounds playful and exuberant in his delivery, a quantum shift from the mood of the preceding tracks. The lyrics paint a picture of a faux Arabian scene, with Bowie exhorting, "You must see the movie—the sand in my eyes. I walk through a desert song when the heroine dies." In addition, at the beginning of verse one he takes the opportunity to name-drop his own previous work, with a reference to the opening song of *Low* in the line "I was running at the speed of life." The faux nature of the song is enhanced by the affectations evident in Bowie's voice, most particularly on the key word "Arabia," which he draws out with an exaggerated cockney twang that ensures the singer sounds as far away from his subject matter as possible. Of all the songs on *"Heroes"* it is "The Secret Life of Arabia" that sounds like it least belongs to the album overall. Nevertheless, with its catchy pop sensibilities and energy, it provides a highly satisfying end.

While still groundbreaking, and clearly a close relative to *Low*, *"Heroes"* is a more accessible album. With the inclusion of more vocal tracks and fewer instrumentals, and especially given that both sides begin and end with relatively conventional songs, the voyage into Bowie and Eno's experimental electronic ambience is lessened, although by no means does this render it less impressive. *"Heroes"* manages to both solidify and advance Bowie's new direction, which was so alarmingly embarked upon with *Low*. In addition, it provides one of the most enduring songs of Bowie's career in its epic title track.

LODGER, 1979

> Another year, another record. Even when playing at superstars, it was always hard to escape the sense of Bowie as tourist. —Jon Savage, *Melody Maker*, May 1979

> The LP is easy to listen to because it rarely challenges the listener; it only baits you with slick and highly embossed surfaces. It is not really a departure from *Low* and *"Heroes,"* but a rejection of their serious nature. . . . You can't help liking parts of it, but if you really liked *Low*, liked '*Heroes*,' and generally like the challenging side of Bowie's previous works, you can't help feeling cheated and dismayed by this one. —Paul Yamada, *New York Rocker*, July 1979

> It was as if the turmoil of the previous records had been focused on to the artwork of *Lodger*, leaving the music itself unsettlingly free of emotion. —Peter Doggett, *The Man Who Sold the World: David Bowie and the 1970s*

Side One	**Side Two**
1. Fantastic Voyage (Bowie/Eno)	1. DJ (Bowie/Eno/Alomar)
2. African Night Flight (Bowie/Eno)	2. Look Back in Anger (Bowie/Eno)
3. Move On	3. Boys Keep Swinging (Bowie/Eno)
4. Yassassin	4. Repetition
5. Red Sails (Bowie/Eno)	5. Red Money (Bowie/Alomar)

Recorded in Switzerland, and thereby rendering the term "Berlin Trilogy" somewhat suspect despite this notion being propagated by Bowie himself at the time, *Lodger* is the album on which Bowie and Brian Eno collaborated the most fully.

Overall, *Lodger* fared a little better than *"Heroes,"* reaching number four in the UK, and twenty in the US. None of the Berlin Trilogy albums had been outstanding successes in the US. Of the singles, the best-performing was "Boys Keep Swinging," which reached number seven in the UK, while "DJ" was the best performer in the US, reaching a modest number twenty-nine.

The cover of *Lodger* is a gatefold design, with Bowie shown from the waist up on the front while the lower part of his body completes the picture only if the cover is fully opened. The picture is immediately disturbing in that Bowie appears not in control of his situation. Bowie's album covers have always given the impression that he is in command of the scenario in which he is shown. On *Lodger*, it appears he is someone to whom something bad may have happened. The white tiles suggest a bathroom, and it appears from the viewer's perspective that he/she has just entered a public bathroom and found the victim lying there in the aftermath of a crime. Yet just what has happened remains unclear as there are components to the image that do not add up. Perhaps the foremost of these is the displacement/distortion of Bowie's nose, which gives the appearance of being squashed beneath glass. Also, one might speculate as to whether the act of apparent violence was carried out by a now-absent assailant or was self-inflicted. In support of the latter, the bandaged right hand suggests Bowie may at some previous point in time have slashed his wrist, and in that same hand he holds an implement. However, it is a comb.

The look on Bowie's face is pained and stressed, his extremely white teeth exposed as his lips are pulled back in a grimace. Adding no support to this, however, his eyebrows are arched high in an extremely unnatural position, seemingly totally unrelated to the overall expression he conveys, given that pain usually causes one's eyebrows to contract and pull downward. This unreal effect is particularly the case with Bowie's right eyebrow, which is positioned too far up on his forehead and falls unnaturally away to the side of his face.

When one opens the gatefold sleeve out fully, the image becomes more bizarre still, as the location of the handbasin to the viewer's left makes it apparent that Bowie is defying the laws of gravity, spread-eagled across the wall and not the floor. But, adding further to the mystery, his feet are not on the floor and thus he has no means of support to be against the wall like he is, and his hair and jacket are falling upward instead of downward. Also adding to the unreality of the scene is the fact that his left arm and leg are turned unnaturally inward toward the right instead of being splayed out naturally to the left as we might expect. Both limbs could perhaps be broken, yet there is no sign of blood upon the white tiles—no outward sign of trauma to account for their unnatural positioning. Further, the shadow cast by the pencil—or whatever the object is that lies above his shoulder to the left of the image—is separated from its cause, and the only apparent explanation for this is that it is somehow hovering in midair above the tiles. There appears no rational explanation for this.

The viewer must speculate on why the postcard is addressed to David Bowie, c/o RCA Records, Bedford Avenue, London WC1, and also why the message simply reads, "Lodger." A lodger is someone who has no home ownership, a tenant, somebody perhaps just passing through. This might well be applicable to Bowie's passing through musical styles, literally a lodger who stays for a time before moving on to something and/or somewhere new. It is almost as if he is acknowledging this vagrancy to his record company. And yet he feels beaten up by this constant change.

The transitory nature of the album title is supported in the connotations of travel contained in the title of the first track, "Fantastic Voyage." However, the lyrics quickly revisit the favorite Bowie concern of nuclear Armageddon brought about by unchecked technological development in the hands of unstable leaders: "It's a moving world, but that's no reason to shoot some of those missiles," he proclaims. Oddly, given the gravitas of the subject matter, the music is presented in a simplistic pop style, understated and upbeat. The musical mood of "Fantastic Voyage" sits in contrast to the challenging experimental textures and moods that predominated on *Low* and *"Heroes."* Bowie's vocal style is dispassionate, quiet, and controlled; matter-of-fact, even, until he finally allows himself full emotional vent on the pessimistic final line of the chorus: "'Cause we'll ["I'll" is substituted in the final chorus] never say anything nice again, how can I?"

The travel theme continues on the following "African Night Flight," a song that stylistically resembles nothing else Bowie had ever done before. Through a rapid and almost rap-like delivery, during which words are spat out with heavy rhythmic emphasis, we hear highly visual snapshots of a world he glimpsed briefly when vacationing in Africa. It is the world of foreign freelance bush pilots who live in bars by night and fly the vast expanses of the African plains and bush by day. "Getting in mood for a Mombasa night flight. Pushing my luck, gonna fly like a mad thing. Bare strip takeoff—skimming over Rhino." The pilots are uniformly dysfunctional, estranged from their own homelands and trapped in a highly unusual dichotomous lifestyle that only alcohol can relieve; so they "slide to the nearest bar." "Sick of you, sick of me," they "lust for the free life," represented by the terrain they fly over each day. But such freedom is something they can only ever observe rather than truly experience. The music of "African Night Flight" is frenetic and literal, with Swahili lyrics and chant, African instruments, and jungle noises utilized throughout like colors on a postcard. One is very hard-pressed to find linkage here of any kind to the prevailing sounds of *Low* or *"Heroes."*

"Move On" furthers the travel theme of the album's title and the first two songs. "Sometimes I feel that I need to move on, so I pack a bag and move on," sings Bowie over a relentless rapid-fire tom-tom beat that sustains throughout the entire song, refusing to settle into stability. The notion of continual movement is presented here as a defense to ward off consequences when things go wrong: "When the chips are down, I'm just a traveling man." Musically, with strummed guitar predominating, unstable percussion, and extensive oohing and ahhing of a dominating backing vocal track, the very sound of "Move On" informs upon its title, being the third sonic palette within as many songs. Of course, it is applicable too in the wider sense—isn't moving on exactly what Bowie has always done? "Move On" links to its immediate predecessor by referencing Africa, which is described as being full of "sleepy people," as well as other travel destinations, including Russia and Cyprus. Employing a deep, calm voice in spite of the restless accompaniment, late in the song Bowie takes on an entirely different tone, seemingly representing, in Doggett's words, "a final outburst of passion as he recognized the obvious: his unrelenting travelling was just a disguise for 'drifting' helplessly in the wind."[7]

The next song, "Yassassin," is reminiscent in feel of "Fame" from *Young Americans*, although built more upon a reggae backbeat. Its title is identified on the album's sleeve notes as being Turkish for "Long Live." The plight of Turkish people in Berlin was explored on *"Heroes"* in the instrumental track, "Neuköln," and here he revisits their displacement: "We came from the farmlands to live in this city . . . Look at this. No second glances. Look at this. No value of love. Look at this. Just sun and steel. Look at this, then look at us." A repeated chant of the song's title is utilized as the primary hook, while a virtuoso violin improvising within Middle Eastern scales depicts Turkishness. This implied geographical departure represents yet another travel destination. But there is conflict here because the Turks are in Germany, not Turkey, and therefore significant racial tension exists in "You want to fight, but I don't want to leave."

Earlier, during "Move On," Bowie suggested that he might "sail at dawn," and here, on "Red Sails," the upbeat closing track of side one, he turns to the sea as his means of travel. The opening lines effectively summarize the album's content to this point and also allude to the cover as the constant shifts to new destinations take a toll: "I feel roughed up, feel a bit frightened. Nearly pin it down some time. Red sail action wake up in the wrong town. Boy, I really get around." The electronic sounds that predominate in "Red Sails" are suggestive of Neu! or Kraftwerk and thereby stylistically link the song more closely to the preceding albums than was the case in the previous four tracks. In addition, the sound is highly reminiscent of the then-current pop favorite in the UK, Gary Numan, who was himself labeled a Bowie clone by music critics. As with every track thus far, travel is viewed as problematic in terms of fitting into a foreign environment: "Struggle with a foreign tongue."

Clearly, Bowie organized the first side with a great deal of fore-thought, with every track relating to travel and thereby aligning with ease to the notion implied by the cover art of "lodging" in different locales.

The first song of side two, however, initially appears to have little to do with any such geographical concerns. The opening lyrics of "DJ" set up a bleak scenario. "I'm home, lost my job, and incurably ill. You think this is easy realism?" From this point on, however, the central protago-nist transforms—in what appears to be a revenge scenario—into a club DJ who requires that everybody, quite literally, dance to his tune(s) as he becomes the sum of his song choices: "I am what I play." This musical dictatorship is directed toward his partner, who has left him at home to go out dancing. It is a musically complex song, the chorus notable for its three five-syllable lines followed by a four-syllable one, a technique that imbues this section with hooks that are simultaneously rhythmic and melodic: "I-am-the-D-J. I-am-what-I-play. I-got-be-liev-ers. Be-liev-ing-me." While on the surface this is commercial and catchy, the song as a whole eschews commercialism. This is evident right from the introduction, which sounds like a series of musical errors, complete with illogical bar lengths and unexpected entry points for both violin and Bowie's vocals. In addition to the personal vendetta outlined in the lyrics, the song clearly comments in a wider sense upon the disproportionate power that DJs hold over musicians. Bowie's voice demonstrates histrionic qualities at times, appearing both desperate and cynical.

Despite having departed from the notion of physical, geographical travel, it is an easy task to extrapolate and conclude that the DJ has the power to travel between musical styles, between musical acts—and can evoke emotional journeys on the part of both himself and his listeners via the music he selects to play. A veritable musical tour guide, in this light, "DJ" remains consistent with the overriding concern of *Lodger* thus far. In addition, such was the cult of the DJ at this time, one might also see the song as a further critique on the notion of celebrity.

The following "Look Back in Anger" is the most upbeat, full-on, rock-oriented song of the album. The theme is that of looking back upon one's life just before death, and this scenario is set up in the opening lines of the first verse when an angel "with crumpled wings" appears, saying, "You know who I am . . . It's time we should be going."

Built on a virtuosic drum part upon which aggressive guitar and synthesizer parts frenziedly come and go, the unrelenting intensity of the instrumental backing ensures no rest. Bowie's vocals too are quick-fire and tormented, and it is only in the group-sung chorus hook line, "Waiting so long—I've been waiting so long," that any sense of respite is felt. The syllables of these words are drawn out and the melody is simple and sing-along compared to all that goes on elsewhere in the song. The inference is that death will at last deliver a longed-for state of peace to the protagonist, who has seemingly been angry all his life. While "Look Back in Anger" does not align to the geographical travel theme of the album's first side, the notion of traveling between the physical world and the spirit world is a clearly aligned deviation, and the crime-scene-like image on the cover might well portray the moment that the transition occurs.

"Heaven loves ya. The clouds part for ya. Nothing stands in your way when you're a boy," promises Bowie in the opening lines of the next track, "Boys Keep Swinging." Though the song initially seems to be a celebratory anthem to young men everywhere, it quickly becomes clear that Bowie has his tongue firmly in his cheek, and the unfolding lyric drips with irony as the images of beckoning manhood that he paints are stereotypical and hollow: "Life is a pop of the cherry . . . you can wear a uniform . . . learn to drive and everything." Indeed it is gender instability that lies at the thematic heart of the song, a fact brought out with clarity in the accompanying promotional video in which the three female backing singers are exposed at the end as being Bowie in drag. The song's title, which doubles as the main chorus lyric and hook, is the biggest clue of all; boys can "keep swinging" between the rigidly fixed gender signifiers, behaviors, and attitudes Bowie lampoons in the lyrics *or* they can break free of such constraints and explore their gender identity. It is the very same thematic area and mode of ironic delivery that the Village People presented so consummately in their hit songs "YMCA" and "In the Navy." The musical backing on "Boys Keep Swinging" is loose and full of parody, with the instrumentalists rather famously required by Bowie to record the song playing each other's instruments rather than those on which they specialized, resulting in the drummer playing bass, the guitarist playing drums, and so on. Just as the theme of travel in the previous song was transformed into the transition between life and death, here too another variation—the extremely fluid line of continuum between male and female—is clearly discernable.

The album's penultimate song, "Repetition," is also one of its most disturbing. Related with a cutting directness in the lyrics and a calculated disinterest through Bowie's monotonal and unemotional delivery, the song tells a story of domestic abuse. Johnny—"he's bigger than you"—takes out the frustrations that he experiences, because his life has not turned out as he would have liked it to, upon his unnamed but long-suffering wife, who must wear long sleeves in order to cover her bruises. All the while, Johnny thinks of how he could have instead married "Anne with the blue silk blouse" and it drives him to further violence: "The food is on the table but the food is cold. Don't hit her." Emotion is absent in the band's performance, too, as swirling, unstable guitar and synthesizer lines sit uncomfortably above metronomic bass and drum lines, the latter featuring snare hits on all four beats of every bar and evincing physical blows. The ambiance created is in complete collusion with the "Repetition" of the song's title, a feeling of inevitability and hopelessness pervading every aspect of the performance. For the first time on the album it is hard to discern any notion of travel or transience such as might fit in with the theme of the album's title. Indeed, the trapped, going-nowhere nature of the situation in which the song's protagonists exist stands in stark contrast to any such possibility. They are not *lodging* in this scenario—they are here forever.

"Red Money" is the last song on *Lodger*. Surprisingly, given that *Low*, *"Heroes*," and *Lodger* hitherto contained only completely new compositions, it is constructed upon the musical bed of "Sister Midnight," his 1976 collaboration with Iggy Pop. Though it is more abrasive than Pop's version, with guitar more to the forefront and the heavy utilization of electronic percussion, Bowie has rewritten both lyrics and melody line for "Red Money." Of all the tracks on *Lodger*, this unexpected finale is the most difficult to penetrate. Just exactly what it is about eludes the listener throughout. The only clue as to meaning—all too evident and therefore feeling like a signpost that Bowie purposely planted—is the repeated phrase "Project canceled." As critics have noted, given that this is the last song of the last album of his self-proclaimed Berlin Trilogy, "Project canceled" sounds very much like a signing off; a dismissal. It is hard to read this any other way, and therefore this small portion, at least, of "Red Money" has an overarching resonance. Yet, in terms of appraising the song in its own right, intrinsic meaning is unfathomable. This, coupled with the cover version inference of using an existing musical bed, has led some critics to regard the track somewhat poorly; David Buckley, for instance, suggests it is "a surprisingly flat ending to a fine album."[8]

As the last sounds of "Red Money" linger in your ears and the arm returns to its cradle, your mind is in something akin to turmoil. Back in 1977 when you first heard *Low* and then, quick on its heels, *"Heroes,"* you were left with the feeling that, although you knew you didn't quite "get it" on all levels, and you sorely missed the boa-sporting glitter-monster that Bowie had been, you could still sense in those releases that something radical was going on; something pioneering and dangerous. That feeling was nowhere near as palpable on *Lodger*. It was, for the most part, an easy listen that required far less of you because all ten songs were, despite the world music instrument borrowings of side one, far more conventional. The incomprehensibility of the album's closing track aside, in the narrative of his lyrics and the utilization of far more standard song structures, there was far less to puzzle over and ponder than Bowie fans had become used to. Doggett has suggested that, "by his own exacting standards, *Lodger* was Bowie's one serious failure of nerve during the 'long seventies.'"[9]

When describing *Lodger* at the time of its release, RCA spokesperson Mel Ilberman suggested, "It would be fair to call it Bowie's *Sergeant Pepper* . . . a concept album that portrays the Lodger as a homeless wanderer, shunned and victimized by life's pressures and technology."[10] While it is true that long-established Bowie themes such as the threat of technology, gender fluidity, alienation, and concepts of identity were expressed through the overarching notion of travel on *Lodger*, the comparatively unchallenging means of their delivery removed an edge from the work. The album cover was indeed the most abrasive aspect of the entire package.

Ironically, had any other major artist apart from Bowie come up with *Lodger*, it would probably have been deemed superb. However, for an artist whose very foundation lay in unconventionality, and with the preceding pairing of *Low* and *"Heroes"* the benchmarks by which it was to be judged, *Lodger* suffered.

8

THE RISE AND FALL OF DAVID BOWIE

*Scary Monsters (and Super Creeps), Let's Dance, Tonight,
Never Let Me Down, Tin Machine,* and
Tin Machine II, 1980–1991

The 1970s had belonged to David Bowie. As Peter Doggett has suggested, "like the Beatles in the decade before him, Bowie was popular culture's most reliable guide to the fever of the seventies."[1] Just as the doomed exploits of Major Tom had farewelled the sixties and ushered in the new decade, so too, with characteristic neatness, would Bowie provide the perfect complementary bookend to the seventies with *Scary Monsters*. With remarkable poignancy, he tied the 1970s up with a bow by surprisingly resurrecting Major Tom in order to illustrate his "look where we are now" summation. On *Scary Monsters (and Super Creeps)*, through the seemingly impossible task of moving forward and backward simultaneously, Bowie melded commercial success (number one in the UK and number twelve in the US) with widespread critical acclaim.

SCARY MONSTERS (AND SUPER CREEPS), 1980

Learning to live with somebody's depression: the man in the clown suit stops running, finds self in back-against-wall situation, attempts to deal with same. —Charles Shaar Murray, *New Musical Express*, September 1980

Slowly, brutally and with a savage, satisfying crunch, David Bowie eats his young. —Debra Rae Cohen, *Rolling Stone*, December 1980

It was me eradicating the feelings within myself that I was uncomfortable with. You have to accommodate your pasts in your persona . . . it's very important to get into them and understand them. It helps you reflect on what you are now. —David Bowie in Nicholas Pegg, *The Complete David Bowie*

Side One	**Side Two**
1. It's No Game (Part 1)	1. Teenage Wildlife
2. Up the Hill Backwards	2. Scream Like a Baby
3. Scary Monsters (and Super Creeps)	3. Kingdom Come (Verlaine)
4. Ashes to Ashes	4. Because You're Young
5. Fashion	5. It's No Game (Part 2)

The "real" David Bowie cannot be found on the front cover of *Scary Monsters (and Super Creeps)*, despite the fact that he is shown twice, as a shadowy silhouette and as a cartoon. The cover is a black-and-white photograph that has been torn in two, and in the space that has been torn away the drawn Bowie stares out at the viewer, his lips shiny and red, traces of blue upon his right temple, and a small black harlequin diamond upon his left cheek. Oddly, the light-blue ruffles of the upper part of his clown costume do not end at the border of the picture but instead flow down over the bottom of the cover, distorting perception and boundaries. The expression on his face is somber. In what is left of the vandalized photograph we are denied access to his head and face and are left to focus our gaze upon his extended right arm and hand, in which a cigarette is held theatrically aloft between index and middle fingers.

Reality is merged with fantasy through the employment of both photograph and drawing, but fantasy wins the day; the cartoon is privileged not only because it shows Bowie's face, but also because it is rendered in color. The inference is: strip away what *should* be the real

Bowie (the photograph) and you will find only a painted construction beneath. Such are his demeanor and expression in the drawing—caught in a moment of reflection and repose, clearly offstage and off-duty—that we have the impression that we are seeing the artist in a candid, genuine moment, despite the fact that we are viewing a drawing. In contrast, it is the glimpse of Bowie's "real" arm and hand that seems staged; a clear reversal of the natural order of things.

On the rear side of the cover, Bowie revisits several of his previous performance personas, reproducing portions of earlier cover art from *Aladdin Sane, Low, "Heroes,"* and *Lodger*. It is a remarkable piece of self-referencing and evidence of Bowie's awareness of, and confidence in, his own performative methodology.

The clunking, clicking, spinning sounds of a reel-to-reel tape player open the album, leading into the abrasive, doom-laden "It's No Game (Part 1)." But it is not Bowie who ushers in the vocals but a Japanese female voice, for which no translation is given in the liner notes. When Bowie does subsequently enter, echoing the album cover imagery with the opening line, "Silhouettes and shadows watch the revolution," it is with a voice rent with hysteria teetering on the limits of control. From here onward Bowie and the woman (Michi Hirota) trade sections over an unrelenting drum-and-guitar-dominated backing. The concerns outlined in Bowie's lyrics include revolution, boredom, assassination, the plight of refugees, media, torture, and fascism. It is a highly moral address, with Bowie repeatedly beseeching the world to wake up to the fact that such events should not be treated lightly, because "it's no game!" Employing a bewildering array of voices and emotion through the song's course, leaving any sense of continuity to his fellow vocalist, the aural assault ends abruptly and violently, with Bowie twice shouting "Shut up!" over a repeating, loudly aggressive guitar figure.

As its title suggests, struggle is the theme of the following "Up the Hill Backwards." The song's musical underpinning alternates between total fragmented collusion with the troubled-state-of-the-world lyrics and offering ironic false hope through the smooth predictability of the pop-inflected repeated sing-along refrain, "Yeah yeah yeah, up the hill backwards. It'll be alright." Bemoaning the existence of "more idols than realities," the desperate and jarring guitar solo that ensues at two minutes and five seconds and sustains until the end occurs atop an awkward, undanceable 7/8 time signature, making it clear that things will *not* be all right.

The upbeat and superbly aggressive title track features third on the album, and in "Scary Monsters (and Super Creeps)" Bowie turns his attention from the travails of the world to a far more personal turmoil. The destructive claustrophobia of an intense and dysfunctional personal relationship is laid out over a "Thriller"-like guitar-dominated intensity. "She had a horror of rooms," we hear first, and from here onward Bowie paints the bleakest of pictures of his girlfriend. "She could've been a killer," he suggests, with threatening depth to his voice, yet despite the fact that he is continually "running scared," he perversely goes on to assure us, "Well I love the little girl and I'll love her till the day I die." Unlikely juxtapositions in myriad forms are a hallmark of Bowie's work, and the psychological conundrum outlined here is a fine example.

"Do you remember a guy that's been in such an early song?" asks Bowie in "Ashes to Ashes" as he prepares to sabotage the memory and reputation of his much-loved creation from 1969, Major Tom. Referencing Bowie's own drug use, which had reached significant levels during the mid- to late seventies, the most famous astronaut in popular music now languishes as a junkie: "Strung out on Heaven's high, hitting an all-time low." The music is simple, funky, and of moderate tempo, leaving center stage for Bowie's vocals as they tell of Major Tom's demise with clarity and appropriate spaciousness. As the title suggests, "Ashes to Ashes" buries the past; Bowie's, certainly, but the song also lays to rest the naïve optimism that existed at the time of Major Tom's space exploits, that somehow the feat of putting a man on the moon would improve humankind. The hope that things would get better after the turbulence of the 1960s had proven unfounded as the 1970s wore on and it became apparent that life on the green planet was simply business as usual. Humans still fought over trivialities, anyone deemed outside mainstream society for any reason suffered alienation, the development of nuclear weaponry continued unabated, and totalitarian regimes still flourished. Such resigned weariness is the pervading emotion in the song, presented in the forlorn guise of the junkie desperately wanting to—yet completely unable to—improve himself. "Time and again I tell myself I'll stay clean tonight," sings Bowie, but to no avail. His man-in-space achievements—considered so important at the peak of the space race when astronauts were international heroes—are reduced to nothingness: "I've never done good things—I've never done bad things." As if to underline the lack of solidity of the human condition, Bowie's vocal tone alters from section to section and even from line to line. Despite these shifts he avoids any display of energy or vitality and the vocals retain an overarching perfunctory quality. Apart from Major Tom's gradual deterioration and resignation, nothing has changed. The taunting, nursery rhyme–styled chorus, with its repetition and rising/falling melody, underlines the childlike immaturity that Bowie is recapitulating, and the Wurlitzer organ sound at the forefront of the backing adds it own sense of weary fairground folly. "Ashes to Ashes" is magnificent in its unforced truisms; anticlimax and nonachievement have never sounded so good and no other rock artist could have delivered this hard-hitting, self-referential, yet universal treatise.

For Bowie fans especially it was surprisingly pleasing to learn that Major Tom was still alive despite his pitiable state. After all, it had seemed for a decade that he had simply drifted off into deep space to a cold and lonely death. That one of the heroes of one's childhood should return from the dead long after youth had been left behind was a strangely potent nostalgic twist. What might we bring back in our own lives that we had abandoned too readily?

"Fashion" completes the first side, doing so emphatically and ironically. Above a funk groove reminiscent of "Golden Years" from *Station to Station* and also "Fame" from *Young Americans*, yet with the same world-weary vocal quality of the previous track, Bowie eschews physical effort in his performance, delivering his scathing critique of fads—be they concerned with fashion, music, or politics—deadpan, like the straight man in a comedy duo who is in on the joke but never admits it. "Turn to the left—turn to the right," he commands, followed by "Listen to me—don't listen to me." We human sheep, Bowie appears to be observing, follow such orders time after time. Fashions, in all guises, come and go with fickleness and inevitability. Mostly a celebration of trivial, fleeting pursuits, "Fashion" lampoons the very medium (popular music) that carries the message. However, in the chorus, when Bowie sings, "We are the goon squad and we're coming to town," a far more serious point is being made, with overtones of totalitarianism, of fascism and violence, that go beyond the transience of pop culture obsessions.

"Teenage Wildlife" opens side two with an autobiographical bomb-shell. Here, Bowie takes stock of his own (senior) status as a youth-cultural icon, while at the same time acknowledging and warning those other artists who have ridden in on his coattails that the life of the rock-star idol is fleeting and dangerous. "Same old thing in brand-new drag comes sweeping into view, oh-ooh . . . You'll take me aside, and say, 'Well, David, what shall I do?'" Directly referencing the current musical fashion, he targets "the new wave boys," suggesting that they "daren't look behind." Ever the loner, seldom has Bowie expressed this with such directness: "I feel like a group of one," he whines. "Teenage Wild-life" is cacophonous in its instrumental assault and unrelenting due to its almost seven-minute duration. Bowie's vocals run the full gamut of his range and stylistic variations, highly theatrical and a commentary on the way in which pop music fads come and go, with cosmetic changes being made each time in order to imply newness. Whereas, in truth, it's just the "same old thing." "Teenage Wildlife" is Bowie at his cynical best.

"Scream like a baby," exhorts Bowie, dripping with alienation in the title line of the following song, his unnamed character hiding under the blankets to avoid the unwanted attentions of the nurse inside some unidentified institution. He mourns the violent passing of his gay friend, Sam, who was "just like me." Society rejected and brutalized them both: "Well they came down hard on the faggots, and they came down hard on the street. They came down harder on Sam, and they all knew he was beat." Pegg regards the song as "a brutal story of mental instability and *Clockwork Orange*–style totalitarianism,"[2] a telling ob-servation especially given the lines late in the song in which, Alex-like, Bowie resignedly accepts the demands of his oppressors, although he can barely bring himself to say the final word: "Now I'm learning to be a part of so-society." The searing synth-and-guitar-dominated backing works in tandem with Bowie's at times tortured vocals, evincing a dis-turbing musical manifestation of Arthur Janov's Primal Therapy.

As seen through his earlier work, at times Bowie includes a cover version on an album, and his interpretation of Tom Verlaine's "King-dom Come" is next up. Bowie never chooses to do a cover version unless it aligns with his own concerns, and in "Kingdom Come" such an alignment is readily observable. "The voice of doom was shining in my room," sings Bowie, feet firmly on familiar ground. Verlaine's song is about being an outcast; a prisoner kept in chains whose plight can be read as either literal or psychological. The rocks he is required to break open may be psychological barriers, societal decrees to be obeyed, or, simply, rocks, as demanded by his guards, because the "sun keeps beating down on me, wall's a mile high. Up in the tower they're watching me hoping I'm gonna die." Bowie's delivery is full of vocal histrionics, bringing a theatrical, tortured-artist quality to his rendition that was absent in the original.

Aligning itself by title to the earlier "Teenage Wildlife" is "Because You're Young." If the former song addressed youth culture at the macro level, then here Bowie addresses in a far more personal manner the plight of an unnamed teenaged girl about to throw away her future on someone she has just met. Bowie warns that "a million dreams" will turn into "a million scars." With a nod to Bowie's own youth, mod hero Pete Townshend of the Who is the guest guitarist, but the style of the song, with organ to the forefront, disappointingly relegates him to the background.

The end of the album is a recapitulation of its opener, with "It's No Game (Part 2)." Here, however, the treatment of the song is quite different, subdued and even lackluster. Some of the lyrics are different, and the Japanese sections have been removed. The guitar lines have become gentler, repetitive, and lacking in attack, and overall the song is now missing the spiky edge that provided such a slap-across-the-face beginning. It is as if world-weariness has drained its architect of all passion and drive and, while he still espouses his antifascist views, any real fight has gone out of him. Simply, on "It's No Game (Part 2)," Bowie sounds spent. And when the reel-to-reel tape sounds with which the album began finally return to herald its exit, it appears to be the end of . . . something. An era? A life? Regardless of whether it was a game or not, it seems that Bowie, in the fine tradition of the antihero, lost. "Draw the blinds on yesterday," he suggests. But if there's one thing we have learned through the passage of *Scary Monsters (and Super Creeps)*, it's not yesterday that is the problem; it is the future. Because now, in 1980, "it's all so much scarier."

Having heard the album in its entirety, another perusal of the cover reveals further synergy with the recorded contents. Bowie's appearance as the rock music version of Pierrot seems especially well chosen. During the course of the ten songs, like the hardest-working of clowns he has given vent to every emotion he can, pulled every face he can, raised every monstrous fear both personal and global, and tried to shake his audience. But now, as the drawing that stands in for the real Bowie on the front cover shows, he is used up, bereft of ideas and energy; literally a shadow of his former self. But it has been a magnificent failure.

Scary Monsters (and Super Creeps) is almost universally loved by fans, and many critics regard it as the most cohesive and best Bowie album of all. The thematic concerns he had established as cornerstones of his work over the passage of his career were all present, and never had he seemed more alienated and vulnerable. The album certainly invited audience engagement by the shovelful as, despite Major Tom's now-pitiable condition, being reintroduced to him a decade since his inception invited reflection on how we, too, had grown and developed during the passage of those ten years. This was powerful magic.

Here, Bowie was not happy. And this was precisely what fans wanted from the master of angst. Few artists could hold a mirror up to society and entertain us with our own failings. But Bowie could, with flair and aplomb.

LET'S DANCE, 1983

> With this album, Bowie seems to have transcended the need to write endlessly about the dramas of being D°A°V°I°D B°O°W°I°E and about all his personal agonies. . . . Powerful, positive music that dances like a dream and makes you feel ten feet tall. —Charles Shaar Murray, *New Musical Express*, April 1983

> "Let's Dance" was a record anyone could have made. —Barney Hoskyns, *The Independent*, June 15, 2002

> "Let's Dance" is an album on which anything remotely resembling a rough edge has been sanded down and polished up until the glare is dazzling . . . he plays it safe in every department. —Nicholas Pegg, *The Complete David Bowie*

> I don't have the urge to play around with musical ideas. At the moment . . . I think I'm just a little tired of experimentation now. —Chris Bohn, *New Musical Express*, April 1983

Side One

1. Modern Love

2. China Girl (Bowie/Pop)

3. Let's Dance

4. Without You

Side Two

1. Ricochet

2. Criminal World (Godwin/Browne/Lyons)

3. Cat People (Putting Out Fire) (Bowie/Moroder)

4. Shake It

Two and a half years passed before Bowie released his next album. Having changed record company from RCA to EMI, and swapped producer Tony Visconti for mainstream pop-production guru Nile Rodgers, in *Let's Dance* he again delivered a work bristling with change. However, the changes were not to the taste of many existing fans. Throughout the seventies Bowie had managed to take his often confused, yet compliant, fan base through stylistic shifts of a magnitude that would have killed other artists, yet fan loyalty remained absolute because the consistency of themes addressed in his music and the prickly nature of their presentation had provided a confidence-inspiring vital core. Despite unprecedented commercial success in reaching number one in the UK and many other countries and number four in the US, and spawning three smash-hit singles in the title track, "China Girl," and "Modern Love," *Let's Dance* would prove a double-edged sword in its suggestion that the outsider was ostensibly moving inside.

Surprisingly, only the words "David Bowie" appear on the front cover, relegating the album's title to the spine. However, a clear inference to the title remains evident in the diagram that traces the choreographed steps of a dance. Bowie, his hair peroxide blonde, is shown naked from the waist up in the guise of a boxer, with his hands at the ready and his gaze fixed to the viewer's left on some unseen target. Bathed in a red glow, his shadow falls upon the wall behind him, upon which a cityscape is evident, a yellow glow suggesting dawn or dusk.

"Modern Love" is an emphatic opener, as good a pop song as one could imagine and chock-full of the kind of production gloss for which producer Nile Rodgers was renowned. Reminiscent of "I'm Still Standing" by Elton John, which was in the charts at the same time, the dance-oriented drums are purely of their time, and such is the unrelenting instrumental onslaught that Bowie's fractured lyrics are relegated to second place. The crux of the lyrical theme seems to lie in the repeated words "God and man," and this certainly revisits the critique-of-faith theme of earlier songs such as "Soul Love" from *Ziggy Stardust*. Here, however, carried on the jaunty, infectious, frothy pop wagon, and with scant other lyrics helping to clarify the territory, any inclination to ruminate on the song's meaning on the part of the listener is quickly passed over in favor of simply singing along and tapping one's foot in acquiescence. Let's dance.

More interesting, if only marginally less catchy, is the following "China Girl," co-written by Bowie and Iggy Pop, which had featured six years earlier on Pop's 1977 album, *The Idiot*. A song of cultural clash told through the desperate story of a white male protagonist's love for an Asian woman, it lays out its territory straightaway. A faux-Asian guitar riff representing the otherness of a foreign culture is the first thing heard, but this is immediately consumed by the subsequent juggernaut of the great Western pop machine. "China Girl" addresses themes far darker than one meets in "normal" pop writing—and certainly this came across clearly in Iggy Pop's earlier incarnation, but once again the music here leaves little room for such introspection. While in earlier years such a juxtaposition may have come across as being full of Bowie-irony, here the playing field is not level enough for that, as the dance rhythms and pop gloss, coupled with Bowie's straightforward vocal delivery, push the lyrics into second place. By all means, continue dancing.

The title track is next, completing an unprecedented tour de force of an album opening, with each of the first three tracks becoming global hits. "Let's Dance" was given particular poignancy and meaning in the accompanying music video shot in the outback of Australia, wherein a young Aboriginal couple become seduced by Western commercialism—signified by the girl's desire for the red shoes—at the expense of their own culture and heritage. In terms of the song's stand-alone merits, however, when removed from the video such a meaning is hard to discern. Nevertheless, there is a degree of unsettling ambiguity that undermines any presumption that the song is simply about dancing and nothing more, in the lines "Let's dance, for fear your grace should fall. Let's dance, for fear tonight is all." Largely built around a call-and-response technique shared between instrumental and vocal phrases, the main hook is as strongly rhythmic as a pop hook can be, the pulse of the two-word phrase "Let's dance" or "Let's sway" being set up on the fourth beat of one bar ("Let's") and resolving most decisively on the first beat of the next ("dance/sway"). Again the accompanying music is quintessential early-eighties dance-pop perfection and the darker nuances within the lyric are easily overlooked.

It seems categorically unfair to criticize David Bowie for attaining such pop perfection; for achieving massive success around the world and opening up his music to a mainstream audience that had not previously valued him. However, Bowie was not like other musicians. His value, as gauged by existing fans, lay in the fact that he was not a follower but a leader. Yet here, in these otherwise sublime pop songs, his traditional point of difference was diluted to the point where it suddenly seemed that he *belonged* in the company of pop stars. What was going on?

Five songs remain on *Let's Dance* but the remaining song of side one, "Without You," with its "also ran" placement after the three hit singles, was always doomed to relative obscurity. This simple love song, charming, unchallenging, and significantly shorter than anything else on the album, simply cannot compete.

"Ricochet" begins side two and is the oddest moment on the album, a crumb of comfort for those who demand of Bowie that he raise their eyebrows. But despite challenging lyrics that address various ills of the world, the wordy song, half spoken and half sung, is plodding and disjointed. For those who purchased *Let's Dance* as their first Bowie album on the strength of its hit singles, one suspects the finger that guided the needle may have bypassed "Ricochet" frequently.

An obscure glam/new wave song from the duo Metro, circa 1977, is next. The lyrics of "Criminal World," with bisexual undertones reflective of glam rock's foundational androgyny, certainly hark back to Bowie's groundbreaking work, but the clinical production and Bowie's perfunctory vocal delivery here combine to disallow any particular synergy with the subject matter, relegating the song to filler status.

The following "Cat People (Putting Out Fire)" was written by Bowie and disco producer Giorgio Moroder for the movie of the same name in 1982. A surprise number-one hit single in New Zealand, Norway, and Sweden that year, but faring more poorly elsewhere, this rerecording pales against the original.

The end of the album comes with "Shake It," another unabashed dance track dominated by drums and synthesizer whose merit lies in providing a summation of the *Let's Dance* album, through a bass line very similar to the title track and lyrics that expound the act of dancing: "We're the kind of people who can shake it if we're feeling blue. When I'm feeling disconnected well I sure know what to do—Shake it baby." Never had a solution suggested by Bowie been so simplistic.

The *Let's Dance* album *is* problematic. Instead of "our man" being the uniting voice of outsiders everywhere, the voice heard on *Let's Dance* is seemingly that of someone who belongs. Suddenly, the smoke and mirrors that Bowie fans loved were gone, the fourth wall had been reinstated, the invitation to "give me your hands" had been withdrawn in favor of shuffling forward to join the majority. Could it be that Bowie had become a paid-up member of the fat-cat rock 'n' roll elite club? Where was the twitchy paranoid clown eternally standing in the rain looking in through the window, frightened by his own reflection? Even the invitation of the album title, *Let's Dance*, appears vacuous compared to the intrigue and danger contained in the likes of *The Man Who Sold the World*, *Aladdin Sane*, *Diamond Dogs*, or *Scary Monsters (and Super Creeps)*. Of course, the invitation to dance could have been ironic, and surely would have been in the hands of an earlier Bowie, but *Let's Dance* instead appeared to be exactly what it purported to be: another dance-pop album in the era of dance pop.

It must be acknowledged that *Let's Dance* almost certainly catered to new fans too young to have known the epiphany of Bowie's seventies work, and they may subsequently have been sufficiently moved to explore his back catalog and become lifelong fans. Nevertheless, long-standing fans lost a sense of ownership with this record, and *our* David Bowie was now *everyone's* David Bowie. *Let's Dance* is the album that non-Bowie fans are most likely to have stashed away in their record collection, perhaps nestled between other releases from the same year, such as Air Supply's *Greatest Hits* and the *Flashdance* soundtrack album. James E. Perone sums it up well, suggesting *Let's Dance* "placed Bowie in somewhat unfamiliar territory as an artist: he was now one of many people doing approximately the same thing."[3] In the "them and us" spirit of rock 'n' roll tribal affiliation, such a thing simply would not do.

But while *Let's Dance* might have set both alarm bells and cash registers ringing, even the most fierce of critics are unable to deny that Bowie "did" mainstream pop exceedingly well and this is the album's saving grace. Unfortunately, the same cannot be said for the following album, *Tonight*.

A clue to Bowie's uncharacteristically un-innovative mind-set can be gleaned in his response to journalist Charles Shaar Murray's question, in an interview conducted during the month that *Tonight* was released, as to whether he felt he could ever provide another major upset in rock music. Bowie replied, "It's hard to come up with another that has that same kind of force that the first one did. For me, the early '70s period was the thing that gave me my opening. I don't think I would ever contribute so aggressively again."[4]

TONIGHT, 1984

If *Let's Dance* . . . had made Bowie bigger than ever in 1983, then 1984 saw the beginnings of a commercial and artistic freefall that took the rest of the decade to halt. —David Buckley, *David Bowie: The Complete Guide to His Music*

Significantly, *Tonight* was the first Bowie album that was manifestly behind its time. —Nicholas Pegg, *The Complete David Bowie*

The relative large number of cover songs and collaborative compositions added to [a] dilution of the Bowie mystique. —James E. Perone, *The Words and Music of David Bowie*

Side One

1. Loving the Alien

2. Don't Look Down (Pop/Williamson)

3. God Only Knows (Wilson/Asher)

4. Tonight (Bowie/Pop)

Side Two

1. Neighborhood Threat (Bowie/Pop/Gardiner)

2. Blue Jean

3. Tumble and Twirl (Bowie/Pop)

4. I Keep Forgetting (Leiber/Stoller)

5. Dancing with the Big Boys
(Bowie/Pop/Alomar)

Propelled by the massive success of *Let's Dance*, on the surface, *Tonight* performed well, reaching number one in the UK and number eleven in the US. But statistics belie the album's critical reception, which was generally poor.

The cover of *Tonight* is a striking image, with Bowie occupying center frame and bathed in dark-blue light except for his painted bright-yellow hair. His upward, search-for-enlightenment gaze possesses enhanced nuance given the implication of stylized, church-like stained-glass windows behind him. The "God and man" catchphrase of "Modern Love" comes to mind immediately as the most recent incarnation of Bowie's ongoing critiques of human faith and religion.

Fueled by this cover imagery, *Tonight* begins with quite some promise, with "Loving the Alien." Rather than any Ziggy-styled alien, here Bowie is tackling exactly what the cover suggests. His target is organized, established religion and, most specifically, the intolerance that one set of religious believers has toward the next: "Thinking of a different time. Palestine a modern problem. Bounty and your wealth in land. Terror in a best-laid plan." With a sound more suggestive of the soulful "Young Americans" era than contemporary 1984 pop sensibilities, despite the fine song writing the music struggles to match the gravitas of his lyrics. Nevertheless, it is refreshing to hear Bowie tackling such a contentious theme.

Unfortunately, the first track somewhat flattered to deceive, and the album goes significantly downhill from this point. While none of the remaining songs are performed badly per se, questions for the listener include: Where has Bowie gone? What's with all the cover versions and collaborations? What do these songs say that Bowie originals could not have said better? What does a reggae version of Iggy Pop's "Don't Look Down" actually mean? In the case of Bowie's previous covers album, *Pin Ups*, the reason for its existence was respectful homage, a fact plainly acknowledged. And when one listened to the work, the claiming of the sixties generation's iconic songs by Ziggy and the gang was an enjoyable and plainly celebratory affair. But not so on *Tonight*, as tracks from the Beach Boys, Chuck Jackson, and three Bowie/Pop collaborations come and go seemingly without purpose, blunted by extravagant, full orchestrations that remove any cutting edge.

Constituting too little too late, a minor saving grace comes with the second, and final, Bowie composition, "Blue Jean." With saxophones and marimba to the fore in a rhythm and blues–styled fifties throwback, the subject matter is simple and timeless as Bowie professes his love for a rock 'n' roll chick, "Blue Jean—I just met me a girl named Blue Jean." Descriptive, but never trying to move beyond its lustful limitations, the song works very well, and was a deserved hit single, reaching number six in the UK and number eight in the US.

All things considered, however, and in spite of its respectable commercial success, *Tonight* was Bowie's biggest failure to date. Asked in an interview three years later if he'd had any major regrets during his career, it was *Tonight* that Bowie singled out, reflecting, "'Tonight' specifically, only because taken individually the tracks are quite good but it doesn't stand up as a cohesive album. That was my fault because I didn't think about it before I went into the studio."[5]

A lengthy two and a half years later, Bowie would attempt to resurrect things with *Never Let Me Down*.

NEVER LET ME DOWN, 1987

> I guess you could say *Never Let Me Down* did just that; let me down. Maybe it'll make a good primer for first-time Bowie students. Maybe they'll go back to *Aladdin Sane*, *Diamond Dogs*, *Young Americans*, even *Scary Monsters*. —Roy Trakin, *Creem*, August 1987

> It used to be easy. Once a year or so, David Bowie would choose a new persona, pick up a fresh batch of pop-culture reference points, borrow a new musical style and release a new album. Then we'd all sit around and figure out who he was this time . . . *Never Let Me Down* isn't so cut and dried. It's an odd, freewheeling pastiche of elements from all the previous Bowies . . . [that] doesn't bode as well for Bowie's present, or his future. —Steve Pond, *Rolling Stone*, June 1987

Side One

1. Day-In Day-Out

Side Two

1. Glass Spider

2. Time Will Crawl

3. Beat of Your Drum

4. Never Let Me Down (Bowie/Alomar)

5. Zeroes

2. Shining Star

3. New York's in Love

4. '87 and Cry

5. Too Dizzy (Bowie/Kizilcay)

6. Bang Bang (Pop/Kral)

Bowie placed much store in writing new songs in order to resurrect his flagging critical fortunes, with eight of the eleven tracks on *Never Let Me Down* being sole-composed. Nevertheless, the album achieved nothing like the success of its two predecessors, reaching number six in the UK but only a lowly thirty-four in the US.

The album cover is carnivalesque, showing Bowie leaping into the air with arms outstretched while engaging the viewer with full eye contact, in the center of what appears to be a cluttered circus tent. He is surrounded by an assortment of disparate objects, including a drum, a cannon, a suitcase, a burning ring of fire, a painting of the sea, a fluffy pink cloud, a cutout of a skyscraper, a string of lights, and other, harder-to-discern items. A multicolored ladder with rungs askew leads upward and out of the picture. Everything relates to a "show," and in vaudeville, just as the imagery promises, variety and change are de rigueur. Even Bowie's name, loud and bold at the top of the cover, projects this quality, with each of the cut-out and pasted letters in a different font from that which precedes or follows it. If the cover is accurately reflective of its musical contents, the album should be quite a mix of styles.

"Day-In Day-Out" is the opening track and while it recalls *Young Americans* in its rhythm and blues roots, the sound is pure midstream 1984 rock, with cavernous percussion, strident trumpet stabs, and ever-present synthesizer. Bowie's voice is strong and emotive but the song is undone by over-repetition throughout its considerable length. It was written with the intention of showcasing the desperate hand-to-mouth existence of America's poorer classes, but the similarity between verse and chorus and the dominance of just two alternating chords result in the listener growing quickly tired of the song, and the attempt at using repetition to paint the subject's hard, monotonous life fails.

Track two, "Time Will Crawl," works very well indeed. While it displays a similarly undelineated verse and chorus, here there is much rhythmic and melodic interest, kept vibrant by highly impressionistic lyrics such as "I saw a black black stream full of white-eyed fish. And a drowning man with no eyes at all." The overall effect harks back to his early to mid-seventies work, with lyrics fragmented to the point that the listener must assemble meaning him/herself.

Later on side one the title track shines as another highlight, with masterful song writing meeting a level of production restraint all too rare on the album. In a fairly standard but beautifully written tribute, which several critics have compared to John Lennon's "Jealous Guy," Bowie pledges his love for the one who has given the same to him: "When all your faith is failing call my name. When you've got nothing coming call my name." On all levels, "Never Let Me Down" works.

From this point onward, however, the rest of *Never Let Me Down* is a disjointed, uncomfortable struggle. "Beat of Your Drum" is a service-able paean to young love/lust that cries out to be freed from the multiple layers of overproduction. A nod to George Harrison is clear in the opening sitar of "Zeroes," but this is quickly relegated to just a passing gimmick in this tribute to the sixties, in which everything is thrown in compositionally, lyrically, and instrumentally, including, at three minutes and eight seconds, the kitchen sink (joke). Again, there is the sense that, if stripped back, this could have been a great track. "Glass Spider," "Shining Star (Makin' My Love)," "New York's in Love," "'87 and Cry," and "Too Dizzy" follow in turn on side two. Each is passable in its own right for an eighties pop song—artists lesser than Bowie would probably have been proud to claim them—and yet as a group they seem inordinately dislocated stylistically and thematically, and all suffer from the stifling production woes that afflict the work as a whole. The album's closer is another Iggy Pop song, "Bang Bang," but anyone familiar with the original struggles to appreciate such a flat, middle-of-the-road treatment. And herein lies the primary fault with the album. Bowie tries as hard as ever to write about weighty, uncomfortable issues well worthy of his attention, and never more so than in "Shining Star," where he tackles, among other things, crack addiction and Hitler. However, the limitations of the restrictive 1980s mainstream pop style could not bear such gravitas, proving unable even to turn the juxtaposition into irony, so often Bowie's ally in the past. Coupled with wholly insensitive production, *Never Let Me Down* is rightly considered, alongside *Tonight*, by many to be the low point of his career.

Widespread commercial success is often the dominant criterion by which a rock artist's value is judged, and therefore, I suggest again that it is perhaps patently unfair that Bowie's work during this period of his career has been so maligned—a state of affairs to which I am well aware of contributing here. By *most* standards, *Let's Dance*, *Tonight*, and *Never Let Me Down* were strikingly successful. But sometimes criteria that apply to the majority do not apply to a minority. And David Bowie, based on the criteria that he himself had set in the previous decade, must be appraised differently than other artists. He is a very different beast from Phil Collins.

> [The unprecedented commercial success] meant absolutely nothing to me. It didn't make me feel good. I felt dissatisfied with everything I was doing, and eventually it started showing in my work. *Let's Dance* was an excellent album in a certain genre, but the next two albums after that showed that my lack of interest in my own work was really becoming transparent. My nadir was *Never Let Me Down*. It was such an awful album. (David Bowie in Ingrid Sischy, "David Bowie," in *Interview* magazine, September 1995)

Following *Never Let Me Down*, Bowie was well aware that something was seriously amiss. As Pegg puts it, "the residual goodwill of even the most loyal fans was wearing a little thin, and there was a growing sense that the shining light of 1970s rock was a spent force."[6] To address this, Bowie made the extraordinary decision to retire from being a solo artist and instead become just another member of a rock band. That one of the world's most successful and influential rock stars could *ever* be seen as just another faceless musician seems ridiculously optimistic, but nevertheless this was Bowie's way of extricating himself from the seemingly out-of-control downward spiral he'd found himself in. Joining forces with Reeves Gabrels and brothers Tony and Hunt Sales, he formed Tin Machine, the band with which he would record two studio albums.

> I had to get passionate again. I couldn't keep going the way I was going. . . . My strength has always been that I never gave a shit about what people thought of what I was doing. I'd be prepared to completely change from album to album and ostracise everybody that may have been pulled in to the last album . . . I'm sort of back to that

again. (David Bowie, in Adrian Deevoy, "Boys Keep Swinging," *Q*, June 1989)

TIN MACHINE, 1989

> The record has a unity—or, viewed another way, a lack of variety— entirely unlike any previous Bowie album, and strikes you first as a purgative exercise in crap-cutting. —Paul Du Noyer, *Q*, May 1989

> *Tin Machine* will repay those potential Bowie fans willing to be taken on a brutal journey far away from the polished musical surfaces of *Let's Dance*. And make no mistake, without Tin Machine, Bowie might well have remained lost in the mainstream wilderness forever. —David Buckley, *David Bowie: The Complete Guide to His Music*

The music of *Tin Machine* was the complete antithesis of Bowie's solo records of the 1980s. Full of unchecked energy and sounding at times straight out of the garage, it was an exercise in music therapy for the band's most famous member. While the focus of this book is Bowie's solo work, and therefore any detailed reading of individual tracks is beyond the project's scope, commonly accepted descriptors including "grunge," "industrial," "independent," "heavy metal," and "punk" have all been applied to *Tin Machine*'s sound with some justification.

TIN MACHINE II, 1991

> It's been obvious for some time that the thin one no longer addresses himself to any one subject long enough to make much sense. . . . But what Tin Machine lack in vision they make up for in sound whose dynamic appears impressive. —Max Bell, *Vox*, October 1991

> Tin Machine's dense, organic hard rock ("We play the music we like," claims Hunt Sales, "and hope that three or four other people will like it") is an extremely conscious reaction against the contemporary rock and dance music which is explicitly designed for the marketplace. —Charles Shaar Murray, *Q*, October 1991

The first Tin Machine album sold over a million copies worldwide, a figure that any "new" band would have surely been thrilled with. EMI, however, for which Bowie had delivered the blockbuster *Let's Dance* first up, was exceedingly worried at the noncommercial direction its star signing was taking. Before *Tin Machine II* was completed, Bowie and EMI parted ways, and so the band released their second album through the London Records label. More crafted and carefully produced than *Tin Machine*, and thereby losing the raw aggression that had characterized their early sound, the result was an odd kind of halfway house that sat somewhere between their debut and the Bowie solo albums that had come immediately before. In retrospect it is possible to see Bowie stirring and growing restless beneath the band's skin, and the resumption of his solo career was imminent.

9

REDISCOVERING THE ALIEN

Black Tie White Noise, The Buddha of Suburbia, Outside, Earthling, and 'hours . . .' 1993–1999

BLACK TIE WHITE NOISE, 1993

The 1980s was not a happy decade for David Bowie. . . . Now he has rediscovered the insistent electro-dance rhythms and sensual synth and sax textures with which he seduced critics and fans alike during the latter part of the 1970s . . . and if any collection of songs could reinstate his godhead status, then this is it. —David Sinclair, *Q*, May 1993

In a strange way, when Bowie was weird, he defined our normalcy. It was inevitable that, when he straightened out, he'd lose our attention. . . . Once he sang "I'm an alligator," and it was easy to believe him. Now he's reduced to begging "wait . . . don't lose faith," and even that moment of pitiful honesty isn't his, because Morrissey wrote the best song in sight. The hunter has finally been caught by the game. —Dave Thompson, *The Rocket*, May 1993

Side One	Side Two
1. The Wedding	1. Miracle Goodnight
2. You've Been Around (Bowie/Gabrels)	2. Don't Let Me Down and Down (Tarha/Valmont)
3. I Feel Free (Bruce/Brown)	3. Looking for Lester

4. Black Tie White Noise

5. Jump They Say

6. Nite Flights (Engels)

7. Pallas Athena

4. I Know It's Gonna Happen
Someday (Morrissey/Nevin)

5. The Wedding Song

Bowie, newly married and rejuvenated, stated that *Black Tie White Noise* was to be his comeback album, picking up where *Scary Monsters* had left off thirteen years earlier. To his mind, through Tin Machine, he had purged the creative decline of the 1980s and was starting again with a clean slate, no longer a slave to public and record company expectations. If such an appeal can be rendered visually, then the front cover of *Black Tie White Noise* is close to perfection. In extreme close-up, the portrait of Bowie is candid and honest. With his head turned slightly to the viewer's left, his face is shown in a manner that fully acknowledges the passage of time, the lines at the corners of his eyes announcing his forty-six years, a hint of stubble visible on his jaw and chin, and faint traces of red blotchiness unhidden upon his cheeks. His eyes, sparkling blue, catch and hold the viewer's gaze in as direct an engagement as is possible to achieve within a picture. "This is the real me, today," Bowie appears to be saying.

Reviews were mixed, on balance mostly positive, but stirring up some fervent detractors. Certainly, in the UK at least, Bowie's return was welcomed with open arms, with the album reaching number one. The US proved far more reticent, however, stalling at number thirty-nine.

Springing a surprise from the outset, side one begins with a lengthy, saxophone-dominated instrumental, "The Wedding," which begins with church bells in homage to his recent marriage to supermodel Iman Abdulmajid. Built around a reworking of music Bowie had written for the wedding ceremony (another such instrumental, "Pallas Athena," also appears on the album), the song is an evocative and punchy opener, with clear traces of Eastern influence merging with hip-hop-styled dance beats and a funky bass groove. The song returns later as the album's closer, retitled "The Wedding Song," with lyrics that convey his love for his new wife: "Heaven is smiling down, heaven's girl in a wedding gown . . . I believe in magic, angel for life."

The second song, the excellent "You've Been Around," is highly autobiographical, with Bowie's frank image on the cover expressing with honesty the theme of having been around a long time and endured the ups and downs of life. The lyrics outline the protagonist's lonely and isolated life being turned around by a lover, and this notion aligns easily to the concept of Bowie's marriage. Amusingly, he takes the opportunity for a moment of self-referencing in the line "But you've changed me, ch-ch-ch-ch-ch-ch-changed me!" The instrumentation features trumpeter Lester Bowie, who is given free range for a searing solo over the track's highly infectious jazz/funk/hip-hop feel.

"I Feel Free" is the first of four cover songs on the album, and whereas the all-too-frequent cover versions on Bowie's eighties albums often begged the question "Why?" here all are given interesting new life. Undoubtedly the riskiest is Morrissey's "I Know It's Gonna Happen Someday," which was written in homage to Bowie himself. The Bowie-sings-Morrissey-sings-Bowie factor is a delight, and the song's aural revisitation of the *Young Americans* era is a highly successful self-parody.

The title track, "Black Tie White Noise," makes a plea for racial harmony in the aftermath of the LA riots of 1992. Funky and energetic despite its slow/medium tempo, Bowie tips his hat firmly to Marvin Gaye, singing, "What's going on?" Bowie and guest vocalist Al B. Sure! effortlessly blend their vocals and Lester Bowie is again a feature on trumpet. Beneath the track's surface, the crackles of a vinyl record on a turntable add atmospheric warmth and a retro touch.

Following the title track is the album's most successful single, "Jump They Say," which reached number nine in the UK and charted elsewhere in Europe but not in the US. Acknowledged by Bowie as being about his half brother, Terry, who committed suicide in 1985 after many years of mental illness, the track is edgy and, quite literally, jumpy, with sudden outbursts of saxophone, trumpet, and guitar breaking its fundamental repetition and replicating the onset of mental anguish and stress. With the pressure ever-building in both lyrics and musical underpinning, Bowie implores the subject to shut the world out: "My friend, don't listen to the crowd. They say 'Jump.'"

Jazz is a major influence on the album, flavoring many tracks, and none more so than the third instrumental, "Looking for Lester," in which both Bowies shine, respectively, on saxophone and trumpet, showing off their chops and chasing each other's licks over a pulsing techno beat.

Despite a few lukewarm reviews, *Black Tie White Noise* was generally well received by media and fans alike, providing the rejuvenated Bowie with exactly the kind of "return to form" reception he had hoped for. For dedicated fans who had exalted in Bowie's seventies work and then watched his artistic fortunes wane in the following decade, this was revelatory. It was hard to think of any other artist who had fallen from grace to the extent that Bowie had. In the eyes of many, he'd become a laughingstock; an irrelevance. But now, here he was once more, innovative, daring, and relevant. Right now, the future looked very bright.

Behind the scenes, while putting the finishing touches to *Black Tie White Noise*, Bowie had also accepted a challenge of a very different nature. He had been asked to write music for the BBC television play of Hanif Kureishi's 1990 novel, *The Buddha of Suburbia*. Already a fan of the work, Bowie seemed a natural choice given that the story dealt with the rite of passage of a London teenager in the 1970s.

THE BUDDHA OF SUBURBIA, 1993

> This disc isn't a must-have, but, for Bowiephiles, it's a must-hear. Also, because of its incorrect labeling as a soundtrack, *The Buddha of Suburbia* has been largely overlooked. Hopefully, this album can finally assume its rightful place in the wildly erratic and ungainly discography of David Bowie. *The Buddha of Suburbia* isn't a lost classic, but it's definitely worth a listen. And, unlike the ten years' worth of releases that came before, you might actually enjoy listening to this album. —Michael Keefe, *PopMatters*

Track Listing

1. Buddha of Suburbia
2. Sex and the Church
3. South Horizon
4. The Mysteries
5. Bleed Like a Craze, Dad
6. Strangers when We Meet
7. Dead Against It
8. Untitled No. 1
9. Ian Fish, U.K. Heir
10. Buddha of Suburbia

Confusion as to the nature of this album continues to this day. Assumed by many to be simply the television soundtrack, apart from the impressive title track, the album is actually a complete reworking and extrapolation drawn from fragments of that material. A genuine stand-alone Bowie album, yet virtually a lost album, it was poorly promoted and even erroneously advertised as a soundtrack, with Bowie's image missing from the original cover and his name appearing only in small print. Unsurprisingly, it sold badly and was forgotten quickly. The title track reached number thirty-five on the UK singles chart, but that was as good as it got for the venture. Because of this, it can hardly be considered essential listening when tracing the David Bowie career story. But it is a hidden gem and anyone seeking out *The Buddha of Suburbia* is in for a most pleasant surprise. Due to the subject matter there are songs that invoke memories of the *Ziggy Stardust* era, particularly the title track and "South Horizon," which at times sounds like *Aladdin Sane* meets *Black Tie White Noise* due to the avant-garde stylings of pianist Mike Garson. Instrumental tracks "The Mysteries" and "Ian Fish, U.K. Heir" (an anagram of "Hanif Kureishi") are pure Berlin-era; "Untitled No. 1" could have been from *Lodger*, and "Dead Against It" from *Station to Station*. Special mention must also be made of "Strangers when We Meet," which sounds like Roxy Music meeting *"Heroes."* Truly, a great album chock-full of surprises that deserved a far better life.

If there is one obvious conclusion to be drawn from the quality of *Black Tie White Noise* and *The Buddha of Suburbia*, it is that Bowie was again feeling confident and inspired. Somebody else who was becoming increasingly impressed with this creative turnaround was Brian Eno, Bowie's close collaborator during the days of the Berlin Trilogy. In 1994 they began collaborating on what would be perhaps Bowie's strangest album of all.

1.OUTSIDE, 1995

No-one who's been listening to rock for less than a dozen years can remember a time when Bowie was good. . . . With this record, he's hard again; his mojo be working, big-time. —Charles Shaar Murray, *MOJO*, October 1995

David Bowie has made a career of being anything and everything other than himself. But *Outside* . . . is way too much of a good thing. Bowie's almost pathological fear of dropping all the masks . . . has driven him into multiple-personality overdrive and forced melodrama. The music . . . feels shoehorned into the script with frustrating rigidity. —David Fricke, *Rolling Stone*, October 1995

Those legions who came in on *Let's Dance* will most certainly be left completely and utterly bewildered. Perhaps, though, that's entirely the point. —Tom Doyle, *Q*, October 1995

Track Listing

1. Leon Takes Us Outside (Bowie/Eno/Gabrels/Garson/Kizilcay/Campbell)

2. Outside (Bowie/Armstrong)

3. The Heart's Filthy Lesson (Bowie/Eno/Gabrels/Garson/Kizilcay/Campbell)

4. A Small Plot of Land (Bowie/Eno/Gabrels/Garson/Kizilcay/Campbell)

5. (Segue) Baby Grace (A Horrid Cassette) (Bowie/Eno/Gabrels/Garson/Kizilcay/Campbell)

6. Hallo Spaceboy (Bowie/Eno)

7. The Motel

8. I Have Not Been to Oxford Town (Bowie/Eno)

9. No Control (Bowie/Eno)

10. (Segue) Algeria Touchshriek (Bowie/Eno/Gabrels/Garson/Kizilcay/Campbell)

11. The Voyeur of Utter Destruction (as Beauty) (Bowie/Eno/Gabrels)

12. (Segue) Ramona A. Stone/I Am with Name (Bowie/Eno/Gabrels/Garson/Kizilcay/Campbell)

13. Wishful Beginnings (Bowie/Eno)

14. We Prick You (Bowie/Eno)

15. (Segue) Nathan Adler (Bowie/Eno/Gabrels/Garson/Kizilcay/Campbell)

16. I'm Deranged (Bowie/Eno)

17. Thru These Architect's Eyes (Bowie/Gabrels)

18. (Segue) Nathan Adler (Bowie/Eno)

19. Strangers when We Meet

Bowie described *1.Outside*, with tongue in cheek, perhaps, as "a nonlinear Gothic drama hypercycle." In plain language this means it is an old-fashioned concept album, much in the manner of *Ziggy Stardust* or *Diamond Dogs*, that requires a degree of assemblage from an audience rather than being laid out like a picture book. In her *Billboard* review of the album, Melinda Newman chose the telling headline "David Bowie Returns to Drama," yet Bowie had never really left drama. However, through the 1980s most especially, this defining quality had certainly been more haphazard, presented only within individual songs, or visible in mere portions of albums rather than being present throughout a fully unified album-length work. On *1.Outside*, as on those early seventies conceptual titles, the entire work is unified, if not by strict chronology of action, then by threads of thematic consistency. With that said, *1.Outside* does demand more of the listener than those early career works.

Set in a dystopian 1999, the plot of *1.Outside* is bleak and noirish, following art detective Nathan Adler's investigation into the murder of Baby Grace Blue, a fourteen-year-old whose dismembered but electronically reconfigured body was found decorating the doorway of a museum. For this evident art crime, Adler's task is not so much to find out "whodunit" in the usual detective-mystery sense as to determine whether the murder qualifies as art. In total, seven characters are involved in the plot, and Bowie plays them all, delineating difference through the use of different vocal stylings, studio effects, and contrasting musical styles. A glance at the writing credits across the daunting nineteen-song track listing shows the highly collaborative nature of the work's composition, so it is very seldom that we hear one man's vision, and this is surely one of the primary reasons for the unprecedented stylistic variety. If the result is a sometimes bewildering mash-up, all is nevertheless linked at the most fundamental of levels by the dark, doom-laden underlying mood. In addition, however, there are vocal and other aural segues between tracks that further maintain a sense of continuity.

The CD cover plays a very important role in ensuring the listener is able to discern the aural action, making the album something of a multimedia piece. Information included in the accompanying booklet includes Adler's diary entries, gruesome photographs of severed body parts, and so on, and images of the characters, upon each of which Bowie's own face has been eerily superimposed. The front cover is one of Bowie's most disturbing: an acrylic-on-canvas self-portrait that obliquely recalls the violence of the *Lodger* cover. Bowie's face is heavily distorted and indistinct, with careless purple swaths indicating the location of his mouth, eyebrows, and nostrils, and plain white smears where his eyes should be. He could be alive; he could be dead.

Dismissed by some critics as highly pretentious, although in general garnering highly positive critical appraisals, to those prepared to put effort into their listening (and preferably have the CD booklet open before them throughout), *1.Outside* is a remarkable piece of performance art. A postmodern detective mystery brought to frightening aural life, the work can be seen as an opus of extraordinary depth; or, failing that, one could simply sit back and enjoy individual tracks and forget about trying to take the whole thing in at once. While Bowie was renowned for mixing musical styles—some would say it's his stock-in-trade—it is on *1.Outside* that this penchant reaches its most bewildering zenith. Whether the ambiance of the opening instrumental "Leon Takes Us Outside," the masterful building of intensity to full-on rock of the title track, the frightening drone of "The Heart's Filthy Lesson," the dance rhythms of "We Prick You," the drum-and-piano duet-madness of "A Small Plot of Land," the reworking of "Strangers when We Meet" from *The Buddha of Suburbia*, or the retro reminiscence of "Hallo Spaceboy," in which 1970s Ziggy is updated with aggressive techno/industrial/jungle beats that equip him for the far more dangerous 1990s, there are highlights for every taste in this hugely ambitious album.

Reaching number eight on the UK album charts but only twenty in the US, *1.Outside* shows the clear paradox that now existed for David Bowie. Critical acclaim often did not run parallel with the dizzy heights of commercial success. But one can be sure that Bowie cried no tears over the fact that *1.Outside* did not emulate the chart exploits of *Let's Dance* or *Tonight*. "The music is outside," he sings repeatedly in the title track. And he is right.

Bowie had most emphatically taken his work outside the mainstream once more, again assuming the role of the alienated artist with his face pressed up against the window looking in. This was the Bowie that Bowie fans wanted. Thrilled with both the performance and the vibe of the band he had assembled for the *1.Outside* album and subsequent tour, he determined to record another album with them and set to work writing an album built upon the techno/industrial/jungle-oriented sounds that he considered to be the work's most exciting innovations.

EARTHLING, 1997

On *Earthling*, Bowie lets the songs tell the story. Gone are the spoken interludes and overblown avant-garde flourishes that marred *Outside*; instead, the tracks on *Earthling* are linked only by the power of the turbocharged guitars, the energy and intensity of the skittering drum-and-bass rhythms, the spiritual-technological tug of war in the lyrics and Bowie's signature baritone croon. —Mark Kemp, *Rolling Stone*, February 1997

Where most junglists dab just a pale wash of synthesized strings or the cooings of soft-soul vocalists onto their rhythm beds, Bowie and his band splash samples around with abandon, then pour further layers of rock-hard instrumental playing onto that. He'll undoubtedly come in for some stick for using young folks' musical forms, but wouldn't it be wonderful if all 50-year-old rockers retained such an interest in the future? —Andy Gill, *MOJO*, March 1997

Track Listing

1. Little Wonder (Bowie/Gabrels/Plati)

2. Looking for Satellites (Bowie/Gabrels/Plati)

3. Battle for Britain (The Letter) (Bowie/Gabrels/Plati)

4. Seven Years in Tibet (Bowie/Gabrels)

5. Dead Man Walking (Bowie/Gabrels)

6. Telling Lies

7. The Last Thing You Should Do (Bowie/Gabrels/Plati)

8. I'm Afraid of Americans (Bowie/Eno)

9. Law (Earthlings on Fire) (Bowie/Gabrels)

The cover of *Earthling* is one of Bowie's best. With his back to the camera, he is shown dressed in a slashed and dirtied Union Jack frock coat, standing astride with arms behind his back as he surveys the hyper-colorized, gently meandering green hills of the English countryside beneath the bluest of skies. Despite trading the urban setting of the *Ziggy Stardust* cover for a pastoral one, he is still—all these years later—as out of place as he's ever been. With his exaggerated, arrogant, military stance, and adorned as he is in the ludicrously bright symbolism of the British Empire's banner, which does violence to the tranquility of the otherwise serene country vista, one cannot miss the commentary on the folly of colonization.

Earthling was highly experimental in the sense that it was the first Bowie album to be recorded entirely using digital technology, allowing him to cut and paste instrumental and vocal tracks at will—the ultimate cut-up technique, such that he had experimented with, in his lyrics at least, on and off as far back as his glam rock days. This greatly expanded freedom is something he utilized fully.

Reaching number six in the UK but only thirty-nine in the US, on the surface it would seem that *Earthling* did little to further Bowie's renaissance. Yet as previously noted, for Bowie, sales and artistic credibility were often on different trajectories. The value of *Earthling* does not lie in its chart standings.

"Little Wonder" begins the album in fine style. In the most successful single, reaching number fourteen in the UK, the lyrics are impenetrable even by Bowie's eclecticism. Despite lacking any identifiable narrative or theme, Bowie's words are full of visual imagery and sit almost as decorations above the heavy, driving drum-and-bass-driven pulse beneath. The musical style is close to that of the song "Firestarter" by the Prodigy, a number-one UK hit from the previous year. Bowie's later explanation that he was trying to incorporate the seven dwarves into his song only marginally helps any listener looking for meaning. "Stinky weather, fat shaky hands, Dopey morning, Doc Grumpy-nose," sings Bowie in the opening line. The linking of dwarf names aside, within such a maelstrom of lyric disassociation the track possesses a tenuous science fiction quality through its singular "intergalactic" reference and during the searing chorus, which breaks from the drum-and-bass feel to a full-on rock style during which Bowie repeatedly sings of being "so far away." Beneath these repeated utterances the harmony literally moves higher and higher, painting the imagery. "Little Wonder" is another prime example of Bowie presenting information to an audience and asking them to assemble it and make from it what they will, seeding the song just lightly with pointers both musical and lyrical.

Repeated like the mantra of a lost capitalist society, the cut-and-pasted grouping of the words "nowhere, shampoo, TV, combat, Boyzone, slim tie, showdown, can't stop" forms the hinge around which the following "Looking for Satellites" is built. Solidifying the subtle science fiction nuances of the previous track, here Bowie is on familiar thematic ground, posing to humanity the question "Where do we go from here? There's something in the sky shining in the light, spinning and far away." While the territory is pure Bowie, never before has he presented it through such musical means. The circular, going-nowhere nature of the shuffling rhythm that sits beneath the lyrics implies that, while there might well be something up in space, we humans are ultimately earthbound and doomed to the life we have created for ourselves, of "nowhere, shampoo, TV, combat," and so on. The only implied glimmer of hope that we might break free is provided by a startling guitar solo from Reeves Gabrels that starts out low and gradually soars into the musical stratosphere.

Jungle percussion meshed with classic hard rock is at the fore in "Battle for Britain," a song that draws attention back to the album's cover. But despite the evident linkage between song title and picture, there is almost nothing in the lyrics to further the association, the song instead detailing Bowie's personal reflections on being "a winner . . . a loser . . . a sinner." Nevertheless, it is a very strong song in all other regards, with a wonderful melody and inherent power.

"Seven Years in Tibet" addresses a long-held concern of Bowie's, and initially the pace comes back considerably for this atmospheric tale of a spiritual journey. Over a walking-pace drum loop, other instruments are used as textures that come and go as if Bowie is passing through them on his trek. At the chorus, however, the song erupts into violent mayhem. Bowie asks the big questions that man has always asked about his status on Earth and in the universe, here framed in terms of, for example, "time to question the mountain. Why pigs can fly."

Earthling has opened with four quite outstanding songs and addressed themes that have long lain at the heart of Bowie's best work. This continues with his critique of personal alienation in "Dead Man Walking" and the notion of creating a false public face through lies and exaggeration in the album's most obviously drum-and-bass-driven track, "Telling Lies." The following "The Last Thing You Should Do" laments a lack of physical intimacy in everyday life and is the album's most difficult track to listen to. Full of spiky wave-of-noise musical moments and with repeated five-beat-verse lyric lines set disruptively over the song's 4/4 time signature, it is alienation writ large both musically and lyrically, because "nobody laughs anymore." The provocative "I'm Afraid of Americans" provides the late album highlight. In a critique of McDonald's-styled cultural invasion, once again Bowie employs blistering sectional changes, the memorable and highly catchy chorus venomously exploding at the end of each verse, with every available ounce of industrial power utilized.

Earthling is a mid/late career tour de force in the Bowie catalog. While not a great commercial success, and initially resisted by some fans and critics alike due to his evident co-opting of the sound of younger bands such as Nine Inch Nails and the Prodigy, as time has passed the album has risen in status.

Whether stung by some of the criticism or, simply, stylistically bored and ready to move on in typical Bowie fashion, as quickly as he had adopted and absorbed techno, jungle sounds, and the band-saw qualities of industrial rock, Bowie was, however, about to abandon them.

'HOURS . . .' 1999

His past selves have proved a difficult act to follow . . . after the artful *1.Outside* and the indecent noise terror of *Earthling*, 'hours . . .' crowns a trilogy that represents significantly more than a mere coda to a once-unimpeachable career . . . the album's despairing subtext is all too apparent. What's more, it suits Bowie just fine. —Mark Paytress, *MOJO*, November 1999

He studiously avoids techno, dance, industrial, punk, grunge, jungle; in short, he avoids anything that might sound trendy, or specially aimed at an audience far younger than listeners of his own generation. —James E. Perone, *The Words and Music of David Bowie*

Track Listing

1. Thursday's Child (Bowie/Gabrels)

2. Something in the Air (Bowie/Gabrels)

3. Survive (Bowie/Gabrels)

4. If I'm Dreaming My Life (Bowie/Gabrels)

5. Seven (Bowie/Gabrels)

6. What's Really Happening? (Bowie/Gabrels/Grant)

7. The Pretty Things Are Going to Hell (Bowie/Gabrels)

8. New Angels of Promise (Bowie/Gabrels)

9. Brilliant Adventure (Bowie/Gabrels)

10. The Dreamers (Bowie/Gabrels)

While Bowie's ever-worsening slide in fortune in the US continued unabated, the album reaching only a lowly forty-seven, 'hours . . .' achieved number five in the UK, Bowie's best result since *Black Tie White Noise.*

The presence of acoustic guitars and beautifully constructed melody lines designed to carry the, at times, intimate, personal, and confessional lyrics creates an ambiance that is somewhat reminiscent of *Hunky Dory.* And yet Bowie does not eschew the thoroughly nineties sounds of programmed synthesizers and vocodered vocal effects. In addition, his by now longtime collaborator Reeves Gabrels is a familiar presence, with his signature heavily effected guitar stylings frequently in evidence. Nevertheless, compared to what preceded it throughout the decade, the album is a far softer, gentler work.

There is a gentleness, too, about the artwork on the CD cover, which carries a clear message that Bowie is, quite literally, looking after himself. In the image, a younger, long-haired Bowie sits cradling the head of an older, *Earthling*-era version of himself, who lies prone and seemingly ill in a stark, blue-white futuristic interior. The "o" of "Bowie" sits at the center front of the image, rendered much larger than the other letters and functioning as a portal into the room. Both Bowies wear white clothing, while the oversized jagged-cut collar of the younger one acts as a subtle referent to the lines of the Pierrot costume he wore on *Scary Monsters (and Super Creeps)*, as well as giving the picture an angelic quality. While clearly a futuristic science fiction image, it nevertheless communicates an air of tenderness and tranquility, enhanced by the soft tones of blue and white.

The abrupt change in musical direction is evident from the opening strains of the first track, "Thursday's Child," which reached number sixteen in the UK. While Bowie himself warned against reading too much autobiography into the song, it is extremely difficult to see beyond a fifty-two-year-old man reminiscing about his past in this slow, elegant, and soulful ballad. "Maybe I'm born right out of my time," sings Bowie, "seeing my past to let it go." From this point on it is possible to read Bowie's consideration of his past into almost every track. In the following song, the similarly musically restrained and understated "Something in the Air," the micro-description of the trage- dy of a broken relationship is easily writ large to encompass any number of opportunities lost, or possibilities not taken to fruition. The song has inherent universality, with any listener able to absorb the message and apply it to his/her own life. "Who said time is on my side?" questions Bowie in the second single release, "Survive." Reaching number twen- ty-eight in the UK, the reflective, mid-tempo song refers to the "Beatle Boys," a clear reference to his early, formative, pre-fame days. Howev- er, the song is one of regret for a lover he never had, "the great mistake I never made." Again, a quality of universality dwells in abundance. "If I'm Dreaming My Life" and "Seven" follow in quick succession, and it is at this stage that the listener, while appreciating the candid emotions being expressed and the strong hooks and melodies of a supreme song- writer in action, wishes for a change of both pace and mood. Thankful- ly, things do pick up a little with the more upbeat "What's Really Hap- pening?" notable for the fact that the lyricist, Alex Grant, secured the privilege of contributing to the song as the result of winning a competi- tion that attracted over eighty thousand entries. At least for the numer- ous fans that had been with Bowie since the heady glam rock days of the early seventies, the undoubted highlight of 'hours . . .' is surely "The Pretty Things Are Going to Hell." A thematic merging of Bowie's own "Oh You Pretty Things," Iggy and the Stooges' "Your Pretty Face Is Going to Hell," and the 1960s rhythm and blues group the Pretty Things, the song is enormously self-referencing, very glam-stylized, and simply delightful as a musical parody in the best possible taste, afford- ing the listener a rare smile in an otherwise very serious album. "They wore it out but they wore it well," sings Bowie, about himself, certainly;

but also directing his words at every pimply young glitter-clad fan who ever attended a Bowie, T. Rex, Slade, Sweet, Gary Glitter, Suzi Quatro, New York Dolls, Iggy Pop, or Roxy Music gig. Reminiscences continue with "New Angels of Promise," which sounds like a melding of *Station to Station* with either *Low* or *"Heroes,"* and the instrumental "Brilliant Adventure," with its ambiance and employment of the koto, sounding as if it too were a lost track from the Berlin era. The final track, "The Dreamers," is melancholic, telling an oblique story of a lost soul, a "shallow man" who has no direction and is "just a searcher (So it goes) Lonely soul (So it goes) The last of the dreamers (So it goes)."

On *'hours . . .'* there is something for everyone's taste. Certain tracks stand out as one-off anomalies, such as the uber-glam "The Pretty Things Are Going to Hell" and the ambient instrumental "Brilliant Adventure." But if this seems overtly haphazard in a stylistic sense, one should recall that on *Hunky Dory*, the album to which many critics, perhaps unfairly, compare *'hours . . .'* some tracks stood out as being quite removed from its overall flavor as well, including "Queen Bitch" and "Eight Line Poem."

If there is one thing that is certain as Bowie reached the end of his twentieth-century work, *'hours . . .'* showed, as did the albums that preceded it during the nineties, that he was once again prepared to tackle anything and everything. His artistic mojo was once again restored, nothing was off-limits, and who knew what he would bring to the table in the new century. For his army of loyal fans, the future looked bright indeed.

10

TWENTY-FIRST-CENTURY MAN

Heathen, Reality, and *The Next Day,* 2003–2013

HEATHEN, 2002

Packed with fantastic songs, liberally sprinkled with intriguing touches. . . . It would be wrong to herald *Heathen* as a complete return to 1970s form. . . . But those were records made by a decadent gay saxophone-playing cokehead alien pierrot with an interest in fascism and the occult. *Heathen* is the work of a multi-millionaire 55-year-old father of two. —Alexis Petridis, *The Guardian,* May 2002

David Bowie has exquisitely hip taste. . . . A loose theme runs through these songs, covers included: the search for guiding light in godless night. But the real story is *Heathen*'s perfect casting: Bowie playing Bowie, with class. —David Fricke, *Rolling Stone,* May 2002

Track Listing

1. Sunday

2. Cactus (Francis)

3. Slip Away

4. Slow Burn

5. Afraid

7. I Would Be Your Slave

8. I Took a Trip on a Gemini Spaceship (Odam)

9. 5.15 The Angels Have Gone

10. Everyone Says "Hi"

11. A Better Future

6. I've Been Waiting for You   12. Heathen (The Rays)
(Young)

Heathen was notable not just for being Bowie's first post-millennium album but also because it was founded upon a reunion of particular significance. Producer Tony Visconti, whose last album project with Bowie had been the much-acclaimed *Scary Monsters* in 1980 but who had worked with Bowie on and off from as early as his second album in 1969, was once again at the mixing desk. Having produced some of Bowie's most groundbreaking work, including the Berlin Trilogy, expectations were high. Upon release reaction was extremely positive, with the album acclaimed by the vast majority of critics and also validated in commercial terms, thereby achieving the difficult double that had so often eluded him. Reaching number five in the UK, it also marked a pleasingly solid return to form in the US market, where it reached number fourteen, Bowie's highest-placed album since *Tonight* in 1984.

Immediately locating the album within familiar "Bowie country" was the disturbing cover, which featured a sepia-toned portrait of the artist, immaculately and formally dressed in a suit and tie and with his hair swept back. Unsmilingly serious, he could be just another corporate executive except for his eyes, which completely sabotage the image. Looking up and to the viewer's left, the pupils are glazed and silvery white, leading the viewer to conclude he is either blind, alien, or both. The album title also contributes to the unease, the text printed in red at the bottom of the image, upside-down and reversed. Of particular inference is the inverted "t" that sits at the bottom center of the image, appearing like an inverted cross. Alienation and religiosity, two of Bowie's most oft-visited themes, are highly discernable and are here sowed in the listener's mind before a note of the album's music has been heard. In addition, a quick perusal of the booklet contained within the CD package presents the viewer with imagery of religion-themed artifacts and paintings that have been slashed and defaced.

Sparse and bleak, the first sounds heard on the album belong to the slow, heavily atmospheric, and scene-setting "Sunday," which (re)visits a post-apocalyptic world previously explored with some frequency by Bowie, most notably on *Diamond Dogs*. The opening lines are once again descriptive in an almost filmic way: "Nothing remains. We could run when the rain slows. Look for the cars or signs of life." The lyrics address the cataclysmic changes that have occurred as the result of the unnamed yet clearly catastrophic event, and how mankind might cope with them. Aside from the obvious religious connotation of the song's title, the lyrics throughout pit religious beliefs against secular ones. At the conclusion of the song, following imagery of souls rising up through the clouds, it is to God that Bowie looks for deliverance: "All my trials, Lord will be remembered." Supporting the religious theme is a monastic-styled chant beneath Bowie's voice, so effective that one can almost see hooded monks walking in slow procession, swinging incense as they pass by. A remarkable feature of "Sunday" is the way the full armory of the band is held in reserve for so long, allowing the intense atmosphere and tension to build for a full three minutes and forty-five seconds of the four-minute-and-forty-five-second song. The catastrophic events of 9/11 added much poignancy to the song's meaning, with its central themes of destruction and religiosity rendered suddenly, brutally, apt. Some critics have assumed the song was written specifically in response to this event. After all, Bowie was living in New York at the time. However, while acknowledging the parallels and aptness, he has stated repeatedly that he wrote "Sunday" several weeks before.

As with several of Bowie's best albums, the agenda for *Heathen* is laid out with clarity at the beginning, and subsequent songs expand the point of view in a variety of ways. Here, three cover versions augment Bowie's original songs, and in the first of these, "Cactus" by the Pixies—which is afforded significant status in being placed as the second track on the album—it is faith in human love that is put to the test. The second cover, Neil Young's "I've Been Waiting for You," furthers the theme. The third cover, "I Took a Trip on a Gemini Spaceship," is the most interesting choice. The song was originally written and performed by the Legendary Stardust Cowboy, aka Norman Carl Odam, and its inclusion sees Bowie paying a long-due homage to one of the inspirations for his Ziggy Stardust character from decades earlier. While it sounds corny, there's nothing Bowie fans like more than to hear him singing about spaceships and rockets. It's just . . . right, somehow. On *Heathen*, Odam's song provides one of the lighter moments, certainly. And yet its naïve escapist message, recalling as it does the dreams of space-obsessed space race–era youth, allows it to effortlessly tap into the omnipresent human curiosity about what lies "out there" and whether, even today, space travel might offer escape should catastrophic events occur on Earth, where, perhaps, "nothing remains."

The beautiful ballad, "Slip Away," is a highlight, and with its glimpses of New York life is another track given an enhanced depth in the wake of 9/11. Told through the eyes of two puppets who used to appear on TV's *The Uncle Floyd Show*, the song gracefully reveals its central theme of wistful regret at the passing of youth and of simpler times.

Guest guitarist Pete Townshend lends his considerable talents to "Slow Burn," the album's leading single release. While not particularly successful in that guise, it is a fine album track. Reminiscent of "'Heroes'" but with a harder edge, the lyrics ooze anxiety at every turn: "Here shall we live in this terrible town. Where the price for our minds shall squeeze them tight like a fist." Fear, and how to combat it, is also at the heart of "Afraid," one of the most upbeat songs on the album, during which the protagonist searches for something to believe in. In lines such as "I believe in Beatles" and "If I put my faith in medication," it seems quite likely that at least some of the subject matter has been drawn from Bowie's own experiences.

Heathen is strongly bookended, with the closing title track, "Heathen (The Rays)," relating both musically and thematically to the opening "Sunday." Chilling in the warning contained in its opening lyric, this song too conjures up 9/11 imagery: "Steel on the skyline. Sky made of glass made for a real world. All things must pass." Typically nonlinear in laying out the album's action, "Heathen (The Rays)" appears to be the portent of the events described in the first track. Powerfully evocative, the prominence of synthesizers in the track recalls the Berlin-era bleakness, a self-referential moment.

In all respects, and despite the lack of a hit single, *Heathen* marked a triumphant return for Bowie, the perfect way to begin his post-millennium career.

REALITY, 2003

Reality is a proper album, with a beginning, a middle and an end. It's direct, warm, emotional, honest, even, and the surfeit of pleasingly deceptive musical simplicity allows the irony of the central con-

cept—that there is no such thing as reality anymore—an opportunity
to filter through. —Daryl Easlea, BBC.com, 2003

There's a restlessness to much of the music that not only makes for a
great album but suggests that Bowie is struggling more than ever for
answers. —Steve Morse, *The Boston Globe*, September 2003

Track Listing

1. New Killer Star

2. Pablo Picasso (Richman)

3. Never Get Old

4. The Loneliest Guy

5. Looking for Water

6. She'll Drive the Big Car

7. Days

8. Fall Dog Bombs the Moon

9. Try Some Buy Some (Harrison)

10. Reality

11. Bring Me the Disco King

Reality, initially borne on the success of *Heathen*, debuted and peaked
on the UK album chart at a very impressive number three while also
achieving top-ten success elsewhere throughout Europe. Bowie's post-
millennium resurgence in the US, however, proved more difficult to
sustain, and *Reality* peaked at twenty-nine.

The cover of *Reality* immediately caused something of a stir. With
an unbroken history of using photographs of himself on his album covers—albeit photographs that were frequently doctored in various
ways—the substitution of Bowie's image with an anime character di-
vided fans and critics alike. But, of course, it is simply a case of Bowie
juxtaposing opposites, one of his most effective career-long tactics here
employed in a new way. The use of a cartoon facsimile on an album
titled *Reality* is immediately both oppositional and a form of joke.

New York is established as the geographical location of the album's
first track, "New Killer Star," thereby firmly establishing an immediate
continuity with *Heathen*. "See the great white scar over Battery Park.
Then a flare glides over, but I won't look at that scar," sings Bowie in
the song's opening lines. Such imagery is once again made especially
poignant in the shadow of 9/11, and yet nothing in the song is overtly
about that fateful day. Apart from the emphatic opening to *Reality* that
is provided by such an upbeat, riff-heavy song, clearly Bowie's motivation for its primary placement lies in the way it paints both the album

title and cover art in its literal critique of fantasy and reality: "See my life in a comic."

Following this scene-setter is the first of two cover versions on the album, Jonathan Richman's "Pablo Picasso." "Everything you can imagine is real," Picasso once famously stated, thereby explaining Bowie's motivation for the song's inclusion. Beyond this, however, "Pablo Picasso" is really nothing more than a mildly amusing take on romantic angst: "Well some people try to pick up girls; they get called assholes. This never happened to Pablo Picasso." While the song is given a solid reworking by Bowie, it is perhaps the least essential of all *Reality*'s tracks. The main opposition for this dubious honor is provided by the second cover, George Harrison's "Try Some Buy Some," which features late on the album. While Harrison's lyrics address the passing with age of youthful over-exuberance—appropriate enough material for Bowie's problematizing of his own aging process—the song's rendition lacks the impetus and edge of his own compositions on the album.

Indeed, aging is addressed far more aptly in Bowie's own "Never Get Old." "I think about personal history," he sings, setting up the song's theme. However, his feelings about aging change from line to line, from angst to frustration or resignation: "My head hangs low 'cause it's all over now," sings the fifty-six-year-old. But at times there is also total acceptance of his situation: "I'm looking at the future solid as a rock because of you." The inherently funky nature of the track belies any real notion of self-pity even in the less-than-optimistic lines, as might have been suggested had the song received a less upbeat stylistic treatment. In opposition to this apparent self-acceptance, however, in the song "The Loneliest Guy" his repeated claim that he is actually "the luckiest guy, not the loneliest guy" sounds hollow, ringing falsely throughout the song. The song is beautiful in its construction and piano-led instrumentation; nowhere in his recorded output has Bowie ever sounded as sad as he does on this slow ballad.

The events of 9/11 seemingly resurface briefly in "Looking for Water," yet only the line "But I lost God in a New York minute" carries any clarity. Elsewhere this track is so impressionistic that it is, even by Bowie's standards, too difficult to penetrate. "She'll Drive the Big Car" and "Days" take different tacks on the aging theme: Bowie tells the story of a woman who laments living an unfulfilled life in the former, while taking a first-person perspective and owning up to the self-centeredness of his younger self in the latter. Such self-centeredness is revisited in one of the standout tracks of the album, "Fall Dog Bombs the Moon." "I don't care much—I win anyway," sings Bowie with equal measures of self-loathing and disdain.

The strong title track occupies the penultimate position, the heaviest and most up-tempo of all the tracks on *Reality*. Detailing snippets of sex-and-drugs action between himself and a female groupie, the lyrics paint the unreality of the rock-star lifestyle: "Tragic youth was looking young and sexy . . . the tragic youth was going down on me," before "I sped from Planet X to Planet Alpha, struggling for reality."

The track charged with following this telling critique of a life he once actually led—most obviously during his self-admitted hedonistic early- to mid-seventies glam rock years—is "Bring Me the Disco King." At almost eight minutes long, this heavily jazz-inflected brush-on-snare ballad is as moving an album closer as one could imagine, finding Bowie looking back upon his life and career while also seemingly linking to the previous track in his admission to "killing time in the seventies." The song performs a summative function within the context of the album overall, and in addition to looking back Bowie speculates upon the future; on how he might bow out: "You promised me the ending would be clear. You'd let me know when the time was now."

Overall, *Reality* is, in a musical sense, in much the same vein as *Heathen*. The instrumental blend and sonic territory are for the most part an extension of the former album. However, "Bring Me the Disco King" is something entirely new. More than simply a bookend to *Reality*, the song almost gives the listener the impression of a far larger signing-off. Is it possible that this could be Bowie's swan song?

A variety of health problems surfaced during Bowie's extensive global *Reality* tour undertaken during late 2003 and the first half of 2004. Although none had seemingly been particularly alarming, the sporadic ill health culminated in a frightening way while in Germany, when Bowie was required to undergo emergency heart surgery to clear a blocked artery. To the immense relief of fans the world over, he recovered well and subsequently undertook a lengthy recuperation back at his home with his wife and daughter.

But then, years . . . and more years . . . passed. With no further recordings or live performances apart from the occasional brief guest-star appearance on someone else's recording project or concert bill,

Bowie began increasingly to be described as reclusive. The silence continued on and on. The possibility that he had indeed quietly retired without telling anyone turned more and more into a probability. Could rock's ultimate outcast have *really* settled down to a corduroy Third Age with a nice cup of tea, indoor/outdoor slippers, toast in bed, and a life of familial bliss? Yes, perhaps. Fans quietly grieved but eventually moved on with their lives, makeup brushes lying abandoned and Max Factor stocks hitting an all-time low.

But then . . . BANG! The joke is on us. Bowie ambushes everyone with a brand-new studio album. How *very* Bowie. He always was a scene-stealer. (*Never work with children, animals, or Bowie.*)

THE NEXT DAY, 2013

The Next Day is the comeback Bowie fans feared would never happen. . . . There are loads of musical and lyrical references to his past, as Bowie broods over the places he's gone and the faces he's seen. But he's resolutely aimed at the future. —Rob Sheffield, *Rolling Stone*, February 2013

It is an enormous pleasure to report that the new David Bowie album is an absolute wonder: urgent, sharp-edged, bold, beautiful and baffling, an intellectually stimulating, emotionally charged, musically jagged, electric bolt through his own mythos and the mixed-up, celebrity-obsessed, war-torn world of the 21st century. —Neil McCormick, *The Telegraph*, February 2013

This is a record that while happy to acknowledge Bowie's titanic past and borrow, magpie-like from it, is anything but navel-gazing, self-referential or reverent, instead leaping forward with a restless energy to tomorrow. —Emily Mackay, *New Musical Express*, March 2013

Track Listing

1. The Next Day
2. Dirty Boys
3. The Stars (Are Out Tonight)

8. I'd Rather Be High
9. Boss of Me (Bowie/Leonard)
10. Dancing Out in Space

4. Love Is Lost

5. Where Are We Now?

6. Valentine's Day

7. If You Can See Me

11. How Does the Grass Grow?
(Bowie/Lordan)

12. (You Will) Set the World on
Fire

13. You Feel So Lonely You Could
Die

14. Heat

In the 1970s a new Bowie album was *big* news. In 2013, *The Next Day* returned the artist to the rank of headline-grabber. "The Greatest comeback album in rock 'n' roll history," claimed *The Independent*'s Andy Gill, to quote just one five-star descriptor.

Announced to the world on January 8 on the occasion of his sixty-sixth birthday and released exactly two months later, Bowie's first album in a decade took the world by complete surprise, an unprecedented sneak-up-and-go-"BOO!" coup in an Internet age of electronic eavesdropping and digital tongue-wagging. With Tony Visconti once again in the co-producer's chair, the pairing responsible for some of Bowie's most iconic moments were at it again. Immediate critical acclaim followed the album's release, and success came equally quickly on the commercial front as *The Next Day* shot to the number-one position on the UK album chart and elsewhere throughout the world, ultimately hitting number two in the US.

Equally surprising—shocking, even—was the album's cover, which found Bowie subverting his famous *"Heroes"* cover image by imposing a plain white square over his portrait. On the surface, at least, it might have seemed to be a visual depiction of Bowie cutting himself free from the past. And yet vignettes from the past are clearly observable in the album. To name just two examples of many, the distinctive "Five Years" drum pattern from 1972 appears intact in the coda of "You Feel So Lonely You Could Die," while the names of Bowie's favorite haunts in Berlin permeate the album's leading single release, "Where Are We Now?" The resulting subtext is that while, yes, this is indeed *The Next Day*, none of us, not even David Bowie, can completely deny the past.

Any suggestion that age may have mellowed Bowie is quickly allayed. The music is spiky and aggressive, containing much hard-rock instrumentation and angular sonorities. There is little overt linkage to the musical style or sound of the electronics-dominated " *Heroes*," despite the visual alliance, and "Where Are We Now?" lies nearest to such a recapitulation. Sonically, the album sits closer to *Reality* than to any other work. If one plays "How Does the Grass Grow?" next to "New Killer Star" from *Reality*, the link is clear.

From the opening title track where Bowie sings, "They can't get enough of that doomsday song," and "They can work with Satan while they dress like saints," it's clear there has been no easing up on lyrical themes either. While cornerstones such as religion, personality, and apocalypse are present, the theme of personal mortality is highly evident. "I stumble to the graveyard and I lay down by my parents," on "I'd Rather Be High," or "Your fear is as old as the world," on "Love Is Lost," are but two examples. Given his advancing age this preoccupation is perhaps unsurprising. But the manner in which he approaches mortality makes it clear he is not yet comfortable with it. David Bowie is not ready to surrender and go anywhere just yet, because he is clearly not finished. And that, in essence, is the pivotal quality of *The Next Day*. Bowie is still struggling to know who he is, why he is here, and where he is going, let alone where he has been. He is, therefore, still like the vast majority of us, his fans. He is flawed, curious, ever-changing, and unwilling to hand over the reins to a god or anyone else.

Such inherent tension, channeled so expertly through his art decade after decade, is what has made David Bowie one of the greatest artists in popular-music history. And *this* is precisely why David Bowie is still relevant today. He is articulating, once again, our own fears and insecurities in a way that helps us make sense of them and deal with them. "I don't know who I am," he states in "Heat." It is not so much that David Bowie provides answers; more that, through him, we realize how crucial it is to ask the questions in the first place.

The Next Day is far more an electric chair than an armchair.

EPILOGUE

Throughout this book my goal has been to provide more than simply a series of descriptions of Bowie's albums. Instead I have attempted to convey what these many and varied works have meant to Bowie's fans. My analysis has been, inevitably, underpinned by autoethnography. I am a fan of David Bowie and could never have written such a book while pretending to be otherwise. I am aware, however, that I have written this as a man now in his fifties—and with the benefit of hindsight. I discovered David Bowie when I was twelve years old, in 1972, and would not have been able then to articulate to the extent I have done here the reason for his immense appeal to me and youth like me. He was then extraordinarily appealing, attractive, and revolutionary— and he still is. In these concluding pages, I have attempted to candidly revisit my own fandom through Bowie's career. I did write letters to David Bowie from time to time, pledging my gratitude and devotion and, at times, even conveying my disappointment, as I'm sure many thousands of other fans did throughout the world as they shared the Bowie journey with the artist. While the following letter excerpts are fictional re-creations, the spirit of the words remains accurate—a snapshot, if you will, of myself and Bowie fandom more generally.

September 3, 1972
Dear David,
Hi. You don't know me, but I live in New Zealand and I am twelve years old. *Ziggy Stardust* is the best record I have ever heard in my life. Thanks!

Bye,
Ian

September 27, 1972

Dear David,

Hi. It's Ian here again in New Zealand. I wanted to tell you that I've bought *Hunky Dory* now too and I love it nearly as much as *Ziggy Stardust*. You are different from other pop stars.

Ch, Ch, Ch, Cheers,
Ian

October 15, 1972

Dear David,

Wow! I got a record voucher for my birthday and bought *The Man Who Sold the World*. It's far out. Really different from *Ziggy Stardust* and *Hunky Dory*, but I love it anyway. I've never heard anything like "The Width of a Circle" before. Marc Bolan used to be my favorite pop star but now it's you.

Bye,
Ian

January 18, 1973

Dear David,

I ordered *David Bowie*—your first record—and it took three months to come from England. No offense, but I didn't like it as much as the other three I've got. But I'm still your biggest fan.

Yours sincerely,
Ian

P.S. My dad thinks "Rubber Band" is very funny and keeps going around the house saying "I hope you break your baton."

March 3, 1973

Dear David,

I have your second record now too! I like it more than your first one. I *really* like your "Space Oddity" song. It reminds me of *Ziggy* (which is still my favorite record, by the way). Q: What does "a phallus in pigtails" mean?

Cheers,

Ian

May 2, 1973
Dear David,
I LOVE *Aladdin Sane.* And you look awesome on the cover. The other
day when I was at home by myself I got Mum's makeup and tried to do
my face like yours. It wasn't very good. Please do another record really
soon!
Your biggest fan,
Ian

November 30, 1973
Dear David,
"Sorrow" is number one in New Zealand! Did you know? Congratula-
tions! I love *Pin Ups* and I play it all day. My older brother hates it. He
says the original versions are better. But he's just a grumpy old hippy.
He stills wears beads, ha ha.
Byeee,
Ian

April 15, 1974
Dear David,
Diamond Dogs is SO good! I was worried at first because I heard you
had fired the Spiders from Mars and that made me sad. Wow! I think
you are fantastic David. I can do my own makeup now. I got my sister to
show me. She made me do some of her chores, but that's OK.
Cheers,
Ian

April 13, 1975
Dear David,
Sorry it's been a while since I wrote. I like your new record but I am sad
you are not a glam rock star anymore. I still am. Well, not exactly a star,
I guess. The other day I got into a fight with some boys who said you
were crap. They always pick on me. Anyway, will you please make
another glam rock record?
Cheers,
Ian

March 12, 1976

Dear David,

I have never heard anything like *Station to Station* before. I REALLY like the title track and "TVC15." My dad (he's a bit of a nut) is going around singing "Oh oh oh oh oh." I like that it's rockier than *Young Americans*. I still wish you'd go back to glam rock, but oh well.

Still your biggest fan,

Ian

March 30, 1977

Dear David,

I hope you are well. I've been finding life very difficult lately. No one understands me. Somehow though, if I close my bedroom door and pull my curtains, playing *Low* makes things better. I don't know how that works. But THANKS.

Ian

November 22, 1977

Dear David,

Hi. I am really enjoying *"Heroes."* I especially like "V-2 Schneider." I still play all of your albums a lot (well, except the first one), and I find that different ones suit my different moods. I left school a few months ago and I've started learning the drums. If you ever need a drummer you have my address, even if it's "just for one day," ha ha.

Cheers,

Ian

June 10, 1979

Dear David,

Hi. That was a l-o-n-g gap between albums. But anyway *Lodger* is really good. I like "DJ" best, but "Boys Keep Swinging" is really good too. That's a really weird record cover—did someone beat you up or something? Anyway, I hope you are well. I have a 9–5 job now and don't get as much time for listening to records or playing my drums as I used to.

See you later,

Ian

October 19, 1980

Dear David,

Wow! *Scary Monsters* is blowing my mind. It's my favorite album since *Ziggy*. Or maybe *Diamond Dogs*. It's SO good that Major Tom has returned from the dead, even if he's a junkie, ha ha. Great to see YOU back at the top. Did you know your album is at number one in New Zealand, and "Ashes to Ashes" is at number six? And what a fantastic album cover! What a great way to start the 1980s! (Too many exclamation marks?)

STILL your biggest fan,

Ian

June 2, 1983

Dear David,

Wow, *Let's Dance* is top of the charts everywhere. Congratulations! Remember I told you I'd taken up the drums? Well, after being in a few pretty bad original bands I have joined a covers band that's really good, and guess what? We've learned "Modern Love," "China Girl," *and* "Let's Dance," and they always fill the dance floor. My cousin Lynette always scoffed at what she called my "Bowie obsession," saying you were too freaky. But even *she* has bought *Let's Dance*! Gotta run, sorry, got band practice.

Cheers,

Ian

November 14, 1984

Dear David,

I really like "Blue Jean" from your new album. Remember I told you about my cousin, Lynette? Well I think you have a new fan there—she bought *Tonight* even before I did. Our band has learned "Blue Jean" and we play it in our top-twenty set, along with the *Let's Dance* songs and some Duran Duran and Phil Collins songs and other stuff. I feel bad saying this, but I didn't really connect with the other tracks on the new album. I hope you're not offended.

Cheers,

Ian

August 28, 1987

Dear David,

I was playing my *Ziggy Stardust* album the other day and suddenly realized it's been three years since I wrote to you. Lynette told me you have a new album out at the moment—*Never Let Me Down*, is it called? I must get it. Or maybe Lyn will loan me hers. Hope all is well. Gotta go, sorry. Am flat out with the kids—you know how it is.

Cheers,

Ian

May 12, 1993

Dear David,

Hi! It's Ian here. You probably don't remember me, but I was your biggest "down under" fan back in the '70s and early '80s. I just wanted to say that although I didn't really "get" your Tin Machine stuff (sorry) I saw *Black Tie White Noise* the other day in a record shop and thought, "Wow—what's my fav rock star up to now? I've really missed him." I haven't bought a record in ages, but I went straight in and got it. It's great, David. I heard it's number one in the UK, so that's brilliant.

Regards,

Ian

October 15, 1995

Dear David,

Outside is excellent. I haven't been able to get "Hallo Spaceboy" out of my head. I'm not sure I understand the whole "concept" of the album exactly, but most of the songs are great. My wife is getting annoyed because I am playing it all the time.

Cheers,

Ian

March 2, 1997

Dear David,

When I first played *Earthling*, my son came through to my office to inquire what it was. His name's Ziggy (funny, that!), and he's thirteen and a huge fan of the Prodigy. He sniffed and then left when I told him it was you, but I could tell he was impressed. It's just not cool to like Dad's music, you know? Ha ha.

Keep up the great work,

Ian

October 30, 1999
Dear David,
I bought *'hours . . .'* and I really love it. I can't believe that I'm about to turn forty—and you are fifty-two! Yet when I listen to "The Pretty Things Are Going to Hell," I feel like I am thirteen again, ha ha. How did you *do* that? Did you feel the decades falling away when you and Reeves wrote and recorded it? You just keep on surprising me.
Cheers,
Ian

June 20, 2002
Dear David,
You know, in the last ten years I've had two marriages fall apart, lost both my parents, seen two dogs and one cat buried under the hedge . . . and yet you remain a constant presence in my life. I hope I'm not being weird. I just appreciate it, that's all. *Heathen* is great! It's playing right now, and I am finding bits of myself in your songs. (OK, I admit I've had a few wines.)
Cheers,
Ian

September 29, 2003
Dear David,
Sorry about my last email. I'm sober this time, but even if I was a bit gone last time I really *did* mean what I said. :) Your new album, *Reality*, is a cracker! In my opinion, you and Tony are a dream team. "New Killer Star" is the best song I've heard in years, and my girlfriend plays "Bring Me the Disco King" over and over. I'm so excited that you are bringing your tour to New Zealand next year. I'll be there!
Your biggest fan,
Ian

April 3, 2013
Wow, David. So much has happened in the ten years since I last wrote. I can't tell you how wonderful it is that you've released *The Next Day*. What a fantastic surprise! As the years went by I thought you'd retired

without telling anyone! I saw your concert in Wellington, by the way, back in 2004. It was F.A.N.T.A.S.T.I.C. I was really worried to hear about your heart attack later that year. But here you are, back again and as amazing as ever. Don't stop, OK? You've provided a soundtrack for my life and ditto for millions of other fans all over the world. But, more than that, you've helped us make sense of the "big" issues; helped us face our fears and be prepared to stand out and not run with the herd. And somehow you've managed to articulate the ch-ch-ch-changes (see what I did there? I think I've cracked that joke before, right?) in our lives that we all face as we get older. What I *really* like, though, is that you never profess to have the answers. You just know how to phrase the questions. Brilliant. Like I said, please never stop!
Yours,
Ian

THE MANNEQUINS THAT SCREAMED: THE UNEXPECTED POWER OF *DAVID BOWIE IS*

On Saturday, June 22, 2013, a full forty years after becoming a teenager, I visited the *David Bowie Is* exhibition at the Victoria and Albert Museum in London. Within minutes of clearing the entrance queue I was most emphatically, and unexpectedly, transported back in time. Certainly it is true to say I was predisposed to enjoy the exhibition. I'd been looking forward to the trip for many months. But the impact *David Bowie Is* had upon me far exceeded my expectations. I wasn't prepared for the emotional impact such an immersion in things Bowie would have on me. I was, for all intents and purposes, blown away all over again.

The exhibition contained a wealth of Bowie riches of all descriptions, from original album cover artwork to stage props, hand-drawn sketches, and giant screens showing rare footage. To a lifelong fan, every last item was special. But it was the costumes that hit me the hardest, by far. These costumes had never moved on; had never gotten old. They were frozen in time, as resplendent and magnificent as when inhabited by whatever character he had been portraying at the time. These were the very same costumes I had seen over and over in photographs in magazines and in concert footage. *There* was Ziggy! *There* was Halloween

Jack! *There* was the Thin White Duke! Here I was, face-to-face with an era of my past that, I quickly realized, I missed enormously. Wandering around the rooms of the exhibition, visiting some parts of it again and again, I positively reveled in what was actually a shared past—Bowie's, mine, and many of the exhibition visitors I was literally bumping shoulders with. And above everything else, it was his costumes that gave the occasion an eerie, highly tangible sense of the man's presence.

All visitors wore state-of-the-art Sennheiser headsets, giving us a running commentary that automatically changed according to where we were in the exhibition, explaining details and background on whatever we were viewing at any given time. At other moments, however, such as when watching the video of "Life on Mars," the headsets simply gave us audio of the song. These headsets greatly enhanced the welcome feeling of isolation one experienced from the crowds of people all around. It made for a far more personal engagement with the exhibition—and thus Bowie—than would otherwise have been the case. It also struck me that this served as a great analogy for how Bowie's magic had "worked" for myself and for his millions of other fans over the years. Anyone who felt alienated or different for any one (or more) of a myriad of reasons—even simply the ever-repeating and natural cycle of youth/generational alienation—was empowered by the inclusive inner world that Bowie had created through his art, where difference was desirable rather than problematic; sexy rather than threatening. Shuffling along shoulder-to-shoulder amid hundreds of complete strangers at the V&A, everyone was unified, via our headsets, by a celebration of that same inner world. An unlikely, but very real, community.

I saw people in tears at the exhibition. A single case in point: At the screen for the aforementioned "Life on Mars" video, with Bowie's costume from the shoot alongside, I stood next to a woman who, I would guess, was in her fifties. As she watched Bowie she was singing her heart out and crying, completely oblivious to all around her. Who knew what memories were playing in her head as she traveled back in time? It was so obviously just her and David in the equation. Now I'm not trying to suggest that this was a quasi-religious experience or anything, but the exhibition unquestionably moved some people profoundly. While I'm sure there were disengaged onlookers present—people who were not Bowie fans in particular but who were attending the exhibition simply out of curiosity—clearly, the lifelong, dedicated fans like myself were in abundance, and accordingly I too found myself moist of eye on one or two occasions. And, as I indicated earlier, the most powerful of the emotion-inducing totems were the costumes, such as Kansai Yamamoto's Ziggy Stardust kimono, upon which I gazed with what I can only describe as awe.

It struck me later, as I relived the experience over and over in my head and tried to fathom the depth of the impact I'd felt, that of all rock artists only Bowie's costumes could possibly project such power so many decades after the fact. In the 1970s, Bowie was our rock mannequin—a self-confessed "stand-in" rock star; an actor playing a role; a wonderful fake who rent asunder tired and pompous notions of rock 'n' roll authenticity. The personalities and characteristics of the iconic characters he played were framed by these very costumes. The garments were carefully crafted mirrors to Bowie's internal scripts. So how apt it was to see them now upon the shoulders of thematically aligned simulacra; stand-ins for a stand-in. On the cover of *Aladdin Sane*, Bowie practically *was* a mannequin. He was a canvas upon which we fans were required to fill in the details ourselves, fleshing him out to be whatever *we* wanted or needed him to be. That's why Bowie fans were, and are, so devoted; we each created a personal version of him to suit ourselves. In Bowie, we enjoyed a sense of ownership that other rock stars could never offer us.

And that's how it felt all over again at the V&A exhibition. The blank-faced mannequins were devoid of all personal detail, but so strong were the associations we had with the costumes they wore, it was an easy task to project Bowie into the picture, as we wanted him to be, and thus complete the scene in our heads.

The man himself wasn't at the Victoria and Albert Museum when I witnessed *David Bowie Is*. But that was absolutely fine because, as Bowie fans, we are well used to the concept of absence. And isn't/wasn't that the whole point? Bowie's modus operandi is roles, costumes, make-up, smoke and mirrors. He never wore his clothes like other rock stars did. Sometimes, they wore him. In seeing the intelligently contrived constructivism of Bowie exposed in all its detailed glory at the V&A exhibition, perhaps we saw more of him than if he'd actually been there in the flesh. Superb.

NOTES

INTRODUCTION

1. Simon Frith, "Only Dancing: David Bowie Flirts with the Issues," in *Zoot Suits and Second-Hand Dresses: An Anthology of Fashion and Music*, ed. Angela McRobbie (Boston: Unwin Hyman, 1988), 136.

I. ROCK AND ROLE

1. Barbara C. Mennel, *Cities and Cinema* (New York: Routledge, 2008), 47.
2. Andrew Spicer, *Film Noir* (Harlow, UK: Longman Press, 2002), 48.
3. Mick Rock and David Bowie, *Moonage Daydream: The Life and Times of Ziggy Stardust* (Guilford: Genesis Publications, 2002), 12.
4. Barry Miles, *David Bowie Black Book* (London: Omnibus Press, 1980), 69–70.
5. Dick Hebdige, *Subculture: The Meaning of Style* (London: Methuen, 1979), 61.

2. THE ACTOR EMERGES

1. Nicholas Pegg, *The Complete David Bowie* (London: Reynolds & Hearn, 2002), 33.

3. MUSICAL BEGINNINGS

1. Peter Dogget, *The Man Who Sold the World: David Bowie and the 1970s* (London: Bodley Head, 2011), 356.

2. David Buckley, *Strange Fascination: David Bowie: The Definitive Story* (London: Virgin Publishing, 1999), 35.

3. Mark Paytress, *The Rise and Fall of Ziggy Stardust and the Spiders from Mars* (New York: Schirmer Books, 1998), 10.

4. Paul Du Noyer, "David Bowie: The 1990 Interview," *Q*, April 1990.

4. MESSAGES FROM GROUND CONTROL

1. To add further to the confusion that sometimes still surrounds this album, in 1972 RCA rereleased it under the title of its star single, "Space Oddity." It fared considerably better in this rerelease, borne upon the recent success of *Ziggy Stardust*, reaching number seventeen in the UK and sixteen in the US.

2. Mark Rose, *Alien Encounters: Anatomy of Science Fiction* (Cambridge, MA: Harvard University Press, 1981), 50.

3. James E. Perone, *The Words and Music of David Bowie* (Westport, CT: Praeger Publishers, 2007), 13.

4. Kenneth Pitt, *Bowie: The Pitt Report* (London: Omnibus Press, 1985), 179.

5. Nick Stevenson, *David Bowie: Fame, Sound and Vision* (Cambridge: Polity Press, 2006), 34.

6. Philip Auslander, *Performing Glam Rock: Gender and Theatricality in Popular Music* (Ann Arbor: University of Michigan Press, 2006), 9.

7. Barney Hoskyns, *Glam: Bowie, Bolan and the Glitter Rock Revolution* (London: Faber & Faber, 1998), 5.

8. Frank Moriarty, *Seventies Rock: The Decade of Creative Chaos* (Lanham, MD: Taylor Trade Publishing, 2003), 2.

9. In the US the album was released with a different front cover, consisting of a cartoon drawing by Bowie's friend Michael Weller of a gun-toting cowboy standing in front of London's Cane Hill psychiatric hospital. The site is significant because Bowie's older half brother, Terry Burns, was at times a patient there.

10. Just as Bowie's second album had been rereleased with significantly greater success in the wake of the *Ziggy Stardust* album, so too was *The Man Who Sold the World*. On this 1972 release, RCA Records completely dis-

pensed with the artwork of both the original UK and US covers, opting instead for a topical high-energy black-and-white image of Bowie in Ziggy Stardust mode, caught delivering a high kick live in concert.

11. David Buckley, *Strange Fascination: David Bowie: The Definitive Story* (London: Virgin Publishing, 1999), 100.

12. While "The Man Who Sold the World" was not released as a single by Bowie, its commercial viability was later proven when Scottish singer Lulu took the song to number four on the UK singles chart in 1974, with Bowie actively driving the release, producing the song, and contributing saxophone and backing vocals. Also, in 1994, Nirvana covered the song in their *MTV Unplugged* performance, releasing the track as a promotional single for the subsequent album, to further considerable success.

5. IRRESISTIBLE DECADENCE

1. Nick Stevenson, *David Bowie: Fame, Sound and Vision* (Cambridge: Polity Press, 2006), 65.

2. David Bowie in Peter Doggett, *The Man Who Sold the World: David Bowie and the 1970s* (London: Bodley Head, 2011), 176.

3. Nicholas Pegg, *The Complete David Bowie* (London: Reynolds & Hearn, 2002), 243.

4. James E. Perone, *The Words and Music of David Bowie* (Westport, CT: Praeger Publishers, 2007), 37.

5. Stevenson, *David Bowie*, 65.

6. Tom Fraser and Adam Banks, *Designer's Color Manual: The Complete Guide to Color Theory and Application* (San Francisco: Chronicle Books, 2004), 20.

7. Lesley Hornby, *Twiggy: How I Probably Just Came Along on a White Rabbit at the Right Time, and Met the Smile on the Face of the Tiger* (New York: Hawthorne Books, 1968), 154.

8. Perone, *The Words and Music of David Bowie*, 40.

9. Pegg, *The Complete David Bowie*, 246.

10. Stevenson, *David Bowie*, 66.

6. PLASTIC SOUL AND THE BIRTH OF THE EUROPEAN CANON

1. Peter Doggett, *The Man Who Sold the World: David Bowie and the 1970s* (London: Bodley Head, 2011), 223.

   2. David Bowie in Doggett, *The Man Who Sold the World*, 227.

   3. James E. Perone, *The Words and Music of David Bowie* (Westport, CT: Praeger Publishers, 2007), 49.

   4. Nicholas Pegg, *The Complete David Bowie* (London: Reynolds & Hearn, 2002), 64.

   5. Pegg, *The Complete David Bowie*, 256.

   6. Pegg, *The Complete David Bowie*, 259.

   7. Frank Moriarty, *Seventies Rock: The Decade of Creative Chaos* (Lanham, MD: Taylor Trade Publishing, 2003), 209.

   8. Hugo Wilcken, *Low* (New York: Continuum, 2005), 5.

   9. Bowie in Pegg, *The Complete David Bowie*, 258.

   10. Wilcken, *Low*, 9.

   11. Bowie in Pegg, *The Complete David Bowie*, 258.

   12. Wilcken, *Low*, 9.

   13. Doggett, *The Man Who Sold the World*, 252.

7. THE SOUNDS OF EUROPE

   1. Lorne Murdoch, "Hitting an All-Time Low," in *The Bowie Companion*, ed. Elizabeth Thomson and David Gutman (New York: Da Capo Press, 1996), 149.

   2. Nicholas Pegg, *The Complete David Bowie* (London: Reynolds & Hearn, 2002), 263.

   3. Uncut, "Uncut Interviews: David Bowie on Berlin: The Real 'Uncut' Version," *BowieWonderworld*, accessed October 24, 2007, www.bowiewonderworld.com/features/dbuncut.htm.

   4. Pegg, *The Complete David Bowie*, 22.

   5. Frank Moriarty, *Seventies Rock: The Decade of Creative Chaos* (Lanham, MD: Taylor Trade Publishing, 2003), 222.

   6. David Buckley, *Strange Fascination: David Bowie: The Definitive Story* (London: Virgin Publishing, 1999), 324.

   7. Peter Doggett, *The Man Who Sold the World: David Bowie and the 1970s* (London: Bodley Head, 2011), 301.

   8. David Buckley, *David Bowie: The Complete Guide to His Music* (London: Omnibus Press, 2004), 57.

   9. Dogget, *The Man Who Sold the World*, 306.

   10. Pegg, *The Complete David Bowie*, 270.

8. THE RISE AND FALL OF DAVID BOWIE

1. Peter Doggett, *The Man Who Sold the World: David Bowie and the 1970s* (London: Bodley Head, 2011), 2.

2. Nicholas Pegg, *The Complete David Bowie* (London: Reynolds & Hearn, 2002), 153.

3. James E. Perone, *The Words and Music of David Bowie* (Westport, CT: Praeger Publishers, 2007), 90.

4. Charles Shaar Murray, "Sermon from the Savoy," *New Musical Express*, September 29, 1984.

5. David Bowie in Tricia Jones, "Is the Lad Too Insane for His Own Good?" *i-D CONFiDE*, May 1987.

6. Pegg, *The Complete David Bowie*, 284.

SELECTED READING

Auslander, Philip. *Performing Glam Rock: Gender and Theatricality in Popular Music*. Ann Arbor: University of Michigan Press, 2006. Analyzing Bowie's performative methodology within a logical and accessible academic framework, Auslander's book is a primary text. The author convincingly unpacks the groundbreaking theatrical and gender elements of Bowie's interdisciplinary performance palette of the early 1970s.

Buckley, David. *David Bowie: The Complete Guide to His Music*. London: Omnibus Press, 2004. Conversational and witty, Buckley nicely walks the tightrope between fact and fan opinion in this album-by-album pocket guide.

Buckley, David. *Strange Fascination: David Bowie: The Definitive Story*. London: Virgin Publishing, 1999. Buckley is a passionate and extremely knowledgeable researcher and fan who writes extremely well and leaves his rose-tinted spectacles firmly in their case. An easy and highly informative read, it is this author's favorite Bowie biography.

Cann, Kevin. *Any Day Now: David Bowie: The London Years 1947–1974*. London: Adelita, 2010. The last word on Bowie's early career and an unprecedented visual feast of Bowie photographs, ephemera, album cover artwork, and other treats.

Cann, Kevin. *David Bowie: A Chronology*. London: Vermillion, 1983. A very well-researched and valuable resource for any student of David Bowie.

Dogget, Peter. *The Man Who Sold the World: David Bowie and the 1970s*. London: Bodley Head, 2011. This book is notable for the way the author skillfully situates Bowie's 1970s career against the cultural maelstrom of the era.

Frith, Simon. "Only Dancing: David Bowie Flirts with the Issues." In *Zoot Suits and Second-Hand Dresses: An Anthology of Fashion and Music*, edited by Angela McRobbie. Boston: Unwin Hyman, 1988: 132–140. An excellent article in which the author tackles Bowie's unprecedented balancing act between authenticity, commerce, and art.

Gilman, Leni, and Peter Gilman. *Alias David Bowie*. London: Hodder & Stoughton, 1986. One of the most controversial of the Bowie biographies, with a sometimes very unsympathetic emphasis upon Bowie's mental health, the influence of his family, and the origins of his proclivity for reinvention. This work throws up much interesting biographical material but is, at times, worryingly opinionated.

Hebdige, Dick. *Subculture: The Meaning of Style*. London: Methuen, 1979. A seminal work in (sub)cultural theory and now much challenged, Hebdige's work provides an interesting historical snapshot of Bowie's engagement with youth style.

Hoskyns, Barney. *Glam: Bowie, Bolan and the Glitter Rock Revolution*. London: Faber & Faber, 1998. Bowie's glam rock–era work is here admirably contextualized within the wider milieu of glam rock style, 1971–1975.

Matthew-Walker, Robert. *David Bowie: Theatre of Music.* Buckinghamshire: Kensal Press, 1985. Interesting mainly for its relatively early recognition of Bowie's theatrical foundation, as evidenced by the title. The author, himself a composer of some renown, makes a salient attempt at unpacking some of Bowie's most intriguing early- to mid-career songs.

Miles, Barry. *David Bowie Black Book.* London: Omnibus Press, 1980.

Moriarty, Frank. *Seventies Rock: The Decade of Creative Chaos.* Lanham, MD: Taylor Trade Publishing, 2003. While Bowie is but one of many subjects within this work, the way in which the author positions the artist against the social and cultural conditions of the day is well worth reading.

Murdoch, Lorne. "Hitting an All-Time Low." In *The Bowie Companion,* edited by Elizabeth Thomson and David Gutman. New York: Da Capo Press, 1996: 149–155. An excellent article within a highly valuable compilation of diverse Bowie-related articles.

Paytress, Mark. *The Rise and Fall of Ziggy Stardust and the Spiders from Mars.* New York: Schirmer Books, 1998. A focused critique of Bowie's breakthrough work, with impressive background and contextual content framing the album analysis.

Pegg, Nicholas. *The Complete David Bowie.* London: Reynolds & Hearn, 2002. The most meticulous and far-reaching of all Bowie critiques. A virtual Bowie encyclopedia.

Perone, James E. *The Words and Music of David Bowie.* Westport, CT: Praeger Publishers, 2007. In an extensive critique of Bowie's recorded works, Perone makes some salient observations, although the writing is rather dry and there are occasional errors.

Pitt, Kenneth. *Bowie: The Pitt Report.* London: Omnibus Press, 1985. A valuable "horse's mouth" account of Bowie's early years, written by then-manager Kenneth Pitt.

Rock, Mick, and David Bowie. *Moonage Daydream: The Life and Times of Ziggy Stardust.* Guilford: Genesis Publications, 2002. A beautiful coffee table book, with magnificent photographs married to some wonderful firsthand accounts of the Ziggy Stardust/glam rock years from Bowie himself and his renowned photographer.

Sandford, Christopher. *Bowie: Loving the Alien.* London: Warner Books, 1996. An uneven biography that nevertheless pulls off some impressive coups, including interviewing William Burroughs, among a raft of other interviewees.

Stevenson, Nick. *David Bowie: Fame, Sound and Vision.* Cambridge: Polity Press, 2006. An excellent, insightful, and informative critique of the artist from within a cultural and media studies framework.

Thompson, Dave. *David Bowie: Moonage Daydream.* London: Plexus, 1987. A very solid biography that includes details of concerts and recordings, a discography, and a filmography.

Trynka, Paul. *Starman: David Bowie: The Definitive Biography.* London: Sphere, 2011. Another biographer claiming to offer the "definitive" account of Bowie himself, Trynka is certainly thorough and meticulous in his research, managing to bring new insights to some well-trodden aspects of Bowie's career.

Waldrep, Shelton. *The Aesthetics of Self-Invention: Oscar Wilde to David Bowie.* Minneapolis: University of Minnesota Press, 2004. A rigorous investigation into the precursors of Bowie's Wilde-esque talent for image creation amid the art/commerce divide.

Welch, Chris. *David Bowie: We Could Be Heroes.* New York: Thunders Mouth Press, 1999. An ambitious behind-the-scenes analysis of Bowie's albums and songs, this is well worth a read.

Wilcken, Hugo. *Low.* New York: Continuum, 2005. A short but focused investigation into Bowie's most controversial work.

SELECTED LISTENING

David Bowie released June 1, 1967, Deram Records.
David Bowie (aka *Man of Words/Man of Music* and also *Space Oddity*) released November 4, 1969, Philips Records.
The Man Who Sold the World released November 4, 1970, Mercury Records.
Hunky Dory released December 17, 1971, RCA Records.
The Rise and Fall of Ziggy Stardust and the Spiders from Mars released June 6, 1972, RCA Records.
Aladdin Sane released April 13, 1973, RCA Records.
Pin Ups released October 19, 1973, RCA Records.
Diamond Dogs released April 24, 1974, RCA Records.
Young Americans released March 7, 1975, RCA Records.
Station to Station released January 23, 1976, RCA Records.
Low released January 14, 1977, RCA Records.
"Heroes" released October 14, 1977, RCA Records.
Lodger released May 18, 1979, RCA Records.
Scary Monsters released September 12, 1980, RCA Records.
Let's Dance released April 14, 1983, EMI Records.
Tonight released September 1, 1984, EMI Records.
Never Let Me Down released April 27, 1987, EMI Records.
Tin Machine released May 22, 1989, EMI Records.
Tin Machine II released September 2, 1991, London Records.
Black Tie White Noise released April 5, 1993, Arista Records.
The Buddha of Suburbia released November 8, 1993, Arista Records.
1.Outside released September 26, 1995, RCA Records.
Earthling released February 3, 1997, RCA Records.
'hours . . .' released October 4, 1999, Virgin Records.
Heathen released June 11, 2002, ISO/Columbia Records.
Reality released September 16, 2003, ISO/Columbia Records.
The Next Day released March 8, 2013, ISO/Columbia Records.

INDEX

ABOUT THE AUTHOR

Ian Chapman is an author, performer, and academic. He is currently senior lecturer in popular music at the University of Otago, Dunedin, located deep in the South Island of his native New Zealand. David Bowie was the subject of both his master's and doctoral theses. He has written two previous books: *Glory Days: From Gumboots to Platforms* (2009) and *Kiwi Rock Chicks, Pop Stars and Trailblazers* (2010). Chapman is also co-author of *The Kiwi Fisherman's Guide to Life* (2013), in which he joyfully seizes the opportunity to explore his recreational passion. He describes the "research" for the latter as both intensive and prolonged. Chapman has also written articles and book chapters on glam rock for both academic and popular publications. A vocalist, drummer, and guitarist, he performed frequently in the guise of his alter ego, Dr. Glam, before hanging up the makeup brush in 2014.